Creative Chords

Acknowledgements

The Editors wish to thank the editors and publisher of *Priest and People* for permission to reprint an edited version of the article by Emmanuel Gribben and the *Daily Telegraph* library for assistance with references.

Creative Chords

Studies in Music, Theology and Christian Formation

edited by
Jeff Astley, Timothy Hone and Mark Savage

Gracewing.

First published in 2000

Gracewing
2 Southern Avenue
Leominster
Herefordshire HR6 0QF

ISBN 0 85244 424 9

Typesetting by
Action Publishing Technology Ltd, Gloucester, GL1 1SP

Contents

Contributors

Jeff Astley is Director of the North of England Institute for Christian Education and Honorary Professorial Fellow in Practical Theology and Christian Education in the University of Durham.

Jeremy Begbie is Vice-Principal of Ridley Hall, Cambridge and Director of 'Theology through the Arts', at the Centre for Advanced Religious and Theological Studies, University of Cambridge.

Rosamund Bourke researches in empirical psychology and was formerly Senior Lecturer in Psychology at the Hatfield Polytechnic (University of Hertfordshire).

Coral Davies is a practising musician resident in Cumbria, and was formerly Lecturer in Music Education at the University of Durham.

Gordon Giles is Succentor of St Paul's Cathedral, London.

Emmanuel Gribben lectures in liturgy at Ushaw College Roman Catholic Seminary.

Ian Ground lectures in Philosophy at the Centre for Lifelong Learning of the University of Newcastle upon Tyne.

Bill Hall is Senior Chaplain to the Arts and Recreation in the North East of England.

Martin Haselböck is active as a conductor, organist, composer and scholar, based in Vienna.

Timothy Hone is Master of the Music at the Cathedral Church of St Nicholas, Newcastle and University Organist of the University of Newcastle upon Tyne.

John Inge is a Residentiary Canon of Ely Cathedral.

James MacMillan is a composer and resides in Glasgow; he teaches at the Royal Scottish Academy of Music and Drama and is Visiting Professor at Strathclyde University.

Michael Sadgrove is Provost of Sheffield Cathedral.

Mark Savage is Vicar of Bedlington and a tutor at the University of Newcastle upon Tyne Centre for Lifelong Learning; he was formerly Adult Education Adviser of the Diocese of Newcastle.

John Sloboda is Professor of Psychology and Director of the Unit for the Study of Musical Skill and Development, Keele University.

Preface

This book has its origins in two related projects. For several years Timothy Hone and Mark Savage have been involved in workshops with clergy and adult lay people on the rôle of music in Christian education. More recently, they joined with Jeff Astley to organise a series of residential symposia and study days on the relationship between music, theology and Christian education, sponsored by the North of England Institute for Christian Education (NEICE), the Diocese of Newcastle and the Centre for Theological Research of the University of Durham. The majority of the essays published here were first presented at these occasions.

The editors share the conviction that an inter-disciplinary study of the nature of music and its connections with theological concepts and the practice of Christian formation is greatly needed. Theological reflection on the power and nature of music can elucidate both the musical experience itself and the ways in which it can offer people an experience of revelation, enabling them to know more about the nature of God and of religious experience. Likewise, the exploration of musical creativity can offer profound insights to the theologian. A synoptic view is clearly of great importance here, incorporating psychological, philosophical, educational and other perspectives, and drawing on practical experience and empirical research. This collection of papers seeks to provide just such a resource for reflecting on the relationship between music, theology and Christian learning.

We have brought together in this volume three rather different sorts of material: informal exchanges with music practitioners; academic studies of musical experience from the viewpoint of the disciplines of theology, psychology and philosophy; and reflections focussed on concrete situations of worship and learning. This variety of perspectives, methods, contexts, fields of study, and indeed genres, is now offered in the hope that it may enrich and illuminate theological enquiry and religious reflection on the contribution of music to the life of the human spirit.

We are grateful to all who have assisted with this work, especially the authors for making their work available in this way to a wider public; NEICE and the Diocese of Newcastle for funding support; Ushaw College for hosting our symposia; and Evelyn Jackson, Secretary to NEICE, for preparing the text for the printers.

The Editors
April 2000

Foreword:

Music, Theology and Enchantment

Michael Sadgrove

This book explores the important interface between music and religion. There are books a-plenty on *religious music* – how music has historically enriched the liturgy and how, alongside other performing arts, it continues to enable worship to soar. There are books that explore the rôle of music as a companion on the religious path. There has been some creative writing on how music provides metaphors for doing theology. Much of this is germane to this book. But these concerns, important though they are, do not quite lie at the core of this book. What is addressed here is the more difficult and fundamental question of what music *is* in itself, and what its place is in the divine scheme of things.

Few books venture into these elusive borderlands where theology, psychology, philosophy, aesthetics, semiotics, social anthropology and the history of ideas meet. So this book casts its net widely indeed. Some might say a bit recklessly. The threat is a loss of focus, the danger of broad-brush theories of everything that say nothing specific about anything. But an opportunity was glimpsed some years ago by a group of theologians in the north-east of England who believed that it would be fruitful to examine how these disciplines could interact and what light their meeting might shed on a relatively unexplored theological theme. That is the origin of this collection of papers. Perhaps the most a book like this can hope to do is raise questions, set an agenda. I think the authors will be satisfied if that happens. And certainly there is no denying the sense of enjoyment, excitement, creative *frisson* even, that has been around during the discussions stimulated by these papers when they were originally read.

THEOLOGY AT THE FRONTIER

Why does this debate matter?

A first reason is that there is a genuine theological issue here. To do theology is to reflect on our human experience in the light of faith. All aspects of life provide the raw material for theological reflection that draws on the insights of the Bible, the Christian tradition, and the experience of people of faith down the ages. One of the most creative developments in applied theology this century has been to bring theological perspectives to bear on a variety of 'new' disciplines: cybernetics, for instance, or cosmology or computer science. When the seventeenth-century philosopher Descartes said that God had created the natural numbers on his own, but the rest of mathematics was the work of human beings, he was pointing the way to a characteristically modern way of theologising. His platonistic theory of mathematics may not find many takers nowadays. But his recognition that the enterprises of science, mathematics and philosophy are fundamentally acts of partnership between human beings and God is basic to our way of doing theology today. And while it may sound like a typically Enlightenment attitude to the world, it does have deep roots in the Old Testament.

If science, why not art? It is surprising that music, which, the Yahwist tells us, is as old as the human race (Genesis 4:21), has not attracted the attention of theologians to the same extent. It is true that there is a burgeoning literature on religious and theological perspectives on the arts and aesthetics. But there has been little that focuses specifically on music. Most of what there is in English is referred to, at least by way of footnote, in this book. Deryck Cooke's pathfinding book *The Language of Music* (1959) now strikes us as very much of its age, but it did raise fundamental questions about the nature of music, although not from a theological point of view. That is not to say that there is any such thing as a 'theology *of* music' – those 'theology of ...' phrases sound very odd nowadays. But we do need theological frontiersmen and women who will take those questions on and provide us with creative theological insights into the nature of the musical enterprise: what is going on when musicians compose and perform, and where God is in it all.

That leads to my second reason for welcoming this book. It is that, like many other disciplines, music provides clues to the nature of the theological task. Indeed, to take the definition of theology seriously is to say that every area of human experience is capable of offering 'disclosures', has the potential, in other words, to reveal aspects of God to us. To go back to the disciplines that belong particularly to our own time, it is striking how much they have coloured theological language, given a distinctive twentieth-century nuance to classical theological affirmations, and even provided tools of their own to engage in the theological enterprise. I am not only thinking of natural or life sciences, but of human sciences such as psychology and sociology, information technology, cultural and media studies, literary theory, linguistics ... The list is endless. We are not always aware of how influenced we all are by modernity (and post-modernity, for that matter).

This provision of an array of different 'languages' is to recognise something very important: that 'theology' is not only done through the explicit use of human speech (least of all that of white Anglo-Saxon Protestants!). It also happens through many other forms of 'speech' and behaviour, often unconsciously. Among these, music surely has a prominent place. So to ask, 'How does music speak to us of God?' is not a frivolous question. It may well be absolutely central to how we understand what we are about as theologians and believers. When liturgists say (correctly) that people learn theology, not from Bible reading, creeds, pulpit utterances or liturgical formulae, but from the hymns they sing, they usually mean that the lyrics of hymns and songs tend to lodge far more securely in the memory than texts that are merely spoken. That may be for better or for worse. The logic of that insight points attention to how rhythm, melody and harmony all play a part as 'carriers' of a message, as transmitters of meaning. A 'good' or a 'bad' tune has as much to do with the formation of people's theological minds and hearts as 'good' or 'bad' texts do. In other words, the 'text' lies not only in the words but in the music and its performance. There are considerable hermeneutical ramifications to that.

So music and theology inform each another. And that leads to a third reason for suggesting that this meeting place is both crucial and creative. That is to do with the purpose of theology, which I take it has to do with ultimate meanings. Who are we? Why are we here? What is our destiny? These are the questions to which 'theology' proffers explorations, interpretations and, however tentatively, clues to possible answers. If theology is not about the human condition and its redemption, if it is not about human pain and its healing, if it is not about injustice and reconciliation, if it is not about God and the realisation that we are loved, then it is not about anything that really matters.

THE WORK OF ART

The rest of this foreword can perhaps set the debate in the wider context of art as it relates to this ultimate task of theology. If what I have so far said is near the truth, then the danger is that we try too hard to 'explain' what the artist is up to and what happens when we encounter his or her work. What Isadora Duncan said about dance is true of all the arts: 'If I could tell you what it meant, there would be no point in dancing it.' St Francis told his brothers: 'Preach the gospel. Use words if necessary.' There is some seduction, in a book like this, in collapsing the experience of music down to mere prose. In fact, *Art* is art's own best interpreter. Perhaps I may be allowed to cite as evidence a novel, a poem and a film to help us discover how art in general and music in particular have a fundamental part to play in the growth and nurture of the human spirit and the realisation of our God-given destiny.

Soul?

My novel is perhaps a slightly surprising choice: Nick Hornby's *High Fidelity*. Here is a cameo of a very ordinary encounter in a record shop:

> 'Have you got any soul?' a woman asks ... That depends, I feel like saying; some days yes, some days no. A few days ago I was right out; now I've got loads, too much, more than I can handle. I wish I could spread it a bit more evenly, I want to tell her, get a better balance, but I can't seem to get it sorted. I can see she wouldn't be interested in my internal stock control problems though, so I simply point to where I keep the soul I have, right by the exit, just next to the blues.[1]

Nick Hornby charts (forgive the word) the fortunes of an obsessive. His public world is the record shop; his private one his record collection, his relationships, and the inner complexities of the male psyche. The book is funny, wise and in its off-beat way, disconcertingly accurate on life and art and sexuality: what it means to be a man and know from the inside what lust, longing and love are. Records are both a metaphor of another world and a gateway to it:

> Is it so wrong, wanting to be at home with your record collection? It's not like ... collecting stamps, or beermats, or antique thimbles. There's a whole world in here, a nicer, dirtier, more violent, more peaceful, more colourful, sleazier, more dangerous, more loving world than the world I live in ...[2]

The question that runs through the novel is the woman's question in the shop: 'Have you any soul?' To which the answer is, it depends what you mean by soul, what it means to be a human being. That is art's great question down the centuries. That is religion's great question too.

Hornby stands in a long tradition that grapples with the function of art at an oblique or metaphorical level. Perhaps that is the only level at which it makes sense. The world of his record collection, both lovelier and more depraved than the world of his own experience, is not a fantasy world but the real one. Far from dulling his senses, music awakens in him a deeper awareness of reality just as fairy tales 'enchant' children into discovering at a mythical, symbolic level archetypal truths about the way things are. Whatever else is going on when we listen to music and feel ourselves stirred in some way, there is surely an act of *recognition* taking place, a response, a welcome, an embracing of truth that is too deep for words. We are back to the parallel languages we need in order to do theology.

Guide?

Next, the poem. Nick Hornby and Dante are seven hundred years and an infinity of worlds apart in the society they depict. Yet in a curious way, Hornby's record collection, embracing the entire spectrum of human life, seems to echo Dante's *Divine Comedy,* recognised as one of the universal works of the human spirit. There, Dante uses a literary device to open up the worlds of hell, purgatory and heaven, the worlds, that is, of *ourselves* and our human journey. The *Inferno* opens with a man lost in a dark wood, not knowing which way to turn in order to travel safely. Dante introduces us to the figure of the Roman poet Virgil, who shows him that he must travel through the circles of hell in order to come out the other side, climb the slopes of the mountain of purgatory and reach paradise. The metaphor here is of a journey into the self. Dante must travel 'down' into the dark places of terror, fear and sin that lurk in the human spirit in order to travel 'up' into divine light and grace and glory. We can only know God, Dante is saying, as we are prepared courageously to tackle the hard journey into knowing ourselves as we truly are.

Why Virgil? Why not, as in *Pilgrim's Progress,* an evangelist to point the way? Perhaps because Dante's Virgil does more than point the way. He is travelling companion and guide, the map-reader who helps Dante understand the landscapes he is passing through. He is the interpreter without whom these bewildering, often terrifying worlds don't make sense. And in his choice of Virgil, regarded by medieval

Christendom as not only the greatest of poets but on a par with the Old Testament prophets, Dante reveals an entire theory of the function of art in society. It is not to prettify, but to *illuminate* in the technical sense of the word: to uncover meanings and shed light on human experience. It does this, says Dante, not directly, full-frontally, so to speak, but by 'telling it slant', to use Emily Dickinson's memorable phrase: by means of analogy and metaphor that awaken the imagination and lead the soul into dimensions of truth that didactic prose by itself cannot penetrate.

The last part of the journey, the *Paradiso,* introduces us to a different guide. This is Beatrice, the love of Dante's life, whom he had glimpsed as a young man by the Ponte Vecchio in his native Florence, and was only to encounter once more in his life. Beatrice is Dante's symbol of beauty: glimpsed, perhaps, rather than embraced – for like Beatrice, beauty cannot be trapped and tamed by human beings, made subject to their whims and desires. Again, the message is clear, that beauty is to lead us by the hand into paradise and the vision of God. Only then does she bid farewell to Dante as he looks on him 'who made the sun and the other stars'. When we gaze on the God who embodies all beauty, art's work is done.

There is another echo here. In the literature of the Old Testament, wisdom is portrayed as a lady beckoning human beings into a relationship of truest reward and satisfaction. In this, Lady Wisdom stands in contrast to the prostitute at the street corner who seduces the unwary into the downward spiral of destructiveness and death. In one of the greatest wisdom poems of the Old Testament, she is depicted as the first of God's creative works, standing alongside him as 'master-worker', 'daily his delight . . . rejoicing in his inhabited world and delighting in the human race' (Proverbs 8:22–31). The image of Lady Wisdom dancing amid creation resonates to the themes both of art as a creative act, and as 're-creation' in its own right. She recalls Bruce Chatwin's evocative book *Songlines* where we learn how, in aboriginal cosmology, the world is 'sung' into being. The message is: without music, we could not exist. Like Beatrice, Lady Wisdom is a hypostasis of meaning that lies at the heart of life. We cannot live without wisdom, nor without beauty and art. They are not quite the same thing, but in so far as in Dante art and beauty are meant to make us wise, there is undeniably a close connection.

Redemption?

The film I want finally to mention opens up a different dimension to the rôle of music. Jane Campion's *The Piano* (1993) is rightly regarded as one of the best films of its decade. Set in the nineteenth century in New Zealand, it chronicles the fortunes of a dumb heroine Ada who is married off to a tyrannical and abusive husband. She has three ways of communicating: a writing tablet, her little daughter by a previous affair, and her piano. Both Flora and the piano enable her to break her silence and 'speak'; but the piano is her only vehicle for communicating her passionate emotions, what lies in the depths of this complex, agonised woman's heart. Ada falls in love with another man, Baines, a neighbour. The complex interactions within this triangle of obsession, domination, and redeeming love are resolved when Baines finally takes Ada and Flora with him in a boat away from the island. On the boat, Ada insists that the piano is thrown overboard. She deliberately catches her foot in the ropes holding it, and is pulled under by the instrument. Just in time, she extricates herself and climbs up to the surface to live again and find her own voice and freedom.

If the piano is the real heroine of this film, it is because it is such an eloquent symbol of the human predicament. To be human means to be heard, known and understood. Ada's piano is a complex metaphor of this, a transitional object that enables Ada to cling on to her humanity and keep her soul intact while the forces around her threaten to tear her apart. With her piano, she can move safely from one stage of life to the next. When it has served its purpose, it can 'die', and with it, her old self. The piano works at one level as a symbol of how music makes up for the deficiencies of other forms of speech, whether written words (epitomised by the writing tablet) or oral (her daughter, her mother's surrogate mouthpiece in much the same way as the Old Testament describes Aaron as Moses' spokesman or 'prophet': Exodus 4:16, 7:1). The late works of Beethoven show how *his* beloved piano, too, became just such a mouthpiece in the face of his increasing deafness. Perhaps only a deaf composer could have written, so movingly, the superscription to the *Missa Solemnis*, 'from the heart: may it go to the heart'. Those words perhaps encapsulate one message of *The Piano*.

But precisely because the piano is only a transitional object, there comes a time when there is no further use for it. And without it now (the film implies), Ada achieves resurrection and can speak for herself. So the film can be read in terms of music's redemptive rôle in human destiny. This places it in a long tradition of poetry and drama that does this. One example is John Milton's poem *At a Solemn Musick*, which interprets the entire story of creation (the state of 'perfect diapason'), fall (the 'harsh din' that 'broke the fair music that all creatures made / to their great Lord') and salvation (which is to be brought back 'in tune with heav'n') through the imagery of music.

Another is Wagner's music drama *Die Meistersinger*, set in sixteenth-century Nuremberg, where the prize-winning piece in the annual song contest is a symbol of the new, creative art against the old and the hidebound. But in the drama's story of individual human lives, the prize song is also the means through which love is declared and relationships redeemed. All these works affirm that music is a basic human need and experience in which tragedy is expressed, catharsis takes place and resolution is achieved. In *The Piano*, most clearly, music has a salvific function. Without it, we are less than human, and unable to reach our God-given destiny. That we experience music as gift and re-creation makes it a very apt symbol of divine grace. This is, perhaps, the Augustinian subtext to the film.

That is one reading of the film, perhaps the expected one. A more open-ended reading would take the sinking of the piano to the bottom of the sea, not as a redemptive moment but rather as a symbol that music shares in the ambivalence of things, is a victim of our brokenness, can even have destructive associations. The piano must 'die', and part of Ada with it, if another part of her is to live. When I was a student, in love with Wagner, I was advised by some Christian Union colleagues (who could not have been more fervently evangelical than I was at the time) not to flirt with art associated with Nazism. Associations can colour art: it can be meat offered to idols. Another film, *Amadeus,* raises the issue of how sublime art can derive from a mind so scatological and corrupted as Mozart's – something his greatest theological admirer, Karl Barth, had already commented on. Is the truth that sublimity is achieved *despite* the character of the conduit or the associations it can subsequently come to carry, in much the same way as Paul speaks about God's strength being made perfect in human weakness?

That music belongs to a world that is not yet healed hardly needs stating (and in the Yahwist's story, Jubal, 'the ancestor of all those who play the lyre and pipe' belongs to the progeny of Cain, very much part of a fallen world). What is much more difficult to put into words is the difference between music that catharises darkness, evil and pain (Britten's *War Requiem* for instance, or the late quartets of Beethoven) and music that may seem to reinforce it. Not long ago, a worshipper at the cathedral where I work complained to me about the liturgical mass setting that is something of our choir's party piece – the *Messe Solennelle* by Jean Langlais. This (to me) is a magnificent piece, bold, exhilarating, and driven from beginning to end by a furious energy. To her it was the epitome of our century's contradictions: violent, conflicted, disintegrating, pulling in the opposite direction of a liturgy that is meant to put us back together again as human beings. We agreed on the importance of not denying but offering in worship the angry realities of the world and of our own lives in the way the psalmists do. But we did not succeed in 'reading' the music in the same way. To her it was 'bad enchantment', not because the piece or the composer carried any negative 'associations', and not because it was *kitsch* – another issue again, but because it was intrinsically destructive, demonic even, by its very nature. To me, it was the exact opposite. But what are the theological issues at stake here, and how do we identify them?

This foreword can do no more than raise a few questions, whet the appetite for what is to follow in this book. I do not think it is claiming too much to say that the theme of these essays is far bigger and more central to Christian concerns than a rather *recherché* programme of intellectual logic-chopping. Like all good theology, it turns out to be about the whole of life, and what it means to long for and know and love God. To go back to Nick Hornby, it is about 'soul' – the soul of each of us, of humanity, of the world. It is about what the gospel warns us against losing. This book may help us to recover 'soul' and once again make contact with a lost part of ourselves.

NOTES

[1]   Nick Hornby, *High Fidelity*, London: Cassell, 1996, p. 67.
[2]   *ibid.*, p. 73.

Introduction and Overview

Timothy Hone, Jeff Astley and Mark Savage

> A friend persuaded me to go to Ely Cathedral to hear a performance of Bach's B minor Mass.... The music thrilled me ... until we got to the great SANCTUS. I find this experience difficult to define. It was primarily a warning. I was frightened. I was trembling from head to foot, and wanted to cry. Actually I think I did. I heard no 'voice' except the music; I saw nothing; but the warning was very definite. I was not able to interpret this experience satisfactorily until I read – some months later – Rudolf Otto's *Das Heilige*. Here I found it – the 'Numinous'. I was before the Judgement Seat. I was being 'weighed in the balance and found wanting'. This is an experience I have never forgotten.[1]

Music plays a deep and significant part in our own lives. We are convinced that it has a similar rôle in the lives of others. As Christians, and indeed as human beings, we believe that it is important to reflect on why this should be. In particular we are concerned to understand what the use we make of music reveals about our human nature, and to try to understand our involvement with music in a more theological context.

At the human level, we wish to concern ourselves with all music that has been valued by human societies, and not primarily with pieces that have at some time been labelled 'religious'. Although most of those who have worked with us have an enthusiasm and knowledge of a broad spectrum of serious 'art' music in the western tradition, as it has developed over the last thousand years, it is our conviction that the study of all human involvement with music is of significance. We believe that the skills of discrimination of pitch, metre, rhythm, timbre, and the recognition of formal devices such as repetition and variation, are shared in some measure by most human beings, and that on this basis it is appropriate to regard musical skills as being part of our human identity.[2] Therefore, in examining musical experiences critically, we need to ask what implications they might have for an understanding of our own nature.

In trying to approach music from a theological standpoint our concern has not been to begin with any dogmatic position, but rather to ask what the experience of music might reveal of the nature of God, in whose image we were created. All that we can realistically attempt is to reflect on musical experiences that have been meaningful to us, and hope that these might 'strike chords' for others. Our search, then, is for the theology implicit in musical encounters, as we hold them up to the light of God.

CONVERSATIONS

When we began to investigate the issues surrounding the place of music in our lives, it seemed important to start with some understanding of music on its own terms. We hoped that the insights of those involved with music as composer, performer and listener might provide a jumping-off point for a more wide-ranging discussion. Although it would have been possible to assemble a selection of quotations drawn from musicians who have previously allowed their thinking about music to be preserved in some permanent form, our preferred option was to identify individuals who might be prepared to engage with us in conversation, and to see where this might lead.

James MacMillan is a composer whose music has attracted great attention. His observations about the process of composition make a substantial contribution towards understanding the way in which a composer works with his or her material. The interview also brings into the foreground the concerns of a musician whose work clearly has the power to communicate with a large public, across a broad cross-section of age, and cultural and social backgrounds. A number of critics have seized on his unashamed espousal of religious and socio-political issues as an explanation for the enthusiastic reception his music has received. However, the nature of the music itself reveals why his work communicates so strongly: his distinctive musical voice uses melodic, harmonic and rhythmic language which has perceptible roots in other music of the twentieth-century mainstream. His compositions are evolutionary rather than revolutionary and his formal procedures are coherent. While some listeners may be unaware of the carefully calculated compositional procedures which lie concealed beneath the surface of music, its visceral impact provokes a direct and deeply satisfying response.

Martin Haselböck is a highly versatile musician working in Vienna. He is active as scholar, composer, organist, continuo-player and conductor. In a wide-ranging conversation he produced many fascinating insights. Performers have the highly responsible task of acting as intermediaries between composers and listeners. This is not a neutral rôle, since even the most carefully notated score is only a means which enables a pre-determined pattern of sounds to be brought into being. It is that pattern of sounds which is the music itself. While it is inevitable that performers will contribute to the musical experience from their own (re-)creative instincts, Haselböck shows great respect for the score. He suggests that a responsible reading needs to be made in the context of the possibilities which remain when inappropriate stylistic accretions have been stripped away. At the same time, he makes clear that each performance should be the result of a wide range of skills and experiences. Haselböck is also skilled as an improviser, and he makes fascinating comments about the difference he perceives between the acts of composition and improvisation.

The primary involvement with music for most people remains that represented by the rôle of listener. Our society tends to assume that listening is a passive function, and one to be taken for granted; we frequently relegate music to the background, and treat it as aural wallpaper. By contrast, it is vital for our purposes that we assert a positive and active rôle for the listener. **Mark Savage's** account of the impact of music in his own development may stimulate reflections by all of us for whom music seems an important, even essential, part of our daily living. The act of listening provides an immediate encounter with music, caught in the very moment of its performance, whether in the 'live' situation of a concert or as preserved in a recording. Savage argues that listening, too, is a creative process, to which we need to bring an active attention, as well as the willingness to become vulnerable to the potentially transforming experience it can offer. For those who are not primarily performers or composers, it is with the act of listening that the search for God in music begins.

These three conversations are not merely a backdrop for the more academic discussions which follow. We hope that they contain observations which will interact with and clarify the more analytical and formal work of the other contributors. In addition to their insights into the various aspects of musical engagement, they offer some illumination of the elusive process of creation which may be a key in understanding the relationship of music to other disciplines.

PERSPECTIVES

In order to develop our musical exploration, we have attempted in this volume to draw on a range of other disciplines and fields of study, believing that inter-disciplinary reflection is essential to a deeper understanding of the central place which music seems to occupy.

> Our minds are not infinite; and as the volume of the world's knowledge increases, we tend more and more to confine ourselves, each to his special sphere of interest and to the specialised metaphor belonging to it. The analytic bias of the last three centuries has immensely encouraged this tendency, and it is now very difficult for the artist to speak the language of the theologian, or the scientist the language of either. But the attempt must be made and there are signs everywhere that the human mind is once more beginning to move towards a synthesis of experience.[3]

Jeremy Begbie's paper shows that music can make an important contribution to our understanding of the self-communication of the triune God. In particular, he suggests ways in which an understanding of musical repetition can lead to a better understanding of two theological fields: multiple fulfilments of divine promises and multiple enactments of the Eucharist. First, he demonstrates the way in which music exists in time, and a musical composition creates its own virtual time which it structures in extreme detail through a control of metre. In this way music articulates our experience of time. At its most complex it can enable us to hear the flow of time in a series of layers, each moving with its own rhythmic characteristics, independent yet co-existing with the others. The hope it offers of being able to understand time in a sense other than the purely linear one is of profound interest from a theological point of view. He suggests that 'music "takes" our time and "returns it" to us re-shaped'. Secondly, Begbie's discussion of repetition in the Eucharist is profoundly valuable in reminding us that liturgy is something which is 'performed' – it is not simply words on a page but a means whereby the community renews its understanding of its relationship with God. Here repetition leads to renewal. In conclusion, Begbie suggests other areas where music offers the possibility of fresh understanding: a theological treatment of time itself; an understanding that the physical world is essentially time-bound, that temporality is part of God's dispensation; and a recognition that human beings are bodily creatures, whose behavioural rhythms reveal a fundamental relationship with time. Finally he raises questions about musical repetition in relation to wider social and cultural practices, and hints at the implications for the use of music in worship.

The reception of a theological text has been compared with the way in which we hear and respond to music, and the relationship between the Bible and its interpreter analysed in terms of the analogy of musical score and musician.[4] **Gordon Giles'** critique of the part that 'authentic' performance practice plays in our contemporary musical debate, and of the parallels with the reading of a biblical text, draws on the writings of the musicologist and performer Richard Taruskin. Taruskin suggests that our current pursuit of musical 'authenticity' may reveal more about our own preferences for performances which are 'clean-cut' and well regimented (a performance style which he suggests derives more from Stravinsky than the known habits of seventeenth- or eighteenth-century musicians) than they do about the past. By the same token, Giles suggests that an 'attempt to get back to basic Bible interpretation is symptomatic of a current trend, and reflects a "modernist" theology rather than any "historical" tradition'. It is important to be aware of this danger. Because musical works were first created at a point in history, they have a sense of belonging in part to that time and place. When they are re-created in our time and place they take on new meaning for us; but they are also potentially nostalgic, seeming to offer us a glimpse of worlds only accessible through music, together with the visual and literary arts. There are obvious connections and warnings here about the way in which we can similarly view Christianity, and in particular early Christian communities and our own earlier experience of Christian faith, with a similar nostalgia.

The philosopher can offer a valuable alternative way of looking at music. In his paper **Ian Ground** examines the basis of the claim that music expresses what cannot be put into words, the ineffable, and thus allows us to experience the transcendental. Drawing on Kant's *Critique of Judgement*, he argues strongly for a distinction between music *simpliciter*, and intentionally created musical works of art. Such works, he argues, are capable of 'being heard as meant' and demand (and reward) aesthetic contemplation. Not all music, he argues, belongs in this exclusive category: 'clearly most musical works are not works of art'. Although this may seem unnecessarily restrictive, the underlying suggestion that the use of music is not limited to providing a reward for aesthetic attention is implicit in several other papers in the collection. Finally, Ground makes an observation which shows the frailty of human beings as they attempt to communicate to one another their reactions to a piece of music. Perhaps it is when we feel that we have truly shared what we have really heard, that music has helped us to grasp the transcendental.

Within the social sciences, **John Sloboda's** paper presents the so closely follows the centenary of the birth of Duke Ellington, whose work was the inspiration for the liturgical events which are at the centre of this account.

A shared response, implicit or explicit, to a musical experience can be instrumental in bringing about communication between people. This may be more profound if people actually sing or play together. For this reason the place of music within the general education curriculum is crucial. **Coral Davies** reviews the recent history of music education and discusses practical work with young children in schools in a paper which shows the way in which music may be instinctively employed as a way of absorbing, intensifying and learning to cope with intense life experiences. Singing is a particularly natural form of human creativity, and these accounts of children singing their way into a deeper understanding of themselves and of the world in which they live, and which they share with others, remind us of what may be lost without this kind of educational opportunity.

Music has an important part to play in Christian education, understood as Christian formation, and the implications of this for adult learning are discussed fully in the paper by **Jeff Astley** and **Mark Savage**. The composer/performer/listener relationship is suggested as a model for understanding that between tradition, educator and learner. A discussion about the ways in which music helps us to structure reality and to acknowledge emotional response in a positive way leads into a plea for a Christian education that engages the whole person, through both the cognitive and the affective aspects of brain functioning. The authors revisit aspects of communication and revelation, and take seriously the questions which music raises for issues of hermeneutics in theological studies. In addition, they take note of the possibilities raised by music as a theological metaphor, expanding the categories explored by Begbie and others. Finally they offer an exploration of some of the ways in which music can be used in the practice of Christian education in the context of the claim that music enables essential Christian values, such as love, compassion, hope, contrition, and even faith itself, to be expressed more tellingly for the listener than can the words of traditional theological formulation.

As the opening quotation reveals, music can be a locus of the numinous: an overwhelmingly intense experience in which the 'Other' comes close, sometimes frighteningly or disturbingly, sometimes (and often at the same time) with exhilaration, entrancement and even with ecstasy. Ultimately, all our contributors point back to the musical encounter. In so doing, they may lead us beyond the music to an encounter with the Other, in whatever form that may take.

NOTES

[1]   Quoted by Alister Hardy in *The Spiritual Nature of Man*, Oxford: Oxford University Press, 1979, p. 85.

[2]   See John Blacking, *How Musical is Man?*, Seattle: University of Washington Press, 1973.

[3]   Dorothy Sayers, *The Mind of the Maker*, 1941, reprinted in The Library of Anglican Spirituality, London: Mowbray, 1994, p. 24

[4]   See Nicholas Lash, 'Performing the Scriptures', in *Theology on the Way to Emmaus*, London: SCM, 1986 and Frances Young, *The Art of Performance: Towards a Theology of Holy Scripture*, London: Darton, Longman and Todd, 1990.

PART ONE:
CONVERSATIONS
on the Practice of
Creation in Music

1

Creation and the Composer

An Interview with James MacMillan

In your 'Contemporaries of Christ' radio talk [15 March 1994] *you began by saying 'I have been a composer since I was ten years old. By that I mean that the urge to create music was a simultaneous experience with picking up my first musical instrument. Wanting to be a musician has always meant wanting to write music.' I wonder if you can tell us something of how it feels to have the urge to create in that particular way.*

I was thinking about this earlier and was trying to remember a time before I played an instrument – before I was a musician – and tried to think back to those childhood days to see if I had changed at all in picking up an instrument. I have come to the conclusion that being given access to a musical instrument channelled a creativity which was there anyway, a creativity which I think is in everyone and perhaps could have manifested itself in many different ways. With me it was obviously going to be manifested in music. I think that as a child, teenage and adult composer, the one binding element common to every stage of the creativity has something to do with wanting to give vent to that dream-like state which only a child knows. They say an ideal childhood is one in which you seem to exist in a kind of dream-like state until you are about ten years old. Then other important parts of the psyche, other parts of the personality have to open up, otherwise you don't function as a normal human being. But for me, and I think for many creative people, that dream-like childishness never disappears, it never closes up. When I think about composing, a lot of my thoughts turn to something very childlike in essence, giving vent to that kind of wild reverie which, through education, has allowed itself to channel itself into structured forms of music.

What was your first instrument? Were you a pianist?

I started playing recorder, trumpet and piano all more or less simultaneously. But I think the recorder was first, and within days of being given access to that instrument I wanted to write music for it, to create my own themes, melodies and so on, and in any way possible to write those things down.

So the writing down is actually quite an important part of it. It's not just that you wanted to improvise, experiment and doodle with the instrument in the way that so many youngsters do?

The urge to improvise and to be physical with the instrument was certainly there, but I suppose that what edged me into something as disciplined as classical music, rather than becoming a jazz or rock musician, was that I needed to have some kind of literate control over what this physical thing was.

What kinds of music were around? What sort of musical influences were you hearing in the home?

My mother had been a pianist at school, although she had given up playing by the time I started. She had had a bad experience when she had been pushed into music by an over-zealous father, who thought she was going to be the musician in the family when she wasn't. She refused to have a piano in the house for years. I asked for a piano and that was a surprise to her. Then certain gates opened: there was music I was unaware of in the house, which she had kept hidden. I gained access to composers who interested me: Mozart, Beethoven and Haydn in those early days. Because I am Scottish, people sometimes ask me if there was traditional music in the background. There wasn't, and an interest in that came much later. For me it was the classics right at the beginning.

Do your early pieces sound like James MacMillan or a little like Bach, Beethoven or Brahms?

They sound like a child's doodlings, I suppose. I look back with surprised pride at some of them; there's a little piano piece in A minor for example that comes back to me, I remember every note. But I found some old scores from when I was about ten or eleven, and it is quite clear I was wanting to emulate my heroes: Mozart, Beethoven, Haydn, Wagner. There is even a piece I wrote at the age of eleven called *Tribute to Richard Wagner* for Six Tubas and Orchestra!

*How did you grow away from that? Did someone say, 'Come on,
you can't just go on sounding like Wagner for the rest of your life'?
Or was it something in you that began to take a different direction?*

Right up to the time I went to university I had no idea what it really
meant to be a composer – what it meant in the day to day living of
your life. Was there a career in it? Could you make money at it?
These things never occurred to me; I wasn't actually interested in
them. It was only when I left university and I knew I still wanted to
compose, it was the one thing I wanted to do in life. I began to realise
it wasn't an easy road to take and that perhaps I had to be engaged in
complementary work in order to make a living. The urge has never
left me, and it's an urge I haven't abandoned and would never
abandon now.

*So at the university stage you didn't necessarily see yourself as a
composer; composition was just something you did alongside other
musical activities?*

Yes, although it was the one aspect of music I was interested in above
all others. I had no idea that it would be a life-long activity, but it was
certainly the one thing as an obsessive teenager, adolescent and young
adult, that I was pursuing all the time regardless of career prospects.

What were the main influences on your development at university?

I was an undergraduate at Edinburgh University and my teachers there
were people like Kenneth Leighton, one of many people involved with
church music. My style and influences, I suppose, came through him.
The English tradition meant a lot to me at that stage. Gradually
throughout university I became interested in different types of music;
not just music of our own western classical tradition, but music of
other cultures from the other side of the world: the classical cultures
of India and Asia, and folk traditions as well, from all over the world
including those of my own Scottish background. For any classical
musician, any composer whose tastes and influences were being
broadened so dramatically in that way, the real draw was towards the
avant-garde, or the remnants of the avant-garde, because it was within
that small ghetto-esque community that one found like-minded people
with boundless curiosity in every form of musical invention. So I
began to be interested in the European avant-garde and the great
figures like Boulez, Berio and, from America, Cage – all these people
bringing a new aesthetic and a new mind-expanding experience. I
have since come to see that whole experience as perhaps not neces-

sarily as mind-expanding as it might have been. In many ways, once it became an orthodoxy it was quite restrictive. It is like any revolutionary thread in culture – it cannot always maintain its revolutionary aspect and some day it will become an orthodoxy itself. That is why in a sense I turned away from it, and why many composers are looking for ways to develop their creativity in ways proscribed to them by avant-garde orthodoxy.

I was going to ask what your starting point for a piece of music is. In view of what you have just said I guess at different times you have had different ways of starting: that at times your starting point has been the impact of other things you have heard and at others an idea from outside. Sometimes, presumably, you just experience the urge to put down this particular piece on paper because you can hear it in your head and actually need to do something with it. Is that a fair way of looking at it?

Yes; to give as broad a picture as possible of the starting points available to me, it's an accurate picture. Sometimes the inspiration, the starting point, is as boring or undescriptive as a series of notes, and it's down to the composer to make of that raw material something transcendent. On other occasions the starting point has been something completely extra-musical: something literary perhaps, or historical – even contemporary-historical, political. Alternatively, some aspect of religious faith, tradition or liturgy can provide the starting point.

Assuming the starting point is a series of notes, where do the notes come from? If we are not talking about a piece like Veni, Veni, Emmanuel *where the notes already exist, where does the basic first idea come from?*

A very good question. If one doesn't have a musical *objet trouvé* like a piece of plainsong or a folk song and has to start with nothing, one has to inject and envelop the raw material with substance and integrity, interest and worth which don't come from any other source. For me, in those pieces that have begun like that (there are moments in the orchestral piece *Tryst* for example), the antecedents lie in the avant-garde, or the Second Viennese School which started with the raw material of reorganised pitch but not necessarily connected to any mode or scale. The organisation of pitches has always been fascinating to me – the fact that Schoenberg, Webern and Berg were able to work with that raw material. For me the most interesting aspect of the Second Viennese School was when that revolutionary treatment of pitch-handling nevertheless seemed to have a resonance of the tradition from which they came. Of the three, I think Berg is probably the figure of most interest to me. So when I handled my series, my twelve-note rows, they always had a connection, not so much with tonality, but with triadic music. Instead of using twelve notes in a row, I would use perhaps twelve chords, twelve triads each of which would have its basis on the twelve notes of the chromatic scale, which would set off resonances which touched the music of the past, known to us through tradition and experience, through listening to it and loving it.

Are you saying that if you are selecting something like a twelve-note row it is a question of organising notes into a row, rather than having the row appear complete as an inspiration? Or is it that the row is almost arbitrary, because it is the processes of organisation that come after it exists that really interest you?

I think the process of working with the material is crucial to me. It does not necessarily mean that the music resulting from that intricate abstract working is any less inspired or emotional in its potential than music which has its inbuilt resonances of the past and its roots in emotion and easy, facile – perhaps surface – human feeling. I think the composer can, through integrity, touch deeply into the human spirit regardless of his musical material, whether it is purely manufactured or absorbed from other sources known more to us.

I would like to push you a little further. At one point the page is blank. At some point, however much later, you have this basic material. How do you know you have chosen the basic material you want to work with? Do you recognise at some point that it is okay, and you can go on to the rest of the piece because you know the basic material will serve the purposes you want?

You have to live with your material until it's completely familiar and at one with you, until that material, no matter how abstractly organised, can become a source of expression to you on a par with any given melody from any other source, from the past or from tradition.

By way of contrast, when you have taken an idea or a subject as a starting point how long does it take before that subject gives you a musical basis? Does it suggest a form, a texture?

It can change and it can be different from piece to piece. The extra-musical impulse is most potent when the composer feels that the extra-musical story, message or point has enlivened his creativity so much that he burns with passion for dealing with that subject, so much so that it will live with him and inspire every aspect of the composition. So there has to be, right from the word go, something which causes an initial burst of inspiration, a burning burst of inspiration which will send its shock waves through the more mundane nitty-gritty working of the music. It has to sustain itself.

Visitatio Sepulchri is based on the Easter morning story of the visit of the Marys to the Tomb. At what point did that subject suggest to you musical ideas?

That was easy in the sense that there is a whole wealth of plainsong associated with the *Visitatio Sepulchri* drama and my musical *objet trouvé* in that case was some of the plainsong – certain allusions from plainsong, certain remembrances of what a plainsong does musically – and a sense of the static drama that could be made from such a dramatic encounter. There is a balance therefore between that which is purely abstract and that which is purely dramatic. These balances must be dealt with, handled and balanced all the way through.

A little later in the radio talk I referred to at the start of this conversation you discussed your faith in these words: 'I have always regarded myself as an averagely unembarrassingly neutral kind of Catholic – observant but not unorthodoxly zealous, practising but not pious. My spirituality has always been cosily and privately under wraps, inoffensively imperceived by those in contact with me. The words "composer" and "Catholic" for most of my life have seemed entirely unrelated, fairly and squarely compartmentalised. The music I wrote in my twenties, for example, has no religious dimension whatever.' What sort of music was that? I think we are talking about pieces up to about 1989.

Yes. This was music which had been written through the influence of teachers, and through experiences of other composers whose work I admired greatly – composers of the avant-garde, of the last twenty to thirty years, who seemed through their techniques to indicate to younger composers that a good solid grounding in compositional technique had to be acquired before anything more mature could really be addressed. So as a student I was concerned foremost and fundamentally with the basic stuff of musical technique: how do you organise the raw material of sound and music into a coherent musical shape and do that regardless of outside ideological impingement? I still maintain that any composer, regardless of what motivates him ideologically and extra-musically, has to have as secure a degree of control as possible over his raw material – over any given material he choses to use from one piece to the next. It is that logical side of the composer's nature which has to sustain any non-logical or arbitrary or freer decisions and impulses which may arise at any time in a creative person's life and inspiration.

Did it ever occur to you then, or has it since, that those creative patterns actually have a kind of theological dimension in themselves, in that they actually show what it is to create, what it is to develop; and that that perhaps has something to offer in terms of theological insight as well?

This is where you will have to probe as hard as you can. I am not an academic in any sense of the word. My interest in theology, little as it is, is inspired because of my background, because of recent trends which have shown to me there is obviously some kind of connection between faith and music.

Having formerly kept these two areas compartmentalised, why did you suddenly allow the two to come together?

I think it is something to do with maturity. There are more than just two compartments, but the two you mention are the fact that I suppose I am a religious being with a definite spiritual dimension to my life and the fact that I am a creative musician; until very recently those compartments didn't seem to have any connection whatsoever. There were other compartments as well – the fact I was interested in other musical cultures, the fact that I was a folk musician for a while. I used to play round about the folk clubs and bars in Scotland with a little folk band, and that was quite extra to the experience of being a classical musician. But that didn't seen to have any connection with the serious business of writing serious music, or for that matter any religious connection. There is also the fact that I was a political animal as well, interested in politics and active politically, and that was yet another compartment that seemed to be completely disconnected with any other. For a while I thought that was the way it was going to be, that I had to lead a schizophrenic life in which there would be pockets of experience, pockets of friendships made and pockets of associations formed, but these associations were entirely unrelated. For some reason – I don't know whether I can describe it just now – those barriers between the compartments, the walls separating them, began to disappear so that one aspect of life began to cross-fertilise another and I began more naturally to see an ability or potential, for example to use my interest in folk culture in an artistic or high-art serious music way. I began to see the potential to unembarrassedly and unself-consciously express the religious dimension and also the political dimension in the so-called serious business of composing. It is something to do with maturity, a growing confidence and realisation that the compartments are not necessarily mutually exclusive, that they can cross-fertilise. But there are always dangers in expressing a religious point of view or a religious metaphor in music, or a political point of view. There are pitfalls for the composer who chooses to do that.

Can you identify works in which there is a religious or political dimension for the first time?

The first time it worked for me successfully was a piece called *Búsqueda* which is Spanish for 'search'. It is a music-theatre piece written as a companion piece to Berio's *Laborintus 2*, an example of the avant-garde at its most labyrinthine and a work which has always fascinated me, but which on another level has repelled me because of its deliberately obfuscatory complexity. I was asked to write a piece for the same event at which I would be acting as a joint associate conductor for the Berio. For my companion piece I decided to use text from the Mothers of the Disappeared from Argentina, women whose loved ones have been taken away and, as we now know, murdered by the regime there. These women wrote very simple poems. They are not great sophisticates, they are simple peasant women who under other circumstances would not have written any poetry whatsoever. To see the simplicity and beauty and emotional defiance of the poems caused that initial burst of inspiration for me. I suppose that was a revelation for me, because I saw the possibility of expressing both a political standpoint – that is, an act of solidarity with people oppressed – and combining that with a religious potential: the possibility of writing a piece which would give full flood, full vent to a religious faith. I suppose the fact of these simple peasant women who were devout believers, devout Christians, being drawn into the political process was an inspirational thing for me. So the piece uses the words of these women interlaced, intermingled with the text of the Latin Mass. There were points in the poems where I could find distinct correlations between the words of the Kyrie, or the Gloria or the Credo, and what the women were saying in their poems. So the possibility of writing a piece simultaneously political and spiritual in a very deep way, but also giving me scope to pursue musical complexities, all came about together; this was the way forward for me, the way of breaking down the barriers between the different compartments.

Were you aware at that concert of an audience which was expecting one kind of piece from James MacMillan and actually got another kind?

I was very young. I don't know if people in the audience knew James MacMillan's previous music.

It is clear that because of the kind of music you write, and perhaps as a result of bringing these elements together, you get audiences who react very strongly to your work. You aren't the kind of composer who has a very small cult following, while nobody else takes their music on board at all. You are actually writing music people enjoy or value – they turn up, they listen to it, they buy recordings of it. Do you think that's just a musical thing going on there or is it partly because the ideas themselves are helping people to have something to latch on to?

It is hard to say. I certainly have met like-minded souls in audiences. There are many different types of people who feel open to my music and all for different reasons: fellow Christians there for a spiritual aspect; also agnostic or atheistic politically minded people who are there for the politics they perceive in it, or for the sense of standing with the dispossessed – it's not just Christians who take that stance. There is also, back home, a sense amongst the cultural community of 'Well, we've never had many classical composers who've come from within our midst who have had music performed elsewhere. We should be perhaps looking at this.' Of course there is a sort of cultural renaissance in Scotland which is partly to do with looking again at what it is to be Scottish and finding out more about the identity of Scotland and its people – perhaps indulging in a bit of navel-gazing. But there are some positive aspects to that as well as negative. So there are many different reasons why people come to a particular composer. I suppose it is, getting back to these compartments again, the fact that I happen to have many interests and many different experiences in musical and general cultural life and a wide range of associates.

From the kind of political and religious ideas you have hinted at, presumably it is very much part of your concern that you should not just write music for an élite. I assume you actually hope to write music which can touch all sorts of people. With that in mind what sort of changes in musical education would you hope for as a composer?

As a classical composer who is fundamentally interested in the serious western tradition, and as someone from a background which normally had no access to that tradition – from the industrial or post-industrial working class – I see that, regardless of class, people should have access to the best music. Now that class barriers are beginning to disappear there should be some evangelical work done for music, going into the grass roots and taking this great culture of ours to people who like me would not normally have had access to it. There needs to be a social rôle for the composer, then. Not all composers have that facility or aspect of their character. Most composers are very shy. I cannot imagine someone like Messiaen, for example, going into schools and doing workshops. I am also very shy, but I have been able to overcome that because of the necessity to evangelise on behalf of music, both the western tradition and contemporary music. So although these have been rather patchy developments, the whole new notion of composers working with orchestras, education authorities and schools and taking this culture of ours to the grass roots to schools, communities that don't get access to it, is greatly to be admired and encouraged.

How do you relate to the rock/pop scene?

I have a rather ambiguous attitude to it now. As a teenager, I played in a rock band and I suppose for a while I maintained an interest in popular culture because I enjoyed feeling part of it. Now I sometimes feel my interest in pop culture is simply the necessity of needing to 'know your enemy'. In many ways pop culture is our greatest hurdle, that easy, facile, candy-floss culture flung at people the world over. A culture like ours has its integrity deep inside itself, not immediately visible in technicolour; we have a really strong phobia to that superficial gloss, but we need to know what it is about in order to counteract it.

Presumably in educational terms you would hope that a composer going into school could actually help people to create things with more worth, substance and interest than most of the music young people listen to most of the time.

I think so. It is being creative from square one that I would like to see encouraged. I think I've already indicated, when talking about creativity and childhood, that every child is inherently creative, and it sometimes can take a composer or another artist acting as a catalyst, an *animateur* rather than a teacher – the rôles should not be confused – which can sometimes provoke a young person out of the lethargy in which popular culture sometimes confines them.

What do you hope people will hear in your music? How do you want an audience to respond?

For me there has to be a balance between that which is overtly of the heart and that which is directly from the head, and to allow one to get out of synch, out of balance with the other causes an imperfection in the music. I think this has been a problem with a lot of the cerebral avant-garde experience, that the musical roots in emotion and spirit became blurred and perhaps even rejected. On the other hand, music which simply wears its heart on its sleeve with no real logical, cerebral control can be flabby, can lose itself, can be short-lived, short-circuited. The balance, I hope, will communicate itself to an audience listening to my music: music which I hope moves them, which will appeal and relate to them and touch them at different levels, but without ever wanting to proselytise, without ever wanting to preach and allow that music to become a kind of Christian agitprop. The responsibilities on the Christian composer are to open up windows on the divine, windows on the things hidden to normal everyday experience for most listeners, for most music lovers.

Is that something you plan to happen, as you write the music, or is it something you hope happens of itself?

If you plan to make it happen it becomes a form of proselytisation; if you allow it to become a conscious priority in what you do, there are problems, I think. For me it is relying on instinct, on a kind of spiritual antenna which is at work anyway, forcing me and inspiring me to write. Hopefully that antenna will generate a link through the communication process to the listener.

Does it worry you that most people aren't going to hear the kind of organisational things that you probably spend a great deal of your time planning and which have actually formed a large part of writing the piece ? Or do you assume that they notice them at a level without being able to recognise and verbalise about them?

I think a listener subconsciously feels whether a piece has been strenuously organised or not. A listener, even an unsophisticated listener, can feel a piece falling to bits from within. A listener is then perceiving the failure of abstract forces at work in the music, constructive things that are not working. Conversely, he can feel when those constructive aspects are working and it can aid all the deeper levels of communication, the emotional communication, the spiritual aspect of musical communication. If the constructivist aspects are working well, everything else can be channelled well.

Let's turn to a more specific discussion of your work Tryst. *Could you tell us what was in your mind as you were writing the central section?*

The starting point for that section was a love poem by William Soutar, a Scottish poet who died in the 1950s. He wrote in two languages, English and Scots. His intellectually explorative work was done in the English language but his more intimate work, where he addressed the beloved or God, was done in the Scots tongue. These are very beautiful, very simple poems giving a resonance of centuries ago. When I saw the poems I decided to try and set them as songs, but in a way which would provide a kind of musical counterpart to the words, that is, a musical style which also exuded something of the ancient Scottish ballad tradition. They were a result of my involvement with folk music: I wrote these songs and was proud that people thought they were ancient Scottish songs – that was the point of them. But when I finished with the folk band the life of these songs was redundant, I suppose. But I had on another hand given myself a kind of *objet trouvé* to work with, a *cantus firmus* if you like. What I have done in the middle section is to take one of the melodies I used for the Soutar poem 'The Tryst' and subject it to a kind of extension/augmentation of the durations of the intervalic sequences, going over and over little intervalic cells, back and forth, just enjoying the sound of one intervalic leap to the other before moving on and extending the whole process of the melody over a much longer time-span, embellishing the result of the augmentation as I went. I suppose it was a kind of improvisation on the page, taking a melody and doing on the page that which a jazz musician would do live; in a sense being improvisational over a period of weeks or months in the way a jazz musician might be improvisational over a period of minutes. The Soutar love song setting provided me with a *cantus firmus* round which I wrapped another layer of musical flesh. But at the core of this body is a kind of skeleton or heart, which because of its history is deliberately rooted in a tradition, that great reservoir of Celtic traditional music. It is almost as if I wanted to orientate myself in this piece and acknowledge that I am writing the music in the late part of the twentieth century, a music which makes me want to be proud in its invention, to be as creative and innovative with the given material as possible, knowing it has its backbone deeply rooted in something very ancient. I suppose what I am trying to do with this and many other pieces – instead of being a kind of musical iconoclast (as the avant-garde were in trying to dig up the past and ignore it) – is to show that one can have a relationship with tradition which is not necessarily reactionary, which still has one face looking to the present and open to the future, while at the same time looking over one's shoulder to the past and feel it is a valid artistic position to be in. It's not a conservative position to take up.

What are the other elements that are going on there? The harmonic style creates a real moment of stillness right at the heart of the piece as a whole. Rhythmically it is very different from the ostinatos and almost Stravinskian Rite of Spring-*like rhythms that are going on elsewhere.*

The piece has five sections and we are discussing the third of them. The outer sections 1, 2, 4 and 5 are much more propelled by rhythmic considerations, polyrhythms and irregular rhythms. I wanted a piece which was not necessarily symphonic in its design. It's quite episodic and doesn't give the impression of being a symphonic through-composed organic piece at all. But there was a necessity for an element of contrast, so that after two sections of music in which the fundamental priority was perhaps rhythm, there is now a section which dispenses with obvious rhythmic interaction and deals with texture and melody as its priority. Even although the melodies are quite obscure, hidden and inter-woven, the mode of working is initially a melodic one.

With a big piece like this with a duration of about twenty-seven minutes, what came first? Did you write in detail one section at a time, or did the overall design come first?

Soutar's love song was the genesis of it and that pre-dated the composition of the orchestral piece by a few years. The song has lived through various other forms: there is a little violin and piano piece for example called *After the Tryst* which was the next stage down the line from the song – the first working of the given material. This piece is the second stage. It is almost as if you start with one thing, expand it into something else and then expand that thing into some other thing.

It could go on. There is a clarinet quintet which used the same procedures and the basic sound material, although by that stage it was much
more into my bones and I wasn't needing to think of it too self-
consciously. I was able to work it more as I would anything else.

*I suppose in a sense you could say that that central section has a
very spiritual kind of atmosphere, a spiritual kind of sound, but it is
a very different kind of music from the kind of spiritual music which
has become very fashionable at the moment, the spiritual pieces
which have entered the best-seller charts, those of Tavener and Arvo
Pärt and Górecki's* 3rd Symphony. *How do you see that kind of
music? It seems to me that that style is something you've not exactly
embraced and yet are you perhaps doing something parallel to it?*

The first thing I think I need to say is that I find that music very beautiful – seductively so. I would defend it passionately in a company of
avant-garde-ists who disparage it as playing to the gallery and playing
down to the lowest common denominator principles in audience taste.
However, I have obviously got to think about how I relate to that
music as a fellow composer and why my music is different from what
they do, and the fact that that music seems to want to set up a static
transcendent state all the time, in which there is no dialectic in the
normal western sense. I suppose they have deliberately turned their
backs on the dialectic organic process that takes place in western
music, to go for a kind of iconic effect in sound – the static image in
sound. You are right to notice a difference, because in my music there
is conflict – there is violence a lot of the time; there is, even in a
serene piece like the central section of *Tryst*, conflict between the
different battling tonalities. It is not as serene and floating a tranquil-
lity as one might get in Górecki or Pärt. I think the way I think about
it is that they have deliberately turned their back on a particular tradition and, thinking about it in spiritual terms, on the corporeal nature
of man's humanity. I think they aim for post-struggle vision – it's a
vision of the Resurrection. I can understand it in Tavener's case which
is very much an Orthodox thing, the icon of the resurrection, the transcendent Christ. I have heard Tavener himself say that he feels very
uncomfortable with the image of the crucified Christ which he sees as
an image of defeat, something which has to be re-interpreted or re-
drawn. I have come to terms with the fact that as a Catholic one
cannot escape from this rather violent image in western Christianity.
One has to deal with it, come to terms with it, and in coming to
terms with it in music one has the violence of the crucifixion, the
conflict and the unpalatable, before the resolution and liberation of

resurrection. I would say there is definitely a redemptive aspect or potential to my music, but it needs to have that conflict gone through and fought through before it's reached.

Presumably, people listening to it are going to engage with that conflict in a way which may well be more helpful to them because it relates much more to life as it is lived, rather than simply offering them a 'cloud nine' spiritual alternative to real life.

Your words, not mine. As I say, it is music which I love dearly, but it is music which seems to achieve a spiritual 'feel good' factor in quite an immediate easy way. Perhaps that is part of the aesthetic, that's the intention and I wouldn't want to disparage it at all. Perhaps it has come from a tradition which is not mine and it can be discussed and explained by a different set of cultural criteria.

Certainly I have heard Tavener say that he writes that way out of necessity now, because he sees it as the only way in which he as an Orthodox composer can write. He in fact very much disparages his own earlier music because he sees it as having taken a wrong turning – which is perhaps fine for him as an individual. The problem can be that some people think that there is now only one way of writing religious music – the emphasis is entirely on getting this spiritual other-worldly dimension into the music in order to offer a kind of escapist route to God. Your music actually shows a very different approach, one which I feel is very welcome.

Can I ask you now, how important are performers? What do they do to your music?

Mostly, if the communication and relationship are right, they bring it to life and interpret the mere symbols (that's all the music on the page is) and breathe life into it. The music must become a living organic entity which needs their input. I have generally had a very good relationship with performing musicians. There is a residual suspicion of the living composer that has to be obliterated from any musician who has lived through the avant-garde and has had to deal with some very complex scores which are not easy to interpret. I am not saying my music is easy on any level – it is hard to play, it keeps them busy, it taxes them. But I would like to think they are able to feel that the pain of working hard at a piece of music can bear fruit, and the communication of the emotion and depth of the music is all the more potent and alive if that stretching of their ability and musicianship has been undertaken.

Have you sometimes been surprised when you have heard a piece for the first time, especially an orchestral piece? However carefully you calculate and however finely you can hear the textures as you write it, have you ever been surprised by the effect 'in the flesh'?

'Surprised' isn't the word. I am too busy worrying, when I first hear a piece of music, about whether things are going to work as they come alive in sound. I get elated when things do work and disappointed when they don't. If something doesn't work I go back to the drawing board and change it. Large chunks of pieces have suddenly gone because they messed up the structure of the piece. It is usually large chunks of music which go, rather than playing about with little details.

And that is something you only realise at the point when you hear the whole piece?

More or less, although after it happens a few times you begin to get an instinctive feel for what is right and hope to make more of a success of large- or small-scale design with every subsequent piece.

If a performer turns a phrase in a particular way, with that little hesitation that you hadn't planned, does that irritate you or does it add a whole different dimension and you are glad that it continues the creative process?

Mostly I am delighted by it. I've never really been irritated by an interpretation. I usually am quite willing to let go of a piece emotionally. It is like letting a child go. You either let it go reluctantly (there are problems in a kind of father/child relationship) or you are mature enough to let it go naturally. When I hear a piece of music coming to life in many different guises, with many different types of performers and interpreters, that just fills me with delight.

If you perform it yourself do you react to it differently when you start to play?

Yes, there is a flip side of creativity that has to take over, a different set of disciplines has to be brought in in communicating with players, to get structures to work and get an ensemble to work. In a sense I can be quite detached from the fact that I was the composer of the piece. I think you have got to be.

Lastly, how do you feel about music in church? You presumably go to your local Catholic church. Does it distress you, what is happening in church music? Are you encouraged?

It depends. Mostly I am distressed, I must admit. I see the principles of Vatican II being thoroughly misrepresented and the tradition of the church being thrown out. It is almost as if they've thrown the baby out with the bath water. There has been an iconoclasm in the Catholic Church about what it means to be Catholic in a cultural sense, in a musical sense. For the last ten years (a bit longer in Scotland – it may be different in England) there has been an embarrassment about the great wealth of Catholic tradition, and that was never meant to be. If you look through the Vatican II documents, plainsong, for example, is held up to be one of the most spiritual channels of music and a music suitable to be used in a modern liturgy. The great choral tradition is also discussed as an aid for the faithful to a deeper spiritual understanding, and that seems to be disappearing as well. There are cultural problems as well, the fact that the Catholic Church in Scotland has always been a workers' church. It has been a poor community, and access to music lessons in the past has never really been very easy, so you don't tend to find professional musicians within the Catholic community in Scotland. That's a very practical reason why music is in decline.

Is that something you as a composer feel you want to address, or do you feel that the kind of music you want to write needs a different kind of public – that essentially you need a concert-going public to appreciate what you are doing?

I would like to think that I as an individual composer was able to turn my hand to various things, to be an artist as well as an artisan. To write good church music, good liturgical music, whether for congregation or for choir, one has to have an understanding of tradition and recent tradition and the reasons why there have been changes in liturgy and the need for the congregation to feel more part of the liturgy. Many musicians, you may have found this yourself, get suspected of being Tridentinists because they talk about tradition favourably and it's not the case. I'm a great supporter of Vatican II but I don't see why the fact of being supportive of the changes should have edged me out into a cultural wilderness. That's where a lot of Catholics want to see me!

2

Creation and the Performer

An Interview with Martin Haselböck

What is your earliest musical memory?

I come from a family where music played a major part. My father is in the same profession, my mother was a professional musician and teacher, so there has always been music around. I had two prime experiences as a very small child. One was to hear a recording of a trumpet concerto which I think, looking back, pushed me into the baroque craze. The other was strange: a strong musical experience which I had as a very small child when I went with cousins to the circus. It was not a normal circus band, it must have played some higher class music, and some of the tunes stayed in my head. These were my first impressions of music, but it is hard to tell because there was always music around in the family.

What was your first instrument?

I started early in two directions. I learned the recorder as all small children do, but later I found a very good teacher and developed my playing. Then came piano lessons from the age of four or five. My first teacher may have been the strongest: when I switched full time to organ when I was about twelve I had the feeling that my piano standard was already as good as it was to be later on. I didn't learn very much more about piano playing after that.

Who was your first piano teacher?

A lady in Vienna who specialised in work with children, but she had a few students who later developed into famous concert pianists. Her name was Miss Riegler. She was very strict, but never gave you the impression that it was really hard work. She always made it seem natural to work.

Your father is a professional church musician?

He is now in his last years as Professor of Organ at the Church Music Department in Vienna – a professional church musician. He did a lot for German language church music in Austria. I am very much formed by my family, although his background was so totally different. He came from a very poor farm family and it was impossible for him to have professional teaching. When the war came he was sent to a school without music teaching, so he was one of the very few autodidactic educated musicians I really knew. He had his first music lesson when he was eighteen and his final diploma as a concert organist at twenty. Then he had bad luck. After the war, when he was a very young man, all the positions were given away to young musicians. Two to three years later, when he was trying to enter the profession, there was nothing. So he did a doctorate in Latin and German Literature and worked as a teacher at the university in Aberfeld. Then he won the prestigious improvisation contest in Haarlem in Holland three times, and this brought him back to music. But he always gave me the impression that it would be senseless to concentrate only on music; he believed it was necessary to do something else. Until I was twenty to twenty-five he was even sure that I would not be a professional musician. In some ways this gave me a very good attitude because I never felt pushed. My early training was supervised only by my mother and he never interfered. On the other side, there was always the example of my father doing the same things which I also happened to do, but I always told myself that I did things differently. That was true really, because he plays very differently. He has a different repertoire and he does different things.

So was he ever your organ teacher at any point?

Never. The Vienna School was divided into two groups, two different styles of playing. In the beginning I worked with Anton Heiller, a composer and church musician, and then with a student of his, who is now a leading figure in the performance of early music: Michael Radulescu. He was my major teacher and his style was totally different from my father's. My way was somewhere between their two styles, and that made me feel independent in some ways too!

You also went to Paris, I think, to study with Langlais.

Yes, with Langlais and Daniel Roth.

That must have been a different kind of tradition.

This was again very different, because the organ world has changed very much on the continent.

When I was educated there was a school of playing in Paris with a national style, even though there were many foreign students – especially from the USA. I think it was the same in England. The next generation obtained a lot of international contacts and their horizons opened up. The advantage was that they knew a lot about other styles; but there was also the disadvantage that these national schools started to disappear. I was the first of the young Austrians to go to Paris: this was because French was my first language in school and I was also in France several times as a child. I knew the organists. For me this was very important. It was even more important to get the atmosphere of living for six months in another city. However, the lessons and teaching were also important, certainly.

You had already won an important organ competition when you were only eighteen I think, the Vienna-Melk competition.

I had a strange experience with competitions. There were fewer competitions than today. I finished my education very early and won this one competition. Then I wanted to compete in others but, for the two years after my graduation, there was not a single competition where my father was not on the jury, so I couldn't enter! I went to the only one in the following year: this was the Nürnberg competition, where I got the second prize. After that, I went once to Haarlem, where I did not have such good luck as my father, then I gave up. In the end competitions were not necessary, I found other ways. But the situation with competitions has always been crazy. It's the same for my students right now. It has made me question my attitude to competitions.

You seemed to be studying at the same time as your career as a soloist had already begun.

For me the situation was beautiful, and unusual too. I finished my training in Vienna very early. One of my earlier colleagues, Peter Planyavsky, did the same thing. The programme in the Hochschule usually starts when you are eighteen, but Planyavsky obtained special permission to start when he was twelve. I said I wanted to do the same, so I obtained my three diplomas at eighteen, nineteen and twenty, while the others were still starting out.

When exactly did you start at the Hochschule?

I started in a children's programme (with piano and other things) first in the conservatorium, then, aged ten, in the Hochschule. I started with the full church music and organ programme when I was twelve, which is crazy. I was lucky to be good enough in school and I had tolerant teachers. The Hochschule was right in front of the school I attended and so I would ask my teachers if I could leave my maths class early in order to go to a music theory class, or whatever. This was fun for me; it wasn't planned like that by my family, they just intended that I should have organ lessons. Then I started to go to other classes including the choral conducting class, and so I was through quite early! I didn't have problems with the school programme so it was possible for me to do things in this way.

In general terms, how do you see the rôle of a performer? What does a performer do?

I had a helpful conversation with the English conductor John Carewe, who was conducting in Germany at the time. He told me in two to three sentences what I had been thinking for quite a long time. He says that a producer in the opera is someone who can re-create the piece, who is free, who is independent. A performer is always confronted with a musical mind which is stronger than his own. He feels there is always someone [the composer] who knows the music he is playing better than he does, someone who had a stronger idea about it. That approach teaches you a lot of humility.

As a performer you are always between two poles. On one side is the pole of your own will, what you want in your head – you see some meaning in this notation and you have to translate it into sound. In order to make this translation you need your musical will, your own ideas. On the other side is the fact that you are always confronted with physical and technical limitations: there are always some things you cannot do as you want to do them, because your fingers don't do it well enough, or because the acoustic or the instrument are not ideal. For me the ideal performing situation is one which is, as Jean Langlais says, *l'idéal fugitif*, one which is always running away in front of you, which you have to pursue without getting tired or relaxing but which, as with anything human, you cannot reach as a final goal – happily enough, or life would end!

I think you have to be taught humility to accept that the things which have been left as musical notation should be some kind of a law for you. On the other side you still have to have your own personality, to be your own person, in order to translate the notation into sound as well as you know how, and to make your instrument sound well in the acoustical situation which we call a concert.

For me, to be an organist is something different again: you need to be something between an ordinary performer (such as a pianist or violinist, for instance) and a producer. For the organist, the question of sound is of particular significance. I have worked with many composers and several of them have been very influential, like Ernst Krenek, who died in 1991. There is always the question of what the composer wanted in terms of sound. We organists have the challenge and the opportunity to re-create the basic sound of the music through our choice of registration. This can change the music to an extreme extent, even in Bach interpretation. If you hear Bach on a Silbermann or on an English Romantic instrument it becomes like another piece. As a result, it is not just the sound of the piece which changes, but also the structure. You can make the structure stronger than that which the composer had in mind, or you can hide the structure, just because of your instrument. As organists we have more power to change the will of the composer than any other musicians. This gives us a particular duty: to get as close as possible to the will of the composer.

But in many cases the composer hasn't left explicit instructions about the sounds he had in mind.

There are two approaches. There are certainly the organist-composers who write down every registration, as Messiaen did when he specified each registration change in terms of the exact stops available to him at the church of La Trinité. Then there are other composers who just write down more or less ideal sound colours. Composers have different attitudes to this situation. There are the famous letters of Arnold Schoenberg, in which he spoke of trying to interdict further performance of the Organ Variations, because he was so frustrated that he did not hear what he wrote down. On the other hand I talked to Krenek about the problem. He told me there was once an organist who came and said to him, 'Do you want this sound for this measure here?' He said, 'Yes.' Then the organist suggested, 'Oh, but I can do it differently. Do you want *this* sound?' He had six or seven different proposals. In the end Krenek said, 'It's your job to do the registration: it's mine to compose the music.'

I feel it's the same with composers in general. When you are a performer and you meet a composer who really knows what he wrote and can hear what is happening to it in performance – my extreme example would be György Ligeti, who can come into a performance of one of his most complicated choral pieces and say to the fourth tenors, 'Flat! Lift it higher!' – then you accept his will as law. But there are certainly many composers, and I talk as someone who also composes and knows about the problems of hearing one's own music, who don't hear their own structures very well, who cannot follow what is happening or re-create the things which they wrote down. There you sometimes feel that you have to help them by making the music better than it is, or making the structures clearer than they are.

So the composer also shares the idéal fugitif?

Yes, I am sure. In a double way. Beethoven said, 'You should control the notes, they should not control you.' That is the first step, the technical facility which is needed to create things. The second stage is to control the music in performance. There are very few composers who can actually do that in an exact way.

In very general terms, then, how sure can you be that you understand the composer's intention?

This is maybe the central question in our time. We live in a very strange period at the moment where music in general is so easily transformed into sound that we can live in a very escapist world. We can have a whole library of music complete on CD or tape and this changes our spirit totally. For us, for musicians and for the general audience, four bars of a Vivaldi concerto have become more important than the latest big piece of Pierre Boulez. This is very strange. The performance of any music right now is controlled by fashion. Certainly, as a performer, I don't have a telephone line so that I can ask Bach how he wants his music played. But I now have access, if I want it, to more information about the history of interpretation, more knowledge about where what I think of as the mistakes in performance practice began. The first development was that orchestras became bigger and bigger, the sound became less articulated, resulting in the long flat lines which were characteristic of the performance of Bach around the time of Mendelssohn. Then the next direction was a reaction against that style. I have a theory that the history of performance is like a series of waves. You always have a certain development, then somebody comes and counteracts this development. Certainly I cannot tell how a piece *should* be played, by Bach or even by a living composer, but I can give many examples of how it should *not* be played. So my interpretation is based, in many ways, on a system of excluding more and more wrong things, until you come to a field or group of ideas – a centre – where you think you might discover the right possibilities.

Presumably you would allow yourself more freedom say with a piece by Liszt than a piece of Bach?

Not really. The freedom in Liszt is a freedom which is very controlled. In a way, that is harder to achieve. For me, Liszt is a free composer, his pieces are *rubato* music. But, from the viewpoint of a performer, to create this *rubato* spirit needs more feeling and more knowledge than to create a straight movement in a Vivaldi concerto. My problem at the moment is that there are many colleagues on the early music scene who, like teachers in a school, are able to give yes or no answers. They have the advantage because they can always say, 'This *must* be like that' or 'This must *not* be like that.' I cannot give those kinds of answers. For me, even in teaching, I can only show possibilities. I can show a whole package of knowledge about this field, about this music, but I cannot tell a student he should play in a certain way. I can give examples, I can give corrections because I can tell him that certain things are not possible, or that a certain way of playing will lead to a particular kind of result. Life is not so easy that you can give yes or no questions in performance practice. Certainly there is free music in all periods. I have played a lot of Liszt. For me, Liszt's music is related to Bach's *Fantasia in G minor* [BWV 542] or to certain pieces of Krenek. The only difference is that in the free music pieces you are allowed to show more personality than in other pieces. The personal interpretations have to be as good, as sincere and controlled as in a strict piece.

But it is presumably more important that your own personality does show in a performance of a piece of Liszt?

The same thing happens with the performance of pieces written in the *stylus phantasticus* which is a major feature of baroque organ music. Johann Mattheson says that in the *stylus phantasticus* the *Takt*, the beat, is 'on holiday'. The same thing happens with Liszt's music, but I think you can make many things go wrong in a Liszt piece if you don't know how to control it. But it is certainly virtuoso music, and so you have to show more personality. You're right.

Is there a difference when you are studying a completely new piece which has not received a previous performance. For instance, if you are about to perform a piece of Bach, even if it is new to your repertoire, you probably already have the sound of the piece in your head. But if the piece is completely new and all you have are the dots on the paper, is it harder to understand the music which lies behind the notation?

Usually I think the approach to learning any new piece is the same. I tell my students it's just like putting a frame over a picture: by drawing lines you begin to control the material more and more. The lines become more and more narrow, so that in the end your overall view is filled out in complete detail. It's always the question of experience. No new piece contains only totally new ideas and new material. There's always some point which you can relate to some tradition of composition, where you say, 'Oh yes, he's writing that a little bit like that', and so on. You look for these relationships. When I think of music and performing I am very much aware of myself as being no more than a point in time, and I always want to relate in some way to the past. I do that with historic music and with modern music. Even with pieces which are at first surprising, because they seem to stand outside their own tradition, you begin to realise that their starting point is maybe from jazz or ethnic music. I always try to find these traces at first in order to have something I can hold on to. Then I ask myself why the composer wrote that, why did he do that, what meaning does he want to reach through the music?

What kind of elements do you see as being continuous?

There is always a connection between horizontal and vertical structures in music. The horizontal structure is to do with how you build a melody. Usually there are standards for melody – rising tension, relaxation – which result in a continuum of thought. Then there is always the rhythmic consequence. There are two traditions of rhythm; the European idea of rhythm which consists of the sub-division of a big unit. Then, in the music of Messiaen and some other modern composers, there is what I would call the African tradition, where complex rhythms are the result of small additional note values.

Music has had common elements for centuries. Another feature of our eclectic age is that when you flick the switch of a CD player to hear a piece by Machaut, you discover that Machaut's music is not so far away from music which was written ten years ago. For me, as in Paris when I started to study the organ, the atmosphere, the inspiration of things outside the music, is sometimes as important as the writing itself. For me the encounter with some of the personalities – in the way in which I was for some time very close to Alfred Schnittke, or Krenek – has given me strength and a lot of inspiration.

Improvisation has always been a feature of your performing activity. In a sense it is a kind of instant composition. Can you give us some idea of how improvisation works? What actually goes through your mind?

I now make more and more connections between improvisation and composition. When I began, I saw improvisation as something totally different from composition. To put it simply, improvisation begins as a musical form which is then filled with notes; in composition you begin with the material and you expand it until you reach a form. When I start to compose I see a theme. I am trained and have practised, so I know how to create, let us say, a three-part prelude and fugue out of this material. For me improvisation, although it is instant music as you said, is *less* spontaneous than the way I compose. When I sit down to compose, although I need much more time, I develop from a little piece of material a bigger form – and I don't know what the final result is going to be. When I improvise (and I think this is true of many well-known improvisers) the overall scope of the improvisation is decided from the outset – otherwise the result would be chaotic. However, improvisation has two sides: the free side, the free fantasy where you really let yourself go and meander around; and the improvisation which is usual in a service or a recital, which has to reach a goal. In service playing, you have to know the point the priest has to reach, or maybe the improvisation has to introduce the chorale, or it has to be a certain length. In concert, you know from experience what will be effective. Certainly, there is always something which goes in a different way and you have to react to it, but I think I improvise better when I have practised for some time. Maybe it's because of my French training where there is a strict division between *improvisation libre* (which is not *libre*!) and improvisation in the old style, which was just an art which you could learn through training. I think I have my personal style of improvisation. I know the harmonies which I use. But my style of improvisation is much more traditional than my composing. Composing is my laboratory; my improvising stays more on safe ground.

Is there a sense in which the habits of the fingers actually play a very big part in improvising?

A very good point. There are different kinds of improvisers and I tell my students they have to find out how they can develop their own harmonies. One way is that you can actually improvise as if you were going to write the music down. There are some people who really can do that. Another way is more like the way in which a guitar player uses tablature: from the positions of the hands you know that a certain sound will result. This is the result of training. Certainly I know jazz pianists who work in that way too. You then have a standard repertoire of harmonies which you can combine in new ways.

Does improvisation play an important part in your performances of baroque music?

Yes. I love to play my own continuo, and always do so. From improvisation, I know exactly how the thing has to work. Conductors of baroque music have typically been either string or keyboard players who turn into conductors. The advantage for the keyboard people is that they have lived always with ornamentation, with continuo playing and with improvisation. I think this is a very important part of the musical language.

In your performances you seem to use less added ornamentation than is common with some other performers, someone like Ton Koopman for instance.

In Bach, do you mean? For me, there's a big difference between Bach, Mozart and the rest of the world. Bach had these big problems – he was criticised by his contemporary Scheibe for writing everything in! So, for me, there are relatively few pieces where I use ornaments in Bach. But when I use them I use them a lot. Free ornamentation of this kind was an Italian invention and I certainly use ornaments in Bach's transcriptions of the Vivaldi concertos. When I play the F major fugue [BWV 540] or the D minor [BWV 538], which are composed in the *stile antico* with long notes, I play versions with lots of embellishments. These come from the generation of Bach's children – they felt that the style needed some ornaments to make it less boring. However, in Bach's orchestral music there are few places where I think it is necessary actually to add something.

Usually, in order to draw the line, it is necessary to ask what would have been played in Bach's time. I think in a *stile antico* piece performers would still have played in the strict way without ornaments. All the ornaments which we have written down come from the generation after Bach. It's the same problem with theory books: they always come from the following generation, but talk about the generation before. Very few theory books actually deal with their own time because it is not necessary. It is clear what to do.

Do you think there was a sense in which Bach himself went back and looked at earlier pieces and revised them in the light of a new taste?

Certainly. The problem with Bach was, in contrast with the French composers, that he had very few pieces printed in his lifetime: almost no organ music, only three collections of organ chorales. So, as is the case with the so-called *Eighteen Chorales*, there are several chorale preludes where he took an earlier manuscript and rewrote it. As a result there are a number of valid versions of some pieces: for instance with *O Lamm Gottes* [BWV 656] there is no real final version. This is because the music was never published in a printed form.

We have talked quite a lot about your respect for the composer and the re-creative rôle of the performer. How much responsibility do you feel towards the listener? What part does the listener play in the musical experience?

At the moment, musical life in general is changing in a very radical way. As I see it, this is the result of the combination of computer technology and CD. For the first time with CD you have the transformation of sound into a sound library. It is possible to buy the complete works of Mozart or Bach. You have them in your library and can recall at the switch of a button each piece in every interpretation. For the first time the performer not only has to play to the standard which is necessary, but to compete with colleagues of the past. So when I bring out a recording of Haydn it is compared with one by Antal Dorati, recorded thirty years ago, or even with performances by Mengelberg and others recorded fifty years ago. 28,000 classical CDs came out in the last two years, which is frightening. The bad side is that the listener, especially in Vienna where there are so many concerts, becomes spoilt. Music is no longer something elemental for him. The listener in the baroque period, or in the time of Mozart, had the elemental feeling of noise, of novelty, of surprise. We read about people collapsing in a concert just from the effect of the music. That this is no longer possible remains a problem which we cannot resolve. There is another problem which Walter Benjamin has identified: that of the art work being duplicated and repeated many times. Again, I try to find answers from outside musical life. It is the same with my children watching TV. How much can I allow them to dig into a world where everything is possible, where you can buy everything, you can have everything? That is the situation in music, too.

The area of making the connection with the listener is the one about which I am the most pessimistic at the moment. I feel we cannot create the feeling of musical poverty naturally any more. We have to force people to become concentrated once more. In order to concentrate, they may need to reduce the amount of music to which they listen. They may need to decide what they want to hear, to prepare more for a concert, for instance. For me, there is a major educational need to bring people back to an attitude of listening where music is not something superficial, or something to be heard in the background, but where it becomes something elemental and important again. I don't know any more how to handle a situation where you can hear classics, the best pieces written in the world, as background music in a shop, or where you can get hits of the classics on CDs. I hope that the positive side will be that, with the sheer number of CDs available, listening at home will become less important, and the event more important again. That's what I hope: that people will leave their houses to go to real concerts where they can experience the sound played by human beings. This is my hope: to re-awaken the interest of the listener.

In an attempt to draw theological comparisons with the musical experience it is tempting to see the composer as a creative figure who, like God the Father, creates from the beginning ex nihilo. *It is easy to see the performer as a kind of incarnational figure, someone who lives out the Word, the musical text. Is there any sense in which the listener needs to work in a rather more inward way, rather like the Holy Spirit?*

If you continue the thought and try to examine it in terms of our society, you come to feel that the creator is a powerless creator, less and less powerful. When a living composer writes a piece, he finds he doesn't get any response. He finds a tiny number of people who are willing to accept what he is writing. He is confronted with creations written many years ago, multiplied by technical means which are controlling the musical world right now. When Boulez, who is so powerful a modern composer, writes a new piece it comes out on Deutsche Grammophon, it sells perhaps 15,000 CDs and might be played in Salzburg, Paris, Vienna and London. By contrast, Nigel Kennedy can record another set of Vivaldi's *Four Seasons* and sell ten times as many discs.

I think that the distinction between composer/creator and performer/incarnator is not always as clear as you suggest, because in much music the creator and the performer are the same; but in general it is possible to see parallels. But the question of the listener is more difficult. Modern Roman Catholic theology has raised the question of whether someone sitting in a church and listening to a classical Mass-setting is really part of the service. Or does he have to sing and to act himself, to stand up and give the responses, in order really to play a full part? Is it necessary to be interactive?

Does the question of participation actually limit church music in Austria?

Yes, very much. I often run into the problem in church. Even a former cardinal wanted the liturgy to be changed, because he said that it was not a real service since people did not sing the psalm or make the responses themselves. For me, this was almost a reason to leave that church. I thought this was an insult to people who come into church to sit and meditate and pray in silence while they hear a Bruckner *Credo*.

In general, I don't know what we should expect of our listeners – we don't know who they are. For me it is easier to make connections between composer and performer. It is harder to work out the nature of the connection with the listener. In earlier times quite a lot of music was written without any listeners in mind. All the late Bach works were *musica speculativa*, written just for himself. Similarly, many modern pieces were just written without any listener in mind. For me this is something which is not just negative, it has a positive side too. We don't always have to address somebody, to direct our meanings, to set them an example. On the other hand, in earlier times many listeners were just accidentally present when music was being played. The idea of an audience sitting in a concert hall concentrating on music is a nineteenth-century attitude. In general, the whole idea of the listener towards music is not clear or very easy to answer. It can be someone sitting at home just listening to a machine, it can be someone who goes to a concert because of the desire to appear beforehand in a social situation, or it can be somebody who really wants to absorb the music.

But is there also the problem that we undervalue listening, and that participation is something that people in church have misunderstood?

This is a general problem with the church, especially towards large-scale Roman Catholic church music. My church in Vienna has a big balcony, with a fence and a curtain, because all the people came when the opera singers were singing, they applauded and so on. In this church, the Augustiniankirche, two thousand or more people attend on every Sunday. The priest didn't like it because he thought they just came because they wanted to hear the big music. I said, 'Don't be silly, these people attend, they are a community, they are a congregation, they listen to the sermon. This provides a chance, an opportunity.' When there is a desire to force every church to do the same kind of liturgy, without any provision for the totally different styles of adoration which are possible, it results in a kind of poverty. I think this trend will be reversed; there are signs of hope right now.

3

Creation and the Listener

An Interview with Mark Savage

What are your earliest musical memories?

My memory of music during my early childhood days is hazy. The sound of many people coming together in church to sing was exciting and moving; but whether it was just the music that moved me or the sense of common purpose I am not sure. The context in which music was performed certainly had a powerful effect on me. A sense of space was particularly important. A shiver of delight and anticipation ran down my spine when I heard the distant approaching drums and bugles of the massed bands that led our Whitsuntide Procession of Witness through the streets of Burnley. They always sounded more compelling when still out of sight. My expectation and excitement combined to make a strong cocktail of emotion.

Older, and bound by the convention that males ought not display certain emotions in public, I became ashamed and almost fearful of the intense feelings that large-scale public events still stir up in me: a combination of joy, exhilaration and wistful sadness. Before I learned 'to control myself', I felt no such fear. My mother remembers that when I was about three I sat in an empty church listening to the organ, in rapt silence, tears streaming down my face. She thought that something had upset me and rushed to comfort me. Nothing was wrong, I was crying because the music was 'so beautiful'.

During my primary school years, I was attracted to music with a strong beat, music that made me want to get up and move to it. I was born in 1955 and was hooked, along with most of my friends, by the rock music revolution. Budding groups took over from the brass band on Sunday afternoons in our local park (both sounded more exciting half a mile away than close to), and I successfully pestered my parents into buying me a plastic 'Beatles' guitar. Classical music was shunned by most right-thinking nine-year-old boys of my acquaintance and I didn't want to be different; and yet there were moments when, almost in spite of myself, I fell under its spell. I particularly remember one lunchtime broadcast of Brahms's second symphony. I was moved deeply by its long melodic lines and richly autumnal sound world. Once my attention was caught, time stood still. Only the music seemed to matter.

When we moved to a suburb of Liverpool in 1966 I felt free to discover my own taste in music. In that November I was taken to my first orchestral concert. Boult conducted the Royal Liverpool Philharmonic Orchestra in a programme of Brahms's *Academic Festival Overture*, a Haydn symphony and Holst's suite *The Planets*. I was bowled over. It was as near a conversion experience as I have ever had. The sheer colour and impact of the sound was thrilling, but it was the all-embracing sensation of listening which took hold of me: a large number of people giving total attention to something that made intellectual and emotional demands on them and which, like my recollection of the Brahms broadcast, created its own time-frame. Thereafter I grabbed every opportunity to listen to and absorb classical orchestral music. The rock and pop groups were at first quietly forgotten and then, with all the unreasonable zeal of a new convert, despised.

First of all I devoured my parents' old and dusty collection of 78s, played on a battered machine borrowed from church. I had already bought my first LP – Ansermet's recording of Beethoven's ninth symphony – when a new record player was bought. I soon managed to persuade my parents to let the player stay in my room. At first I think my parents were not too unhappy, but as music became my constant companion I suspect they may have wished that they had exercised a stronger control.

One consequence was a threat to my schoolwork. I still find it difficult to listen and to pay attention to something else at the same time, and I cannot easily allow music to become a background noise. I would escape to my room, put on a record and listen. Homework took second place. At the time I protested that I could manage both. In fact the music took precedence.

Did you learn to play a musical instrument?

I had my first piano lessons before my fifth birthday. Unfortunately, these only continued for a few months. The teacher moved away, and wasn't replaced. I seem to remember that I enjoyed the lessons, but clearly didn't show such promise or enthusiasm that a new teacher had to be found. Much later, at the age of eleven, I began violin lessons at school and made steady if slow and somewhat erratic progress. Time practising meant less time listening and my efforts did not bring me the all-embracing and emotional involvement I gained through listening. I wanted to play Bruch's first violin concerto before I had passed Grade 1. I never gained the discipline that might have led me to be able to play competently and I now regret it; but at the time music mattered more and what I played was not remotely good enough. I often wonder whether if I had continued with the piano I might have been able to bridge the gap more adequately between my experience of music as a performer and as a listener.

I confess that I often feel jealous of the composer and performer. I cannot help feeling that they have a privileged access to musical meaning from which I am largely excluded. This may just be a knee-jerk reaction to society's assumption that if you claim to be 'musical', you must know something about the mechanics of musical form (I know precious little) or you must be able to play an instrument. My jealousy is probably misplaced. I have often found singing in large choirs immensely therapeutic. The sense of achievement has been great and the exhilaration of being able to participate in making music has been powerful, but the communication of the meaning in the music itself has not been any greater than in those occasions when I 'just' listen.

The very act of listening brings its own deeply satisfying sense of creativity as the music is re-created in the unique circumstances of that person, moment and place. This sense of creativity is, for me, hugely more immediate, therefore, in the experiencing of live music-making, through participating in an act which can never be repeated, which imposes its own framework of time and space, and which is enormously influenced by the unspoken interplay between the performers and listeners. This interplay may easily become a communion and is not always, of course, restricted to the performance of music: I well remember a theologian, who not infrequently cried and sweated profusely whilst giving a lecture. Those of us who listened soon recognised that this was because his subject mattered so deeply to him that it was literally a matter of life and death. Many of us who were moved by his struggle became convicted of the same passion – it became something shared at a deep and unspoken level (words alone were certainly inadequate to express this shared struggle). But this profound sense of communion and of journeying together can be even more vivid in the shared experience of live music. I shall, for example, never forget a concern given many years ago in Birmingham by The Beaux Arts Trio. As an encore, they played a movement from Dvořák's *Trio in E minor* Op. 90 (the *Dumky*). The members of the trio played without looking at their fingers. They concentrated on each other; and their faces mirrored the deep pathos of the music which combines in such an extraordinary way joy and tragedy. As I became caught up in the music and in their reaction to it as it unfolded, I learned something new, and though I later bought a superb recording of the piece, played by the same artists (a disc which I love and listen to often), that special sense of communion and of sharing in truths too deep for words is absent.

As for my envy of the composer, it is largely because I am aware how poor my own imagination is in comparison. If I have my own music in me, it is recessed deeply in my subconscious. I have only rarely felt the frustration of not being able to translate it into a score. I suppose that my enduring envy of performers is based in the feeling that they have a greater access to music than I do, and they are able to facilitate music-making in a way that is closed to me.

What prompted you to begin to reflect on the rôle of music in your life and to begin to make connections with other parts of your experience?

My reflections really began when at the age of eighteen I went away to university in Birmingham and found accommodation at Woodbrooke College. Woodbrooke is an international study-centre run by and for the Society of Friends, but at that time was also willing to take in other students.

I found a rather good hi-fi system in the large, airy drawing room, and soon learned that I could play my wholesome classical records on it almost as often as I liked, as long as I stood up at dinner and offered the enterprise as a record recital open to everyone. One or two older and wiser souls persuaded me to talk about my love of music to smaller groups, and on one occasion I was urged to bring a piece to Sunday Meeting and play it. It was implied, but not actually spelled out, that to do so would be an act of prayer. This was the first time such a possibility had occurred to me. In truth, I was unconvinced. The music in question was the opening scene of Verdi's *Otello*, which I'd been studying as part of a project on Shakespeare and music and which appealed to me in a rather basic way because the sheer noisiness of it, cannons and all, was rather exciting.

I found the experience of playing Verdi at the meeting embarrassing, faintly ridiculous and disturbing. I was embarrassed because I wanted to say, 'Hold on, there are other pieces of music which mean a lot more to me'; but my sense of unease was because I found my concept of prayer more challenged than the significance for me of music. I felt that I understood the music; but my understanding of prayer was incredibly shallow and yet, for the first time, I knew that there was a connection between the two. It was a turning point not only in coming to terms with my love of music, but in my faith: almost another conversion experience.

From then on I began a process of reflection, intermittent and mostly unstructured, in which I attempted to bring together my experiences of music and of Christian faith.

What are the roots of your faith and how do they relate to your experiencing of music?

My father was a Baptist minister. His own faith was supported by rigorous scholarship and the worship he led, whilst never cold, appealed more to the intellect than to the emotions. I grew up with a faith that prized words, reading, reasoned argument and structure. In music I found a medium which ordered experience in a structured way, which was capable of a profound intellectual content and yet which integrated the emotions and liberated the imagination. Until my challenge at Woodbrooke I had never dreamed of the possibility of a spirituality which allowed space for the affections and imagination which did not merely 'degenerate' into a kind of charismatic mush which, once met, I took considerable steps to avoid. (I found that I could not cope with what seemed to be unstructured emotion unsupported by intellectual content.)

How do you now relate your experiences of faith and of music?

I have learned to trust my musical experience more and to see that it could enliven my arid spirituality. A wise Franciscan challenged me to consider whether music had become a substitute for prayer altogether. I was quick to say that of course it hadn't; but I am not entirely sure that my reply was honest. I now feel that if prayer is expressive of a relationship between God, the world and me, then music tells me more about the truth of all three than anything else. I have inherited and am grateful for a faith that trusts the intellect and traditional theological scholarship; but most often it is music that shows me that my literate God is incomplete.

As you look back, what was it that attracted you to particular styles of music? How was your musical 'taste' formed?

From the music that I discovered in my early teens, certain composers and pieces have continued to engage and to entrance me. I have had an enduring passion for the music of Berlioz. As a child suffering in bed

from one of the spotty illnesses that result in a long quarantine, I heard
the 'March to the Scaffold' from the *Symphonie Fantastique*. The
rhythm excited me and the melody engaged my romantic imagination,
taking me into a dream world far more vivid than any book or film. It
was not so much Berlioz's programme that so enthralled me, but my
own.

As I listened more, my tastes formed. I found that much music repaid
attention even if it was not immediately attractive. I was willing to listen
to any programme offered by the RLPO and so encountered music of
many different styles. I warmed far more readily to music that was
romantic or expressive than to music of the classical or pre-classical
periods. I admired the craft of pre-nineteenth-century music, but was
largely unmoved by it. Heavy, Sargentesque performances of Handel's
Messiah by the Liverpool Welsh Choral Union came closer to trying my
patience than anything else. They were almost unalloyed tedium.

*Why did you feel that music was worth paying attention to, even
when you were bored by it or could not understand it?*

I well remember hearing Schoenberg's *Pierrot Lunaire* for the first
time. I have to admit that deep down I didn't much care for it; but I
was deeply embarrassed by the rejection of it by a large part of the
audience. They simply got up and walked out. I was puzzled and
dismayed by their action. I sensed that the music was being performed
superbly and, for me, compellingly, by the London Sinfonietta under
David Atherton, and I recognised that it expressed something important that I had not experienced before and which was beyond the scope
of any other medium. I had to stay and listen. Apart from that, I
thought (maybe rather prudishly) that it was incredibly rude to walk
out on musicians who were clearly doing their utmost to communicate
something they believed to be important.

On another occasion I shared the non-comprehension of most of the
audience at an early performance of Lutoslawski's second symphony.
Again many people walked out, even though I think the composer was
present. I stayed in my seat, but was relieved when the work ended.
Twenty-five years later, as I listen to a recording of the symphony, I
find it hard to know what was so puzzling.

I recognise that some intellectual effort is needed to 'stick with'
difficult new music. Music is able to shock and to disturb, but the
strangeness of the new is often sufficient to deter concert-goers. In the
same year that I heard the Lutoslawski symphony I heard for the first
time a performance of Bartók's *Concerto for Orchestra*. I was
enthralled by that wonderful score and bubbled out my enthusiasm to

my father, who had come to collect me after the concert. He told me that he had been present at a concert in Manchester twenty years earlier, one of the first performances of the work in Britain. It met with the same non-comprehension as I had witnessed with the Lutoslawski so recently.

James MacMillan's delight in the 'boundless curiosity' shown by the remnants of the avant-garde echoes strongly in me. It drives me to listen to music which, occasionally on first hearing, has left me cold. I want to find out what it is that the music is trying to tell me; and more often than not I have found the effort of listening has been richly rewarding. The disappointments and frustrations have been relatively few.

As you have listened more, has the rôle that music plays in your life changed too?

My taste has certainly broadened, but the rôles played by music in my life has altered little. Music affects me now in much the same way it did when my horizons were rapidly expanding during my teenage years. For example, the great symphonies of Mahler and then Shostakovich continue to present the world to me in its many contradictions: noble, uplifting, passionate, bizarre, trite and vicious, they seem perhaps a little less vivid than they once were, but I continue to find subtleties, ironies and delights that I had previously missed.

I am, by nature, an optimist, but especially as I get older I find music which is unfailingly optimistic deeply unsatisfying. Short pieces, including Strauss waltzes, I enjoy greatly; long bouts of cheerfulness, such as some of the major works of George Lloyd, leave me cold. I need to be able to be helped to face the world and to see that my optimism can be rooted in a struggle to come to terms with the world as it really is. Mahler and Shostakovitch help me to do that; Lloyd does not. Similarly, I find long stretches of unalleviated self-pity deeply unsatisfying. I am grateful that my acquaintance with the symphonies of Allan Pettersson is brief. Even more, I have great difficulty in listening to repetitive, minimalist music, no matter how mellifluous it may sometimes be. The idea of the symphony or sonata which explored and works through material in a rigorous and searching way is enormously important. One moving example is Josef Suk's symphony *Asreal*, which I first heard in a radio broadcast of Vaclav Tallich's recording from the early 1950s but which, to my great disappointment, was unavailable on disc for many years. I believe that this work, which plumbs the depths of despair and which yet manages to achieve a genuine sense of acceptance and even of hope, is a masterpiece which is only just now beginning to get the recognition it deserves.

Berlioz's music continues to offer me something else. It touches a deep vein of passion within me and excites my imagination. It also unlocks a nostalgic yearning; and if that is an escape from the particularities of daily life, I find it a uniquely satisfying and healing one.

Some music also has the power to evoke a sense of wonder in me, in that it points quite beyond itself. At times, music is the locus of the numinous, when everything seems intense, distant and yet, at the same time, peculiarly immediate. I have felt a sense of trembling awe when listening to the first movement of Mahler's third symphony and most of his eighth, but also many times in the two gentle middle movements of Brahms's third symphony – a work for which I have the deepest affection.

As I have got older, I have given more attention to the more intimate musical forms, and have found in them a breadth and depth no less engaging than in the big, arresting orchestral scores which first attracted me.

Martin Haselböck argues that we may need to reduce the amount of music to which people listen, if it is to become something elemental and important again. Do you agree?

No, I don't. My main concern, however, is that the music to which people are exposed so much is already too restricted to a shortlist of 'classic-pops'. Classic FM has certainly done a great deal to make music accessible to many people who find the cultural baggage surrounding serious music-making deeply intimidating; but having whetted the appetite, I worry that it doesn't encourage people to listen to works that might be more challenging. I worry that the 'bleeding chunks' which flow thick and fast from such stations produce a culture in which only the highlights are played – another aspect of the 'sound-bite' culture. This, I think is the heart of the problem; for the highlights are only truly such if you listen to them in the context of a whole work. I would hope that there would be a growing demand to hear live music, but this does not seem to be happening. Concert programming is too often conservative, and audiences for anything other than the narrow standard repertory are disappointingly low. If we are to make a real difference, we will have to change far more than people's access to music, we need to accept that the culture in which we live finds it difficult to give sustained attention to anything. Although serious music-making will, I fear, remain a minority activity, and whilst I accept that one of the reasons for the decline of the western churches has been a real failure to come alongside popular culture with sensitivity and insight, I am utterly convinced that we must not be tempted to ditch the truths that only serious music can adequately convey in a headlong, unconsidered rush for inculturation.

Today, I continue to learn through music what the world is like, in all its emotional and intellectual contradictions. Music still, and indeed ever more deeply, reveals to me the truth about the way things really are. When I compare this with what my Christian faith tells me, I see that the essential foundations of truth, love, compassion, hope and even faith itself can often be more tellingly expressed in music than in theological formulations. After the prime and essential experience of relationships with other people, nothing moves or excites me more than music.

PART TWO: PERSPECTIVES

on Music from the Disciplines of
Theology, Psychology and Philosophy

4

Play It (Again):
Music, Theology and Divine Communication

Jeremy Begbie

The world of music offers immense possibilities for any theologian engaging with the theme of the communication of God.[1] There are, admittedly, substantial obstacles. To begin with, despite the saturation of our culture with music, and despite widespread and deeply-held convictions about music and its capacity to communicate (not least in the church), musical communication is in fact an immensely complex and little understood process. It has not been a prominent topic in communication theory. *That* music is one of the most powerful communicative media in human history is incontestable; but claims about *how* music communicates or *what* is communicated need to be somewhat tentative.

Moreover, in modern theological writing, the interaction between music and systematic theology is conspicuous by its absence.[2] More often than not, the theologian's stance towards music has been characterised by hesitation and suspicion, with the result that what scant theological treatment of music there has been habitually gravitates towards ethics, the moral propriety of this or that form of music. In this century at least, the conversation between theology and music has hardly begun.

Nevertheless, there are good reasons to believe that the mutual neglect is highly regrettable, as we hope to show. The purpose of this paper is not to aspire to a theology of musical communication, nor a theology of music, but to demonstrate something of music's capacity to generate fresh and fruitful resources for exploring and articulating dimensions of the self-communication of the triune God. Jacques Attali, in his book *Noise*, declares that 'Music is more than an object of study: it is a way of perceiving the world. My intention is . . . not only to theorise *about* music, but to theorise *through* music.'[3] My concern here is to ask what it might mean to theologise not simply *about* music but *through* music.[4] I have chosen one main theme, which has strong resonances in theology: that of *repetition*. We shall concentrate on two theological fields in which repetition comes to the fore: multiple fulfilments of divine promises, and multiple enactments of the Eucharist.

For reasons of space, I concentrate principally on one major tradition of music – broadly speaking the 'tonal' tradition, which has shaped the majority of western music for the last three hundred years or so, and shows little sign of waning. This restriction of itself need not imply cultural hegemony, nor any particular value judgements about forms of music outside the tonal tradition. Nor, indeed, should it be read as discounting the possibility of other types of music being deployed fruitfully in theology.

Further, we shall focus most of the discussion on music without words. For much of the history of western music and in many non-western societies, speech and music are closely intertwined. But here, in order to foreground some of the theological capabilities especially distinctive of music, the prime interest will be in non-texted music.

MUSICAL REPETITION

The topic of repetition has attracted enormous interest within 'post-modern' cultural theory. The perceived tilt towards 'sameness' and homogenisation in some currents of late modernity has raised a series of critical questions about what constitutes 'original' reality. It is argued that, with the proliferation of processes for the replication of products, texts and information, we are witnessing a diminution in the authority of ideas of originality.[5] Music is sometimes alluded to in this discussion, with special reference to the increasing sophistication of musical reproductive technology – in what does the 'original' consist when the vast majority of music heard today is multiply processed?[6]

However, there has been comparatively little attention shown in this discourse to repetitive processes *within music itself*. Even Theodor Adorno, who had so much to say about the dangers of musical repetition in mass culture, devoted relatively little sustained work to repetitive processes within particular pieces and forms of music.[7] Modern 'worship songs' are frequently attacked for being repetitive – yet it is forgotten that on one level they are no more repetitive than many works by, say, Vivaldi. Deeper understanding only comes if we attend more closely to repetitive procedures internal to music itself.

To state the obvious, every piece of music, to some extent, integrates 'sameness' with 'difference'. It must have sameness (similarity, association) in order to be *a* piece, and difference in order to avoid complete monotony. Middleton posits a spectrum of musical structural types between two poles, ranging from the 'monadic' – most nearly approached by silence or by a single, unchanging, unending sound, to the 'infinite set' – most nearly approached by pieces whose aim is that nothing be heard twice. Absolute monadic sameness and absolute non-recurring difference are, of course, impossible to achieve. Further, sameness and difference are mutually dependent and can only be mediated through each other.

What is striking about music is that relations of sameness would appear to play a more crucial part than relations of difference. Music 'tends towards' the pole of absolute sameness, and this is borne out more than anything else by the extraordinary prominence of repetition in music (compared to the other arts). Musical temporality is usually dependent on a more or less regular, repeated pulse. Repetition, whether small or large-scale, is the prime form-building agent of music. The 'repeat sign' on a score can prescribe the reiteration of long stretches of music, note for note. Apparently 'music can never have enough of saying over again what has already been said'.[8] In so-called 'popular music', this is especially so.[9] Peter Kivy asserts bluntly (but uncontroversially) that music 'from Bach to Brahms, and before and beyond, consists to a large, although of course varying degree, in quite literal repetition of what has been heard before'.[10]

The commonest way of accounting for the pervasiveness of repetition in music is to point to music's deficiency in denotative precision. Its high degree of ambiguity in relation to extra-musical entities means that it 'tends towards' an extreme of total sameness or maximum redundancy. Because it so rarely achieves or attempts specific reference beyond itself, it will, initially at least, tend to 'speak about' itself – what Richard Middleton calls 'introversive signification'.[11] In this light, a high measure of repetition is seen to be psychologically necessary for musical perception. The application of information-theory to musical cognition has shown that without a specific 'object' beyond itself of sufficient clarity to concentrate our minds, and with the limited capacity of short-term memory, repetition becomes vital for imprinting the characteristic shape of its own objects in the memory – motifs, phrases, or whatever – such that when they re-appear after being absent, a sense of coherence and intelligible form may be recognised.[12]

Intelligibility is one thing. But the deeper and more pressing issue is: how can so much repetition be *interesting*?

BEETHOVEN'S SIXTH SYMPHONY: A CASE STUDY

In the first movement of Beethoven's sixth symphony (the *Pastoral*), there occurs a passage in which essentially the same rhythmic motif is repeated forty-eight times without a break. On this rhythm rides a melody which in essential shape remains the same throughout. No sooner have we finished this section than another begins, virtually identical with the earlier, except for being higher in pitch. Here is what seems to be excessive repetition in rhythm, harmony and melody, on the micro- and macro-scale. Why, then, has this music claimed so much attention? What is *novel* amidst the almost obsessive reiteration?[13]

Parallels and analogies with other art-forms do not get us very far. To be sure, carpets and tapestries often display extensive repetition,[14] and in architecture we can find repetition of elements and sometimes of entire formal complexes. But in these cases we have the simultaneous presence of many similar or identical elements. The perception of repetition may not be instantaneous – the eye and perhaps the body must move in order to apprehend it – but the enjoyment depends in large part on being able to set part against part, to wander back and forth, to compare. In music the repetition itself is presented to us in a prescribed, irreversible, unbroken, sequence. In literature, it would seem that repetition is only exceptionally taken to the extremes it is in music.[15] And where it is, it is arguable that we are on the very edges of literature and bordering on music, which only makes us press the question further about music.[16]

Some point to the *different location* of each repetition.[17] In much musical repetition, each repeated unit is perceived as coming after and before music different from that which surrounded its earlier occurrence(s). Hence, we are bound to hear the music differently with each repetition. Sounds may be duplicated; the music *as heard* is not. To be sure, in some cases, this is undoubtedly part of the reason why musical repetition can claim our interest. In Schumann's *Arabesque*, when we hear the second appearance of the main theme (the same theme, note for note), we will likely hear it differently because of the interlude that has preceded it. To say 'it's just the same' would be to misunderstand. However, though this may apply to 'remote' repetition – where an entity recurs after a significant period, it says little about 'immediate' repetition – when the entity is repeated straight away, especially if this repetition is multiple (as in the example from Beethoven's sixth symphony). It is hardly convincing to say that in a string of identical motifs, the fifth will hold our interest because it is surrounded by the fourth and sixth as distinct from, say, the third which is surrounded by the second and fourth!

Undoubtedly, part of the answer lies in the *variation of musical parameters*. In the Beethoven piece, the rhythm of the repeated motif may remain constant, but the form of the melody alters slightly, the timbre changes because of different orchestration, the background harmony shifts, the volume swells and dies. This is an extremely common procedure in music – one parameter remains constant but the others are changed in some way. Even when the changes are not written down, a performer will naturally vary repeated material – by ornamenting it, 'stretching' it in time, and so forth. Much improvised jazz operates according to essentially the same principle – a repeated, relatively constant 'ground' of some sort (harmonic framework, typically) forms a basis over which a number of different improvisations are spun.

Nevertheless, this does not explain how we tolerate (and enjoy) the repetition of large sections of music without any variation – Beethoven wanted the whole of the first part of the opening movement of this symphony to be repeated, note for note.

METRICAL WAVES

The crucial factor – and it is one with potent theological overtones – is metre.[18] Metre is a configuration of beats. In written music it is indicated by a 'time-signature' (e.g. 2/4, 3/4, etc.). Metre collates its beats into groups – bars – each bar containing a certain number of beats. The beats vary in intensity or degree of accentuation – the first is normally strongest, the others weak. What this creates is a type of wave of tension and resolution; there is a force, so to speak, which augments and accumulates energy and a force that closes and resolves.[19] In a three-beat bar, the first beat sets up an implicatory tension which reaches its highest point in between the second and third beats, the third initiating a move towards resolution which is attained at the first beat of the next measure. And so the process of tension and resolution continues in the next measure.

But this process does not work only at one level. The first beats (the '1s') of each bar generate a further wave of tension and resolution at a higher level (a 'hyper-bar'). And the same dynamic is repeated at the next level up: the first beats of the hyper-bars become new 'beats' in another wave. And so the process is extended in still higher hyper-bars, until the whole piece is covered.

These waves of tension and resolution can be articulated, 'marked out' by any or all of the parameters of music – rhythm, harmony, timbre, and so forth.[20] Some waves will be marked out more strongly than others. Music presents us, then, with a multi-layered texture of superordinate and subordinate waves, in which the lower waves of tension and resolution give rise to successively higher waves.[21] This multi-strata format is common to virtually all types of western music in the tonal tradition. If you have heard music today, it will almost certainly have operated in this metrical manner.

It ought to be stressed that the visual representation above could suggest a certain tidiness and predictability, as if music were tied to an utterly regular, pre-given metrical grid. In most cases this is not so. In even the simplest pieces, there will usually be metrical *irregularity* of some sort – at one level, for example, there may be a succession of waves of different lengths; the waves can overlap, conflict, be left 'hanging' in the air, and so on. It is true that these are usually 'regularised'/balanced out at a higher level, thus maintaining metrical continuity, but this still leaves virtually limitless room for novelty and unpredictability at lower levels.

Musical repetition can be seen – or, rather *is heard* – in this context. If we take into account every level in the metric hierarchy, no two beats in a piece have exactly the same accentual quality. Each repeated component of music will have a different dynamic quality because *each occurs in relation to a different configuration of tensions and resolutions.* This is where the fundamental novelty lies within highly repetitive music – two occurrences of the 'same' motif can be sensed as different because each relates to a different combination of metrical tension and resolution. Viewed from the point of view of metre, *everything is 'new'*, 'nothing can ever be the same', we are never 'back where we started'. So, unique location *is* indeed the key to the interest of repetition, but more critical than horizontal positioning of a repeated entity (so to speak) is its location with respect to levels of metrical waves.

In order that this difference in dynamic quality can be sensed, the waves have to be brought into relief, 'etched' by sound. As we have said, this can be done by virtually any parameter of music – melody, harmony, rhythm, and so on. In the Beethoven passage, it is achieved by those slight elements of variation we noted – the changes in orchestration, harmony and volume. These are *not* simply arbitrary ornamentations to add variety and keep people from falling asleep. They are carefully timed to point to something deeper, the patterns of intensification and release in the implicit metrical waves:

> The [notes] do not alter for the sake of variety, that is in order to give the same thing an *appearance* of being different; on the contrary, *because what is apparently the same is basically always different*, the [notes] do not always want to remain the same.[22]

Music's privileging of repetition can now make very much more sense. It is not enough to say that without referential precision, music is forced 'to speak about itself'. More profoundly, repetition is a kind of 'natural state' of music because the very equality of repetitive units brings out with special clarity the inequality (wave patterns) of successive bars and hyper-bars, the manifold differences within the metrical matrix. Music depends on repetition – in some form – to highlight this endlessly different hierarchy of metrical waves.

THE PROMISE OF REPETITION

From what we have observed, on any one metrical level the repetition of a musical figure, section, movement or whatever can function in two different ways, depending on its place in a metrical wave. It can serve *to increase tension*, to accumulate energy, so to speak, but also *to effect resolution*, to establish completion, symmetry and closure.[23] Moreover, because music is always a multi-layered process, a repetition can perform *both functions concurrently*. One level's return is always another's advance. However strong the sense of closure may be at any one level, *there will always be levels in relation to which closure generates an increase in tension, giving rise to a stronger reaching out for further resolution.* Each fulfilment constitutes an increase of promise at a higher level. Every return closes and opens, resolves and intensifies.

Consider a musical theme being stated and then repeatedly 'returning', each return interspersed with different, perhaps contrasting material.[24] Each return marks a 'downbeat' on a metrical wave, the culmination of a resolution of tension on one level. But each return is also a means through which tension is generated, not only at that level, but 'further up' the metrical matrix. Similarly, a group of returns can function as a resolution of tension while concurrently functioning to generate an increasing tension at higher levels, thus intensifying the 'forward directedness' initiated by the first appearance of the theme.

And so to theology. It is hardly fanciful to contend that patterns of promise and (repeated) fulfilment recounted in Scripture display a remarkably similar dynamic to the one we have been uncovering. While not assuming a uniform systematic of promise/fulfilment, it would appear that frequently we are presented with multiple fulfilments of divine promises, such that 'each fulfilment in the past becomes promise for the future'.[25] Each fulfilment resolves something of the tension generated by the initial promise, and of the tension created by the last fulfilment. But each downbeat, while marking the culmination of a resolution process, also gives rise to a further tension demanding completion, not only a tension of the same power at the 'lower level', but of greater (and accumulating) power at upper levels. In this way, hope is intensified, a more potent 'reaching out' engendered.

In the history narrated in Scripture, in part this is because fulfilments are experienced as in some sense inadequate to expectation. Every fulfilment is partial and provisional, and therefore a partial *non*-fulfilment. The 'not yet' of expectation surpasses every fulfilment. And yet, far from diminishing the content of the hope, repeated fulfilments widen their content and extent. In many cases, this higher level of hope is, as it were, marked out by means of a 'drawing out' or an enlargement of the original promise. With each repeated fulfilment, the promise/theme is elaborated or augmented in some fashion, sometimes in highly surprising (though consistent) ways. 'As successive hopes find fulfilment, a tradition of "effective history" or "history of effects" (*Wirkungsgeschichte*) emerges in which horizons of promise become enlarged and filled with new content.'[26] Each downbeat brings an expectation and hope for *more*, so expanding the content and range of the original promise. In musical terms, the original theme is elaborated and developed in some (usually surprising) manner, so as to highlight the 'upper' wave(s) set in motion by its initial appearance.

Hope is also intensified in that each fulfilment is a partial realisation of what will eventually occur in its fullness. Correspondingly, every resolution in a piece of music is a partial realisation of the last resolution; indeed, in much music, the last major resolution is directly anticipated in advance.

By way of illustration, we can relate this to one substantial area of the Old Testament. David Clines has argued at length that the Pentateuch as a whole 'receives its impetus' from the patriarchal promise declared in Gen. 12:1-3, which contains three main elements: posterity, divine-human relationship, and land. He claims that the Pentateuch's 'central conceptual content' is 'divine promise awaiting fulfilment',[27] such that 'the interval between the promise and its redemption is one of tension'.[28] 'The theme of the Pentateuch is the partial fulfilment – which implies also the partial non-fulfilment – of the promise to or blessing of the patriarchs.'[29] Fulfilments carry forward (and sometimes explicitly reiterate) the original promise at another level: 'the partial fulfilments of the triple promise that occur within the Pentateuch have an anticipatory as well as a conclusive function'.[30] Both their inadequacy, and the fact that they are partial realisations of the end engender a reaching out towards a final conclusion. Furthermore, moving one level up the theological metrical waves, so to speak, Clines demonstrates that the patriarchal promise is a re-affirmation of the primal divine intentions for humanity (as expounded in Genesis 1–11),[31] and he also stresses that the Pentateuch as a whole narrates a movement towards a goal yet to be realised – its incompleteness is intrinsic to its meaning.[32]

As we might expect, Christology can be set in a similar light (or sound!). In the New Testament, in a myriad of ways, the advent of Jesus is presented as the completion of multiple implications inherent in the story of Israel, without the assumption that there have been no prior fulfilments. But this very 'conclusion' in Christ, climactic and utterly decisive as it may be, also constitutes an intensification and an enrichment of the promise originally made to Abraham. The first Christians are impelled towards a yet more fervent longing for a yet more glorious future. Again, this arises *both* because of a sense of the provisionality of the fulfilment – the world has not reached its intended end – *and* a sense that in *him* the end has arrived: Jesus Christ is raised as the first-fruits of those who have died (1 Cor.

15:20). Moreover, through the Spirit, there can be 'repeated' provisional fulfilments of the new promise set in motion by Christ (on the
lowest level, as it were), without effacing belief in a terminating
fulfilment in the eschaton, and without effacing the decisiveness of the
fulfilment in Christ. To know Christ by means of the Spirit (repeatedly) outpoured is to know (repeatedly) the 'first-fruits' of the life to
come (Rom. 8:23). The dynamic is expressed with singular power in
the Epistle to the Hebrews, written to a community tempted to fall
away from its eschatological calling and imbued with a theology of
promise (cf. especially 6:13-18). Few parts of the New Testament
stress with such vigour Christ's perfect, complete, finished sacrificial
offering, once-for-all (*ephapax*), culminating in his ascension and
eternal priesthood. This is in contrast to the incomplete and unfinished
character of Jewish priesthood, of which Christ is the decisive
completion. All the same, Old Testament texts about journeying and
waiting are appropriated to remind the readers that they have not yet
achieved eschatological finality and perfection, the divine closing
cadence, the 'rest' only provisionally fulfilled prior to Christ (3:7-
4:11). As Graham Hughes points out in his study *Hebrews and
Hermeneutics*, 'Jesus' exaltation is a *final and definitive form of the
promise* [given to Abraham]'.[33] And Jesus's exaltation is also anticipation of the final goal which the Christian community will enjoy.
Continually (i.e. repeatedly) 'looking to Jesus' now, to the pioneer
and perfecter of our faith (12:2), is therefore to 'venture forth', press
forward in faith, living 'in between' both the promise and fulfilment
enacted in him.[34] (Was the writer to the Hebrews musical?)

Of course, matters are hugely more elaborate than we have space
to indicate here. In both music and scriptural renderings of promises
and fulfilments, we are dealing with interweaving hopes, overlapping
short-term promises, interruptions, aspects of promises dropped, etc.
But enough has been said to indicate something of the theological
potential of musical repetition for enabling us to enter more deeply
into this aspect of God's self-communication. Two points in particular should be highlighted here.

First, much eschatological theology has been vitiated by single-
levelled, 'uniform line' models of temporality, giving rise, for
example, to assumptions that the resolution of promise (or prophecy)
is to be found in a singular, punctiliar, concentrated, and unambigu-
ous happening (or highly compressed cluster of happenings) in the
absence of which we are forced to pronounce the original promise
unfulfilled, void, or at least severely problematic. Musical repetition,
with its concurrent generation and dissolution of tension on different
levels, provides a much more adequate way of understanding, and

indeed *apprehending through sound*, how repeated fulfilments do not lessen but heighten expectation, how divine intention is disclosed through the 'in-tension' of promissory waves.[35] Second, the multi-layered texture of musical temporality if 'heard together' with eschatology in the way we have been attempting, can serve to bring into relief something of the pattern of the *inexhaustibility* of God in his self-communication. In listening to a piece of music for the first time, one never knows how many upper waves are being created. There is always, potentially, a higher wave being generated. There is always an 'overspill' of divine promise which history cannot accommodate, however close the correspondence between the promise and its (repeated) outcomes, an overspill which has its source in the limitlessness and uncontainability of God, 'the sheer inexhaustibility of the God of promise, who never exhausts himself in any historic reality but finally comes "to rest" only in a reality that wholly corresponds to him'.[36] It is instructive to set that quote from Moltmann alongside this description of metre by a musicologist:

> In the temporal component of music, then, we have to deal with a two-faced force, not to say a two-minded force. So far as it is responsible for the organisation of the individual measure, it is perpetually intent upon closing a cycle, reaching a goal; it wills the finite. On the other hand, with its renewed, ever more insistent 'On! Once again!' which hammers out measure after measure, it is a striving without end that accepts no limit, *a willing of the infinite*.[37]

It could be objected that the language of infinity here is misleading hyperbole, its theological attractiveness deceptive. For a piece of music ends; it *does* 'accept' its limits. There *is* a 'highest' wave, and it, along with all the others will 'fall' and converge on the last note or chord, to be succeeded only by silence. Further, it might be said that in this respect music is thoroughly unhelpful if we are to grasp the character of the 'ultimate fulfilment' of creation in relation to God. Indeed, according to at least one prominent reading of musical history, the tidy closures of tonal music betray modernity's questionable confidence in progress towards a goal marked by the ultimate purging of all unresolved implication and dissonance, the harmonisation of all conflict, a 'grand temporal consonance' (Kermode). Much has been written about the theological hazards of this kind of vision, not least its inability to accommodate creation's ultimate participation in the richness and inexhaustibility of God.

To this we reply: the musicologist still has a point. Musical 'finality' is a much more sophisticated business than we might suppose, and when heard theologically, can be highly evocative of God's inexhaustibility and the *telos* of the created world. Final closure is frequently unpredictable, delayed and deferred through a range of techniques, not least repetitive techniques. As we have observed already, this means that, unless one knows the piece well, *one is often uncertain whether or not 'higher' waves of tension are still being established*. Furthermore, there is a very pervasive feature of tonal music – 'modernist' tonal music, no less! – which lends it a specific kind of 'unboundedness'. To speak of music's reaching out 'infinitely' is indeed hyperbole, but it is instructive hyperbole nonetheless. Closures (cadences), even though they may be rhythmically accented, normally occur on *weak* metrical beats; in this sense, they reach out for further resolution. When we consider a piece of music as a whole, specifically those where the main fulfilment is achieved some time before final closure, we find the very last cadence is metrically weak. Thousands of pieces – including most pieces in 'sonata' form – follow this format. We reach a beguiling conclusion: *the piece never finishes* – the 'highest' wave never falls. There is a metrical momentum, articulated by some form of repetition, which cannot be contained or bounded. The music, in a sense, is projected beyond the final cadence into the ensuing silence. Promise 'breaks out' of sound.[38]

EUCHARISTIC REPETITION

To speak of liturgy is inevitably to speak of repetition. Most churches engage in the repeated performance of something akin to a liturgical form (even the most 'non-liturgical'!), and such forms often include a substantial amount of repetition (responses, litanies, etc.). In discussions of liturgical repetition, as with musical repetition, questions of power are rarely far from the surface. The decision about who is authorised to determine the rituals and repetitions of the liturgy 'is among the most far-reaching decisions any church can make'.[39] The fear of imposed liturgical conformity runs very deep in many, together with a fear of the manipulative potential of 'mindless' incantation. Suspicions about 'vain repetition' (cf. Matt. 6:7) often belong to the same circle of ideas.[40]

Perhaps the most schismatic issue in relation to liturgical repetition has been eucharistic repetition, the disagreement focussing not only on the relation between successive eucharistic celebrations, but even more on that between each celebration and God's 'unrepeatable' work in Jesus Christ. Here again, the musical 'grammar' of repetition has a considerable amount to offer.

Every Eucharist will relate to a complex of temporality, which is graciously given and generated by the activity of the triune God in and for the world, and which, we have been suggesting, can be usefully conceived as a multi-layered texture of metrical waves. At the lowest level, each 'down beat' could denote successive Eucharists; the highest wave would represent the over-arching history of God's engagement with the cosmos; and a multitude of waves, interacting and overlapping, lies in between. Insofar as we are bound to Christ through the Spirit, each Eucharist introduces us to, and enables us to participate in this abundant complexity of waves.

In addition, each Eucharist also enmeshes with the actual temporal patterns which shape our lives. Our temporality, it is sometimes said, is subject to a mutual alienation of past, present and future – a matter much discussed in studies of time in modernity and post-modernity. Our time is 'refracted time, time that has broken loose from God'.[41] Every Eucharist is a repeated opportunity *as time-laden creatures* to be incorporated into a temporal context, established in Christ, in which past, present and future co-inhere, in such a way that our identities can be healed, re-shaped and re-formed.[42] (It may be wise to follow Barth in linking this temporality with the dynamic interrelatedness of the triune God.[43]) It is often remarked that music seems to be able to 'transport' us into its own kind of temporality, to demarcate a distinctive temporal 'space' in radical contrast to the temporality of our day to day lives. We submit that while this may be true up to a point, music is of greatest theological significance, as far as temporality is concerned, insofar is it grants us an *engagement* with, and *re-configuring* of our temporality. Music 'takes' our time and 'returns it' to us re-shaped.

With this possibility in mind, and recalling the metrical waves, what happens if we attempt a musical reading of the Eucharist? Again, we can begin by imagining a theme being stated and then repeatedly recurring, each recurrence interspersed with different, perhaps contrasting material. We restrict ourselves to five main points.

(a) *Eucharist repetition both stabilises and de-stabilises.* It is often assumed that repetition is basically a stabilising practice – marking out secure points amidst life's flux. But we have seen that in metrical music, repetition can stabilise *and* de-stabilise: it can both 'close' the wave and provoke a desire for further fulfilment. And it can perform both these functions *concurrently.* The repetition of the Eucharist, we submit, stabilises. It is a means by which God regularly re-calls the Christian community to know again the transforming power of the cross – here the church's generative and inexhaustible theme is heard and sung again, here 'the Lord's death' is proclaimed (1 Cor. 11:26). At every Eucharist, in being opened to Christ by the Spirit, we are opened to his past, bearing upon us. However, the very same eucharistic repetition also de-stabilises – it does not leave us where we are. To be opened out repeatedly to Christ's past is to be opened out to a future anticipated in him, and thus to experience a 're-charging' of God's promise of a new future. It is to be incorporated into a forward momentum of the Spirit, which activates an increased longing – 'until he comes'. To speak of stabilising and de-stabilising here is *not* to speak of a dialectic of opposites set against each other, nor of successive phases of a process (as if we *first* 'look back' and *then* 'look forward'); in music, the accumulated tension at an upper level is *generated by* the repeated 'return' at the lower level(s). Repeated stabilising *gives rise to* instability. To be regularly re-bound to Christ who was crucified and raised from the dead *is* to be drawn into a stronger hope for the world.

I have used the word 'de-stabilise' here primarily because of the way in which this aspect of the Eucharist is to be felt by the church. Repeated eucharistic celebration will properly provide consolation, a rooting again in the forgiveness forged at the cross. But because it 'settles' us *in Christ* crucified and risen, in whom the new humanity of the future has been given in our midst, the Eucharist will provoke a distinct unsettledness, in ourselves and in relation to our surrounding reality, an acute sense that we (and our world) have not reached our 'rest' (Heb. 4). Christopher Rowland, writing of the Latin American Church's experience of poverty and oppression, speaks of every Eucharist as an anticipation of Christ's final judgement. He comments on some of the Pauline and Johannine eucharistic texts: 'One has very little sense here of a ritual occasion which was seen as the messianic banquet reserved only for the elect, cut off from the struggles and misdemeanours of ordinary life ... the identity of the group is not allowed to mask either the costliness of participation in social terms or the activity of God in history ... the Eucharist requires of us a *transformation of our present condition* pre-eminently in the case of the poor.'[44]

(b) *Eucharistic repetition can 'go flat'.* We have seen that repeated musical units – phrases, motifs, or whatever – invite and maintain interest chiefly because each repetition carries a different dynamic quality in relation to a hierarchy of waves. And we saw that in music with a very large amount of repetition, variations of one sort or another are introduced to clarify those waves.

It is quite possible, however, for a composer or performer to fail in this respect. We only need listen to a beginner playing a piece of highly repetitive music. It will often sound 'flat', 'mechanical' and 'dull', precisely because he or she has not yet learned to 'feel', and turn into physical movement those upper levels of metre. This helps us to see part of what might be involved in 'empty' repetition, 'ritualized' ritual as distinct from ritual. Christian history is replete with thousands of one-levelled performances of the Eucharist where each celebration is effectively 'flattened' into one level of significance, with little regard for the diverse layers of theological import involved. There is, for instance, a kind of eucharistic worship over-concerned with closure and completeness, which builds up no tension on any more elevated level than that of its own recurring (and resolved) performances. In such worship there will be an exaggerated sense of stability, little sense of participating in a movement of divine longing beyond this particular act, little sense of being caught up in a work of the Spirit (the 'willing of the infinite'), little sense of being drawn into a larger, wider hope for the world. Eucharists of this kind, ensnared by their own single-level reiterations, quickly become inured against the anguish of the world. This is worship 'without bite of threat or gift'.[45]

Many churches, out of a desire to avoid 'dull' liturgy, make frantic efforts to 'make services more interesting', which often means trying to make every one as different as possible from the last. Ironically, this can lead to a strange kind of 'sameness'. A wiser strategy is to learn from the musician who has learned to develop a heightened sensibility to the many layers of metre. There may well be variation, but the variations, properly employed, will serve the purpose of 'marking out' those upper waves. Whether or not we belong to a tradition which celebrates the church's liturgical year, this is one way of enabling the church to sense something of the multi-layered waves of salvation. As each Eucharist is experienced as occupying a different 'place' in the seasonal waves, it is almost bound to be sensed differently.

(c) *Eucharistic repetition does not efface the temporal integrity of the initial appearance of the theme nor of its repetitions.* The initial sounding of the theme is circumscribed and bounded. It begins and ends. It has its own completeness. A later repetition is not a prolongation or extension of the theme. Moreover, the subsequent repetition of the theme is not a matter of extracting the theme from its temporal relations and relocating it, as if we could wrench it from 'that time' to 'this time'. It is embedded in a field of temporal contingencies – other notes, phrases, elaborations – which are intrinsic to its identity. Most important, it has a unique dynamic quality by virtue of its relation to a hierarchy of metrical waves. No later appearance of the theme will have this same quality. Identical repetition in the 'now' is impossible, not just because *we* are in a different temporal context, but because every musical event relates to a different hierarchical pattern of tension and resolution.

Eucharistic repetition is not a matter of prolongation, continuation or protraction. Nor is it a matter of extracting something from one time to another. The crucifixion of Jesus took place in relation to a specific combination of historical contingencies ('under Pontius Pilate'), and in a quite unique set of relations to different levels of God's salvific purposes. There can therefore be no attempt to extract that occurrence from its situatedness and 'make *it* happen again now'. This is the classic Protestant concern for the completeness, and the particularity of Christ's work.

By the same token, every subsequent repetition of the theme will have *its* own temporal integrity, not only in relation to our temporal context (and we shall deal with this shortly) but also in relation to the unique configuration of tensions and resolutions to which *it* relates in the metrical hierarchy. Similarly with every Eucharist.[46] (Furthermore, in music where the repeated theme is elaborated, we will never hear the original theme the same way after we have heard its elaborations. Every Eucharist relates not only directly in an over-arching wave to the death and resurrection of Christ (proclaiming the Lord's death), but also, via its 'bottom-level' waves to every previous Eucharist. Our reception of any Eucharist will be shaped, sometimes quite radically, by our accumulated experience of previous celebrations.[47])

(d) *Eucharistic repetition entails improvising.* I have said that each appearance of the theme relates to our temporal context. Especially instructive here is musical improvisation on a theme. When you improvise, typically you engage intensely with the particular constraints of the setting – the acoustic of the building, the time of day, the number of people present, their expectations and experience, their audible response as the performance proceeds, and, not least, the music produced by other improvisers. These elements are not accidental to the outcome but constitutive of it – they are incorporated into the improvisation in order that the improvisation can be, so to speak, 'true' and profoundly authentic to this time (and place). The poet Peter Riley speaks of improvisation as 'the exploration of occasion'.[48] To some degree every performer explores the occasion; however, the increased contingency of improvisation obliges the musician to work particularly hard at bringing alive the 'given' music in a way which 'hooks into' this unique occasion, this 'one off' combination of constraints, such that the theme is heard as fruitful in a new way for the present, and, implicitly for the future. Fresh possibilities, inherent in the theme are thereby brought to light. And in the process, the constraints are themselves enhanced, magnified, developed, enabled in some manner to be more fully themselves — players become more skilful, new features of the instrument come to light, we become more aware of the ambience of the setting, and so forth.

John Calvin used to insist that although the Lord's Supper does not mean inviting Christ to share in our spatio-temporality but rather the ascended Christ inviting us to share in his, nevertheless our space and time are not effaced or escaped.[49] Far from it. Our humanity, in union with Christ, with all that time has made us to this day, is redeemed and enhanced in its particularity, brought nearer to its intended end and fruition. And this is the work of the Holy Spirit. It is also, I submit, the work of the skilled improviser – to particularise the theme for *this* occasion. The Spirit is *the* 'explorer of occasion', *the* improviser *par excellence* in every eucharistic repetition.

(e) *Eucharistic repetition depends on and enables a particular kind of interpenetration of past, present and future.* We have seen enough to suggest that because they are set in a metrical field, musical events are probably best conceived as *internally* related in and through time. When we are in the second phase of a two-beat metrical wave, it makes little sense to say the first simply retreats into nothingness. Due to the hierarchy of waves, nothing, as it were, is 'left behind'; in every instance of 'two', the 'one' is also implicated as the partner; 'two' is the symmetrical completion of 'one'. In every bar, therefore, there is a sense in which a musical event's 'entire past is preserved in its present and given directly with it'.[50] Likewise, because of the wave hierarchy, the first beat proceeds towards the second; within the existence of the first is a need for completion. It is not enough to say the second is not yet, the present of 'one' is a present directed towards its future, pregnant with future. And the same applies to the second beat in relation to the first of the next wave. Thus, 'past and future are given with and in the present and are experienced with and in the present; hearing a melody is hearing, having heard, and being about to hear'.[51] As musical occurrences anticipate their future they carry their past; as their future is *un*folded, their past – and ours – is *en*folded.

All this would need very much more justification and qualification than we are able to provide here.[52] But at the very least we can say that a musical construal of the temporal context of eucharistic repetition would appear to be able to take more adequate account of both Jewish and Christian 'remembrance' (*anamnesis*) and the Eucharist's future anticipation than many eucharistic theologies. Robert Jenson has recently argued that ecumenical debates about the Eucharist between Catholics and Protestants – along with many other themes of contention – have been corrupted by a number of flawed assumptions about time and temporal occurrence which have impeded a proper understanding of the character of *anamnesis* and anticipation. We can mention two. First, a one-level linear view of time is assumed, in which events are seen as receding into ever greater remoteness in the memory unless preserved or 'held' in some manner. 'In the Catholic interpretation, some events are left behind as time marches on and others are carried along by *institutionalization*.'[53] The ecclesial institution thus maintains continuity between Christ's finished work and every Eucharist. 'In the Protestant interpretation, time goes on with or without the repetition of any one event; repetition, if it occurs, is occasioned *extrinsically*.'[54] In other words, God, or Christ (or the president?) must repeatedly 'break into' time in order to make the past event 'live' *now* in the Eucharist. Second, 'both interpretations seem to presuppose the mutually extrinsicality ... of time and *events*. Events happen *in* time, by both interpretations, and may or may not be carried along *through* time.'[55]

Whatever hesitations we may have about some of the details of Jenson's assessment, it is intriguing that music effectively subverts these two basic assumptions. First, it should be clear by now that uniform, one-level models will distort our understanding of musical temporality. Repetition in music is not a one-level succession of ever-receding events on a 'straight' time-line, but occurs only in relation to a composite of metrical waves in relation to which musical events cannot be conceived as falling 'backwards' into vacuity. Second, we have seen that time and musical events are intrinsically bound together; notes do not roll down some bowling alley of time (nor are they highlighted by the 'spotlight' of the present). They live and interrelate dynamically in and through time.

Our reflections here can be expanded by reference to Jean-Luc Marion's treatment of the Eucharist in his book *God Without Being*. Marion is especially concerned to stress that eucharistic presence is not a function of the will, attention or consciousness of the church. (This is as much a Protestant error as a Catholic!) The logical extension of this would be the belief that Christ's presence endures only for as long as the community is present; the present becomes the unique and sole horizon of the eucharistic gift: 'presence is valid only in the present, and in the present of the community consciousness'.[56] Marion maintains that this binding of eucharistic presence to 'the immediate consciousness of the collective self' is dependent on a conception of time in which there is an 'ontological overdetermination of a primacy of the present: the past finishes and the future begins as soon as the present begins or finishes. Their respective temporalities count only negatively, as a double nonpresent, even a double nontime.'[57] Countering this, Marion proposes that eucharistic presence be understood chiefly as gift, and according to the order of the gift the eucharistic present is temporalized from past and future, and only finally from the present. From the past it is temporalized as memorial (the present is understood as a today to which alone the memorial, as an actual pledge, gives meaning and reality); from the future as eschatological announcement ('the pledge, which the memorial sets into operation, now anticipates the future, so that the present itself occurs entirely as this anticipation concretely lived'[58]); and then, only finally is the eucharistic present temporalised from the present 'as dailyness and viaticum' (the eucharistic present is never possession, but always gift, to be received anew each instant, each hour, each day).[59]

This would seem remarkably congruent with the temporality disclosed in music. Musical repetition in this context is not, as we have seen, primarily a device whereby we in the (real) present attempt to 'preserve' and carry forward into the (as yet) unknown and unreal future something that otherwise might be lost in oblivion. In music, past and future are not 'blackouts' created by the present, but the very determinants of the present. In the midst of our fractured and distorted temporality, we are given to participate in a temporality such that our past, present and future can be at 'peace', co-inhere. Likewise, repeated Eucharists are not a means by which the Christian community repeatedly attempts to recover in its corporate memory now an ever-retreating event. Eucharistic remembering cannot be a matter of our calling to mind a nonpresence, nor is 'anticipation' a matter of our imagining an utterly discontinuous and unreal future. The Eucharist is the repeated embodiment of God's 'summons', provoking our attention, opening us out to Christ in such a way that what Christ was, suffered and did for us is made ever and again contemporary in its completeness for us who are still 'on the way', and, moreover, in such a way that his past is known not merely as past to us but also future. Put another way, the Holy Spirit opens our present (and us) to Christ's past and future, and, as in the case of music, this does not entail the refusal of 'our' temporality, but its healing and re-shaping.

There is, of course, no pretence here that every stumbling block in eucharistic controversy evaporates in the presence of the sound of music! But enough has been outlined for us to propose that consideration of music might be of singular assistance in freeing us from some conceptions of time which have disfigured the debates.

BROADER IMPLICATIONS

Clearly, there are many issues in connection with the philosophy of repetition that we have been unable to address, and we have dealt with only a very small range of repetitive strategies in music. Nevertheless, we have seen something of the considerable potential of musical repetition for opening up and articulating some of the central temporal characteristics of God's self-communication. In this final part of the paper we indicate something of the wider implications of our discussion. I limit myself to comments in four areas.

(a) One very obvious implication to arise is that informed treatments of music could arguably have an important, even prominent place in *theological treatments of time*. The almost complete absence of any mention of music in modern (and post-modern) theologies of time (despite Augustine!) is extraordinary and perhaps even reprehensible. The philosophy of time is, of course, a subject of notorious and fierce complexity, and conclusions, including those which draw on musical temporality, have of necessity to be tentative. Nevertheless, because of music's especially intimate intertwining with time, issues in the philosophy of time which have proved crucial in theology are raised with exceptional vividness. More than that, we have tried to show that music may well offer assistance in liberating us from certain conjectures about temporality which have corrupted theological tradition. In particular, musical repetition of the kind we have examined, and the temporality upon which it relies and which it brings to sound, raise acute questions about conceptions of time which suggest that only the present is 'real': this is hard to sustain when brought into engagement with the phenomena of music. The paradox here is that music, apparently the most transient and evanescent of the arts (seemingly real only in the 'present moment'), may well in fact be the art-form which most directly and intensively embodies a mutual implication of past, present and future.[60]

(b) Bound up with this, consideration of musical repetition raises crucial issues concerning the *time-laden character of the physical world*. It is frequently said that music is the most 'spiritual' of the arts, and hence the most valuable in explicating the nature of divine communication and the communication of the divine. 'Spiritual' here is frequently understood to denote an evasion of temporality and materiality. So it is assumed by some that music can contribute most theologically insofar as it directs our attention away from time, evoking or approximating to a timeless condition or state.[61] Some support this by a theological rationale which acclaims music's ability to suggest the (purported) 'timelessness' of eternity. In the same circle of ideas is the view that because music is marked by a high degree of impermanence and insubstantiality (where is the melody once it is played?), and because it cannot achieve anything like the same precision of reference to extra-musical physical objects or states of affairs as the other arts and consequently in comparison with other art-forms would seem to have the loosest 'ties' to the physical world, it is especially apt to be drawn into the service of theology. In addition, this is sometimes bolstered by an appeal to the supposed 'inwardness' of music – more than anything else, music, it is said, arises from and is geared towards stimulating our emotional life.[62]

On the contrary, we would maintain that music can contribute most to a theology of divine communication precisely in and through its intense engagement with time, time as an irreducible dimension of created being. Rowan Williams writes: 'if music is the most fundamentally contemplative of the arts, it is *not* because it takes us into the timeless but because *it obliges us to rethink time*'.[63] Our discussion above suggests that music is capable of granting us a peculiarly profound experience of time; not as absolute receptacle or inert background, nor merely as psychological or cultural construction, but time as a function of the interrelationship between physical entities.[64] The Christian faith announces that our experience of temporality corresponds to a dimension of created reality with its own integrity established by the creator. More than this, it announces that this temporality is a gift, such that our interaction with time need not be characterised by struggle, competition, intrusion or invasion. Nor need it be marked by retreat or escape. God's own climactic self-communication in Christ – from which, ultimately, all our discussions about temporality must take their cue – involves an interaction with temporality that neither evades nor attempts to defeat it. Music has the potential to demonstrate that these two broad options do not exhaust the possibilities. (In this music has a good deal to offer to those who would argue that too much theology has been perennially plagued by a suspicion of the goodness and order of time, rendering an adequate grasp of the temporality of God's self-communication highly problematic.) Our findings suggest that music is not *essentially* to do with an escape from (or evasion of) the temporality and temporal relations of the physical world, nor an imposition of a particular kind of time upon a basically atemporal world, but affords the possibility of an interaction with and re-configuration of the temporality of the created world. Through music's presentation of an ordering of and in time, we are enabled to participate in the relation of physical entities in such a way as to bring the possibility of 'peaceful' interaction with the (good) time God confers upon creation. Williams again: 'What we learn, in music as in the contemplative faith of which music is a part and also a symbol, is what it is to work *with* the [temporal] grain of things, to work in the stream of God's wisdom.'[65]

(c) Moreover, we do so as physical, *bodily creatures*, as those who themselves are physical and time-laden. The making and enjoyment of music are profoundly bodily activities. A significant quantity of research into the organismic dimensions of musical rhythms has appeared. It shows that the human neuro-physiological 'clock' against which periodic processes and temporal experiences are measured is intricate in the extreme, integrating very many different time forms associated with different bodily activities.[66] Whatever the intricacies, there is little doubt that musical repetition with its associated metrical waves, is 'lived in' and (in many cases) 'lived out' by the body. (The link between repetition and bodily processes is also confirmed in the way in which fear of repetition in some branches of the church is expressed – a resistance to empty bodily actions not properly linked to 'inner' attitudes and intentions.[67]) One of the differences between responses thought appropriate at a 'classical' music concert and, say, a rock concert is that the quality of the former is often measured by the degree of stillness achieved during performance ('you could have heard a pin drop'), in the latter by the degree of physical movement generated ('I came away exhausted').[68] In popular music, the most commonly learned form of associated movement is dance, and whatever else dance involves, it is a 'living in' and 'living out' of repetitive patterns highlighting metrical waves.

Studies of ritual, of course, come to mind in this connection, a topic of growing theological interest. But this is beyond the scope of this essay. The point to register here is simply that if it is foundational to the Christian faith that the promissory 'waves' of God's self-communication have been embodied, enacted, 'danced' for us in history, supremely in Christ; and if it is integral to Christian freedom that participation in these waves entails (in some manner) the participation of our bodies with their peculiarities and specific capabilities; then there is a vast and largely untapped reservoir of *musical* wisdom which can be drawn upon by theologians to enhance the understanding of this bodily dimension of salvation.

(d) A fourth area opened up by our discussion concerns musical repetition in relation to *wider social and cultural practices*. The field is vast. However, in order to pinpoint some of the issues at stake, we restrict ourselves to some comments on musical repetition in 'popular culture' and its relation to the church. 'It's monotonous'; 'it's predictable'; 'it's all the same' – comments such as these about popular music, including some brands of church music, echo the discussions of the mass culture theorists of the 1930s and 40s. From this point of view, repetition (within a piece of music) can be assimilated to the same category as what Adorno called 'standardization' (as between pieces of music). Undeniably, popular music places heavy reliance on techniques of repetition: 'if music is a syntax of equivalence, much popular music carries the principle to a highpoint'.[69] Undeniably, metre is normally highly regular at every level. And, undeniably, repetition within music, in the hands of a burgeoning music industry, has been used to define and hold markets, to channel types of consumption, and to pre-form response. The church has not been slow to engage in such projects, as a number of critics of worship music are only too keen to point out.[70]

Nevertheless, alongside the proper suspicion, we also require a heightened sensitivity to different forms of repetition, and to the different ways in which repetition is practised and functions within particular settings. In this regard, three points are in order. First, in virtually all contemporary popular music, a high degree of repetition ensures structures which have a large measure of continuity and a relatively low incidence of disruption or radical contrast.[71] It is only very rarely acknowledged by cultural theorists (and even less in Christian attacks on 'post-modern' popular culture) that the multiple visual overwhelming of the 'video/screen culture' is nearly always accompanied by music, and that the metrical/rhythmical structure of the music displays very little of the fragmentation and disjointedness allegedly present in the kaleidoscope of imagery. There may indeed be 'sampling' – the bringing together of sounds from many different sources – but this is tied to a tight and cohesive harmonic and rhythmic structure. In many ways, music provides the continuity absent in the visual display. Second, although repetitive strategies can function to create a sense of direction in music, as we have seen, this is usually so only if the upper levels of metre are brought into prominence. Large amounts of popular music, while privileging repetition, effectively ignore those upper waves, thus subduing directionality and the sense of long-term goals. Dance music from the much-discussed 'rave' culture is an example – now very much alive in some British churches – paralleled in many ways in the sound-world created by 'minimalist' composers (Riley, Reich, Glass).

These observations clearly raise important theological questions about the deployment of music in the service of the church, not least in worship. But they must be held together with a third point. The way in which musical repetition is going to function and be received in any particular context depends on a vast network of constraints, a multiplicity of intersecting variables – acoustics, expectations, the music people are used to hearing, biological make-up, the way the music is introduced, and so forth. A 'theology through music' may indeed highlight theological resonances in musical repetition in a way that is highly instructive for theology, but we need to be very cautious about assuming that we can then instantly translate these resonances into a project which would outlaw certain forms of music and promote others in order to secure some specific desired theological 'effect'. Musical communication is generally more complex (and interesting) than that.

The implicit claim of this paper is that 'theology through music', as a heuristic discipline, has the capacity to *advance* the theological enterprise in highly significant ways, not least as theology seeks to clarify and articulate the inexhaustible depths of God's gracious self-communication. Music holds out sizeable opportunities at a time when artistic questions are increasingly on the theological agenda, and when theological discourse seems all too prone to a certain (repetitive!) weariness. It remains to be seen how far theologians will avail themselves of these opportunities. But if they do, it will not be long before they will be wondering how it is that so much theology has managed to do with so little music.

NOTES

[1]   This article originates from a paper delivered at the annual conference of the Society for the Study of Theology, University of Kent, April, 1997. The theme of the conference was 'The Communication of God'.

[2]   There are some notable exceptions. One of the most recent is Frances Young's book *The Art of Performance*, a penetrating essay in musico-theological hermeneutics (Young, 1990). And there have been a few courageous forays by musicologists into theology: e.g. Mellers (1981, 1983); Chafe (1991).

[3]   Attali (1985), p. 4.

[4]   There have been theologians who, without developing their theology in dialogue with any systematic treatment of music, have nevertheless pursued theology in a

musical manner. Jonathan Edwards is a prime example. Cf. Jenson (1988), pp. 20, 35f., 42, 47ff., 169, 182, 195.

5   Cf. a stream of writers from Benjamin to Baudrillard, see e.g. Deleuze (1969), Derrida (1976).

6   Cf. Attali (1985) on the era of 'repetition'. For Attali, 'repetition' (mass reproduction) is in crisis. Overproduction leads to devolution, even a universalising of cultural power among users, because the enormous accessibility of music threatens all traditional 'uses' of music and communicative codes – music, all music, is just *there*. For much more nuanced discussions, cf. Connor (1997), pp. 165ff. and Middleton (1990), especially chs 2 and 3.

7   Adorno tended to see the enjoyment of repetition as psychotic and infantile; Adorno (1973), pp. 160ff., esp. pp. 178–81. For sensitive treatment of Adorno, see Paddison (1993); and in relation to popular music, Middleton (1990), ch. 2.

8   Zuckerkandl (1956), p. 213.

9   Middleton (1990), pp. 215ff., 267ff.

10 Kivy (1993), p. 328. It was in line with this that Nicolas Ruwet, drawing on R. Jakobson's description of poetry, proposed a whole analytic method – 'paradigmatic analysis' – based on the concept of 'equivalence'; Ruwet (1987). Ruwet believes that the most striking characteristic of musical syntax was the central rôle played by repetition, and by extension of varied repetition or transformation. The strong interest shown by Bright (1963) and Nattiez (1990) in concepts of 'variance' and 'equivalence' signals an implicit confirmation of this.

11 Middleton (1983), p. 236.

12 Barry (1990), pp. 65ff.

13 The fact that some have found and do find this music dull need not alter the point being made. The fact is that millions have found in it an endless source of delight without complaining of boredom, and without any suggestion that Beethoven was experiencing some kind of 'off day'!

14 Kivy (1993), pp. 349ff.

15 In a typical nineteenth-century symphony it is common for the entire first section of a movement (lasting, say, five minutes) to be repeated note for note at the end of the movement. Parallels in literature are few and far between.

16 Writing on the relationship and analogies between music and language abounds; for useful and careful discussions, cf. Nattiez (1990), ch. 5, esp. the section on musical narrativity (pp. 127ff.); Norton (1984), pp. 65–71; Sloboda (1993), ch. 2; Thomas (1995); Brown (1987), ch. 9. Musical repetition is one of the things which strains such analogies to breaking point.

17 Cf. Cone (1968), p. 46, on Chopin's *Polonaise* in A major.

18 What follows is dependent especially on the work of Kramer (1988), Berry (1985), Lester (1986), Hasty (1981) and Zuckerkandl (1956).

19 Zuckerkandl (1956), pp. 174ff.

20 I am employing the word 'tension' in a very wide sense, to describe that which is generated by any musical event that is implicatory, an event which in its context arouses in us a sense of expectation, that matters cannot be left as they are. 'An implicative relationship is one in which an event – be it a motive, a phrase, and so on – is patterned in such a way that reasonable inferences can be made both about its connections with preceding events and about how the event itself might be continued and perhaps reach closure and stability. By "reasonable inferences" I mean those which a competent, experienced listener – one familiar with and sensitive to the particular style – might make' (Meyer, 1973, p. 110). 'Resolution' can consequently also be understood in a broad sense to describe the process of

completion of the implication, the dissipation of the tension generated by the implicatory event. A tension – in our sense – *may* arise through some kind of conflict or antagonism between two or more musical elements – dissonance being an example (where combinations of notes are regarded as conflictual and radically unstable) – but not necessarily so. All that is necessary is the generation of a sense of incompleteness.

21 Zuckerkandl (1956), pp. 152–180; (1959), pp. 98–136; Kramer (1988), ch. 4.

22 Zuckerkandl (1956), p. 222. My italics.

23 For the purposes of the discussion, we leave aside instances where repetition extends over the mid-point of a wave.

24 For the purposes of our argument, the 'return' does not have to be an identical set of notes. The theme may be varied, elaborated, augmented, and so forth; all that matters in this case is that the returns are recognisable as variations or transformations of the original theme.

25 Goldingay (1990), p. 117. Of course, it could be objected that the setting up of a 'tension' is one thing, a promise another; and that in music it is rare to find anything closely resembling a promise directed towards a very specific end. However, we are understanding 'tension' in music in a wide sense, to denote that which is generated by any implicative event (see above, n. 20), and this would certainly include a promise. There may well be a sharp discrepancy or conflict between the promised reality and the context in which the promise is uttered (the promise of return in the midst of Israel's exile, for example), and this will undoubtedly increase the sense of tension and 'longing' for resolution, but such conflict is not essential for the promise to function as such.

26 Thiselton (1995), pp. 150f., paraphrasing Pannenberg.

27 Clines (1994), p. 111. Clines draws on the work of others, notably Zimmerli's treatment of promise and fulfilment (1963, 1971).

28 Clines (1994), p. 116.

29 *ibid.*, p. 29.

30 *ibid.*, p. 117.

31 *ibid.*, pp. 61ff.

32 *ibid.*, pp. 110f. The dynamic is of course considerably richer than I can indicate here; not least because in the Pentateuch not only are we presented with repeated fulfilments, the patriarchal *promise itself* is repeated (and amplified).

33 Hughes (1979), p. 53. My italics.

34 Cf Thiselton (1996), pp. 262ff.

35 In this connection, a case could be made for recommending that the convolutions of Romans 9–11 be read in a similar way. Is this not an appeal from Paul to wrest his hearers away from understanding the historical outworking of the promise to Abraham on one level alone? To believe that the unbelieving Jews are necessarily excluded from the fulfilment of God's promises in Christ is to fail to see that *this very fulfilment* carries forward the original promise to Abraham – that God will form one people without racial exclusion, inclusive of Israel.

36 Moltmann (1967), p. 106.

37 Zuckerkandl (1956), p. 176. My italics.

38 Crucial to this is Kramer's argument in Kramer (1988), pp. 117f.

39 Sykes (1996), p. 158, *et passim.*

40 Speaking of Matt. 6, Sykes remarks: 'It is ironic that the most frequently repeated prayer of all in the Christian tradition [the Lord's Prayer] should follow an injunction against vain repetition' (*ibid.*, p. 160).

41 Torrance (1976), p. 97.

[42] The transformation of human identity in God's new temporal context has recently been stressed by Anthony Thiselton, in a sustained argument against postmodernist construals of the self, especially those which would advocate 'instantaneousness' as a privileged vantage point (Cupitt), and thus create 'insoluble problems about meaning, identity, self and God'. Drawing on Ricoeur and Pannenberg, he writes: '*"who we are" emerges in terms of God's larger purposes and promises for the world, society, for the church and for us*. This purposive anticipation of the future finds expression in our sense of *being called by God to a task within that frame*. We find our identity and meaning when we discover our *vocation*.' Thiselton (1995), p. 151. Significantly, his essay closes with a piece of compressed exegesis of passages from Hebrews (p. 163).

[43] Despite his opacity, Barth is clear in his desire to link a vision of redemption as the integrating of past, present and future with the dynamic interrelatedness of God's triunity. Refusing to define eternity apart from the particular temporality of Jesus, Barth specifies the particular eternity of the triune God as 'pure duration', in which beginning, succession and end do not fall apart, in which there is no conflict between source, movement and goal, but rather mutual co-inherence. The configuration of divine eternity, the trinitarian structure of movement and interplay, is perichoretic not only in itself but also in its reception of history. The economy of salvation thus frees and liberates our history for the perichoresis of eternity without dissolving its character as created being. Barth (1957), pp. 608–640.

[44] Rowland (1995), pp. 207, 208, my italics. For an impressive presentation of a similar dynamic in Old Testament worship, cf. Brueggemann (1988). Even more fundamentally, the Eucharist de-stabilises *our very understanding* of 'our present condition' by situating us in a temporality which is directed towards a new future promised in Christ. This prevents us from making our particular 'present situation' some fixed and immutable point of reference (for God as well as us!). Cf. Thiselton's devastating critique of some pastoral theology, especially its tendency to pivot theological understanding around 'the present situation', in Thiselton (1992), pp. 604ff. Music reminds us that our present is 'temporalized' from past and future. It may be that if more pastoral theologians took music more seriously, some of these problems might not arise!

[45] Brueggemann (1988), p. 45.

[46] As Dr Markus Bockmuehl helpfully pointed out to me, 'remote' repetition of the kind we are considering might not do justice to the revelational and soteriological uniqueness of Christ: the notes of the theme are, after all, still reiterated, however different their dynamic quality. Despite this, the 'remote' repetition does highlight in an illuminating way the differences between successive performances of the Eucharist, even if it is weaker in explicating the difference between these and the foundational 'theme' from which they take their cue.

[47] Rowan Williams, speaking of the biblical text, writes: 'What we are dealing with is a text that has generated an enormous family of contrapuntal elaborations, variations, even inversions – rather like the simple theme given to Bach by Frederick the Great, that forms the core of *The Art of Fugue*. When we have listened to the whole of that extraordinary work, we cannot simply hear the original notes picked out by the King of Prussia as if nothing had happened. We can't avoid saying now: '*This* can be the source of *that*' – and that is a fact of some importance about the simple base motif.' Williams (1989), pp. 93f.

[48] As cited in Dean (1989), p. xvi.

[49] *Institutio* (1559), IV:17, especially pars. 10, 11, 12, 26.

50 Zuckerkandl (1956), p. 225.

51 *ibid.*, p. 235.

52 The case has been argued at great length, against 'projectionist' and 'absolutist' views of time, by Victor Zuckerkandl (1956, esp. chs 1-6).

53 Jenson (1992), p. 110.

54 *ibid.* My italics.

55 *ibid.*

56 Marion (1991), pp. 166f.

57 *ibid.*, p. 170.

58 *ibid.*, p. 174.

59 *ibid.*, p. 172. Critical questions need to be asked about Marion's own version of transubstantiation, in particular whether or not he gives due weight to the particular ministry of the Holy Spirit in preserving the 'distance' between the eucharistic presence and the consciousness of the community, and in uniting us to the One in whom the temporal modes cohere.

60 Of course, the visual diagram of the metrical waves I have deployed could be misunderstood as endorsing a version of the 'myth of passage' view of time – according to which musical events would be understood as 'moving along' its lines, or else a surge of the 'present moment' doing likewise. While acknowledging the dangers, and the unavoidability of metaphors of motion in musical description, we can still employ the diagram to illustrate temporal relations of tension and resolution, and to bring out the asymmetrical, irreversible character of music's engagement with time. What we would need to take care to avoid is any suggestion that this 'directionality' is in distinction to some self-subsistent 'time-scale' external to and independent of musical entities and occurrences.

61 Whatever one makes of the music of John Tavener, his writings strongly advocate the theological appropriateness of developing an immunity in music to the opportunities and threats of time. Cf. Begbie (1996).

62 This broad line of thinking has a venerable history; a subtle version appearing in Hegel. It is the thrust of the philosophy of music developed by the Congregationalist theologian, P. T. Forsyth, drawing heavily on Hegel. Cf. Begbie (1995).

63 Williams (1994), p. 248. My italics.

64 Cf. above, n. 52.

65 Williams (1994), p. 250. I develop these matters at greater length elsewhere: Begbie (1997), and in *Theology, Music and Time*, Cambridge: Cambridge University Press, 2000.

66 Cf. Middleton (1990), pp. 226f.

67 In an important essay on repetition in relation to liturgy, Stephen Sykes, drawing on the work of Mary Douglas, highlights the Protestant inclination towards 'interiority' and its characteristic stress on right intention as a means of opposing certain forms of repetition. There is a tendency to assimilate externals to the realm of 'works' unless they are preceded by the life-changing, interior transformation of one's standing before God. Sykes (1996), p. 162.

68 Frith (1996), p. 124. In fact, we could argue that there *is* movement in the 'classical' concert, an 'inner' movement of mind and heart as the listener is caught up in the temporal lines of the music.

69 Middleton (1990), p. 189.

70 Percy (1996), ch. 4.

71 Middleton (1990), pp. 216f., 268ff. Most post rock 'n' roll songs display varying

proportions of 'lyric' and 'epic' forms, the former marked by symmetrical and binary structures, the latter focussing on repetition and varied repetition. What is relatively rare are structures that privilege difference and the resolution of conflict, especially on the large scale.

REFERENCES

Adorno, Theodor (1973), *Philosophy of Modern Music*, London: Sheed and Ward.

Attali, Jacques (1985), *Noise*, trans. Brian Massumi, Manchester: Manchester University Press.

Barry, Barbara (1990), *Musical Time: The Sense of Order*, Stuyvesant: Pendragon Press.

Barth, Karl (1957), *Church Dogmatics, II/1*, trans. T. H. L. Parker *et al.*, Edinburgh: T. & T. Clark.

Begbie, Jeremy S. (1995), 'The Ambivalent Rainbow: Forsyth, Art and Creation,' in Trevor Hart (ed.), *Justice the True and Only Mercy*, Edinburgh: T. & T. Clark, pp. 197–219.

Begbie, Jeremy S. (1996), 'Theology through Music: Tavener, Time and Eternity,' in David Ford and Dennis Stamps (eds), *Essentials of Christian Community*, Edinburgh: T. & T. Clark, pp. 23–34.

Begbie, Jeremy S. (1997), 'Theology and Music,' in David Ford (ed.), *The Modern Theologians*, Oxford: Blackwell, pp. 686–699.

Berry, Wallace (1985), 'Metric and Rhythmic Articulation in Music,' *Music Theory Spectrum*, 7, pp. 7–33.

Bright, W. (1963), 'Language and Music: Areas for Co-operation,' *Ethnomusicology*, 7, 1, pp. 26–32.

Brown, Calvin (1987), *Music and Literature: A Comparison of the Arts*, Hanover and London: University Press of New England.

Brueggemann, Walter (1988), *Israel's Praise: Doxology against Idolatry and Ideology*, Philadelphia: Fortress Press.

Chafe, Eric (1991), *Tonal Allegory in the Vocal Music of J. S. Bach*, Berkeley: University of California Press.

Clines, David J. A. (1994), *The Theme of the Pentateuch*, Sheffield: Sheffield Academic Press.

Cone, Edward T. (1968), *Musical Form and Musical Performance*, New York: Norton.

Connor, Steven (1997), *Postmodernist Culture*, Oxford: Blackwell.

Dean, Roger (1989), *Creative Improvisation*, Milton Keynes: Open University Press.

Deleuze, G. (1969), *Difference and Repetition*, trans. Paul Patton, London: Athlone Press.

Derrida, Jacques (1976), *Of Grammatology*, trans. Gayatri Chakravorty Spivak, Baltimore and London: John Hopkins University Press.

Frith, Simon (1996), *Performing Rites: On the Value of Popular Music*, Oxford: Oxford University Press.

Hasty, Christopher F. (1981), 'Rhythm in Post-Tonal Music: Preliminary Questions of Duration and Motion,' *Journal of Music Theory*, 25, pp. 183–216.

Hughes, Graham (1979), *Hebrews and Hermeneutics*, Cambridge: Cambridge University Press.

Jenson, Robert W. (1992), *Unbaptised God: The Basic Flaw in Ecumenical Theology*, Minneapolis: Fortress Press.

Kivy, Peter (1993), *The Fine Art of Repetition: Essays in the Philosophy of Music*, Cambridge: Cambridge University Press.

Kramer, Jonathan D. (1988), *The Time of Music*, New York: Schirmer.

Lester, Joel (1986), *The Rhythms of Tonal Music*, Carbondale: Southern Illinois University Press.

Marion, Jean-Luc (1991), *God Without Being: Hors-Texte*, trans. Thomas A. Carlson, Chicago and London: University of Chicago Press.

Mellers, Wilfrid (1980), *Bach and the Dance of God*, London: Faber.

Mellers, Wilfrid (1983), *Beethoven and the Voice of God*, London: Faber.

Meyer, Leonard B. (1973), *Explaining Music*, Berkeley: University of California Press.

Middleton, Richard (1983), "Play it again Same': Some Notes on the Productivity of Repetition in Popular Music', in Richard Middleton and David Horn (eds), *Popular Music 3*, Cambridge: Cambridge University Press, pp. 235–270.

Middleton, Richard (1990), *Studying Popular Music*, Milton Keynes: Open University Press.

Moltmann, Jürgen (1967), *Theology of Hope*, trans. James W. Leitch, London: SCM.

Nattiez, Jean-Jacques (1990), *Music and Discourse: Toward a Semiology of Music*, trans. Carolyn Abbate, Princeton: Princeton University Press.

Norton, Richard (1984), *Tonality in Western Culture: A Critical and Historical Perspective*, University Park and London: Pennsylvania State University Press.

Paddison, Max (1993), *Adorno's Aesthetics of Music*, Cambridge: Cambridge University Press.

Percy, Martyn (1996), *Words, Wonders and Power*, London: SPCK.

Rowland, Christopher (1995), 'Eucharist as Liberation from the Present,' in David Brown and Ann Loades (eds), *The Sense of the Sacramental: Movement and Measure in Art and Music, Place and Time*, London: SPCK, pp. 200–215.

Ruwet, N. (1987), 'Methods of Analysis in Musicology,' *Music Analysis*, 6, 1–2, pp. 11–36.

Sloboda, John (1993), *The Musical Mind*, Oxford: Oxford University Press.

Sykes, Stephen (1996), 'Ritual and the Sacrament of the Word,' in David Brown and Ann Loades (eds), *Christ: The Sacramental Word*, London: SPCK, pp. 157–167.

Thiselton, Anthony C. (1992), *New Horizons in Hermeneutics*, London: Marshall Pickering.

Thiselton, Anthony C. (1995), *Interpreting God and the Postmodern Self: On Meaning, Manipulation and Promise*, Edinburgh: T. & T. Clark.

Thomas, Downing (1995), *Music and the Origins of Language*, Cambridge: Cambridge University Press.

Torrance, T. F. (1976), *Space, Time and Resurrection*, Edinburgh: Handsel Press.

Williams, Rowan (1994), 'Keeping Time,' in his *Open to Judgement*, London: Darton, Longman and Todd, pp. 247–250.

Williams, Rowan (1989), 'Postmodern Theology and the Judgment of the World,' in Frederic B. Burnham (ed.), *Postmodern Theology: Christian Faith in a Pluralist World*, New York: HarperCollins, pp. 92–112.

Young, Francis (1990), *The Art of Performance: Towards a Theology of Holy Scripture*, London: Darton, Longman and Todd.

Zimmerli, Walther (1963), 'Promise and Fulfilment,' in Claus Westermann (ed.), *Essays on Old Testament Interpretation*, London: SCM, pp. 89–122.

Zimmerli, Walther (1971), *Man and his Hope in the Old Testament*, London: SCM.

Zuckerkandl, Victor (1956), *Sound and Symbol: Music and the External World*, London: Routledge & Kegan Paul.
Zuckerkandl, Victor (1959), *The Sense of Music*, Princeton: Princeton University Press.

5

Performing Theology Authentically

Gordon Giles

In this paper I shall discuss the authentic performance of music and
then associate it with issues in theology. In particular, I shall discuss
the claim that 'authentic performance' is in some way 'historical', and
having suggested that authentic performance is not historical at all,
shall briefly consider the related issue of the 'Historical Jesus'. For it
seems that the attempt to be true to history is a phenomenon more
significant for its modernity than for its historicity.

AUTHENTIC PERFORMANCE AND AUTHENTICITY

Many readers will already be familiar with the phenomenon of
'authentic performance'. Rather than offer a definition of it, I think it
will suffice to indicate the recently widespread practice of employing
'period' instruments when performing pieces of music. Fortepianos,
baroque violins and sackbuts have been revived, and it has taken some
time to aquaint ourselves with their unfamilar sound. Authentic or
period performances usually involve a combination of old instruments,
smaller ensembles, lower pitch, less vibrato, more punctuated rhythm,
faster tempi, and thinner sound.

The debate about authentic performance has been confused with
questions about *authenticity*. While authentic performance is about
employing certain resources and producing a certain kind of sound,
authenticity is about something quite different. It is, as the musicologist Richard Taruskin puts it:

> knowing what you mean and whence comes that knowledge. And more
> than that, even, authenticity is knowing what you are, and acting in

accordance with that knowledge. It is what Rousseau called a 'sentiment of being' that is independent of the values, opinions and demands of others.[1]

It is clear that one need not employ authentic instruments in order to produce a performance that possesses the quality of authenticity. The notion of performing on period instruments is a fairly narrow one, and even where such perfomance practice is an end in itself, it must not be confused with the desire that performers on modern instruments also exhibit – to produce a musical experience that is refreshing, vital and valuable.

It is doubly unfortunate that by 'authenticity' some people mean 'authentic performance'. First, as I have suggested, they are not the same thing, and can be usefully distinguished. Secondly, the term 'authenticity' has an evaluative connotation. To say that something is authentic is to praise it, and to deny that it is authentic is to make a negative judgement of it. Thus there lies in the very existence of what may be called the 'authentic performance movement' an implication that alternative approaches are 'inauthentic', or in some way incorrect.

A Debate

Those who defend authentic performance do so on the grounds that it fulfils the composer's intentions, both in terms of what he or she would have expected to hear and in terms of what is stipulated in the manuscript. Implicit here is the view that if the composer has left instructions as to what to do with the work, then those instructions should be followed as accurately as possible. Since we have the resources and ability to employ period instruments, we ought to do so, because the composer knows best how his or her work should be performed. Or, at least, if the composer does not know best, it is not our business to contradict him or her – we should play according to those instructions and let the composer take the blame or credit for the work. It is the job of the performer to 'execute' the work, not to invest it with any personal (re)interpretation which turns the music into something other than what the composer intended it to be. Since the composer took the trouble to express in notation and words what was wanted, it is taken to be a fair assumption that anything which detracts from the score would be frowned upon. And if the composer would frown upon it, then we should not do it.

It is no coincidence that this kind of approach has been described by Taruskin as 'fundamentalism'.[2] For it permits only what has been specified in advance, and forbids anything which is not specifically permitted. So where Berlioz specified and intended ophicleides to be used in performances of the *Symphonie Fantastique,* this means that the use of tubas is not permitted because he did not ask for them. Nor should Beethoven's piano sonatas be played on modern pianos because Beethoven did not say they could be, and so it is therefore forbidden and wrong to do so.

This kind of fundamentalist attitude is one which may be allied to a 'purist' point of view, since it proposes that performers *ought* to honour the composer's intentions, and implies that there is something morally, if not musically, aberrant about someone who seeks to reinterpet the composer's decree. It is *morally* wrong because the composer's wishes have been rejected. It is *musically* wrong because the resulting inauthentic performance of work X is not actually of work X, because an accurate rendition in the light of the composer's intentions renders performance P to be of work X, thus performance P′ is not of work X, and must therefore be of X′, which is to be distinguished from work X. This amounts to the view that if one does not play what the composer stipulated, then one has not only failed to perform the work – one has performed a *different* work.[3]

In the musical world there are plenty of people for whom this does not present a problem – if tuba players are told that they have failed to perform the *Symphonie Fantastique* after all, they will shrug their shoulders and say that they have nevertheless produced a performance which was valued and appreciated by the audience. They may decide that it does not matter what Berlioz thinks as he is dead and it is more important to make his music live today. They may even propose that Berlioz himself would feel the same. To follow the letter of the work is to kill it by fixing it in time – it is the spirit of the work that matters, adherence to which makes performances refreshing and vital. They see no need or value in struggling on old instruments which they cannot play properly, which are out of date, often unreliable, or out of tune.

Purists find the purer, vibrato-less sound of old instruments to be cleaner and less ambiguous. Their effect is simpler, more precise, and although the instruments are harder to play and keep in tune, performers are learning, and audiences and performers soon become used to the harder sound, free as it is of an homogenous 'orchestral' sound that draws everything into itself and makes everything sound not only very pleasant, but very much alike:

The eighteenth-century bassoon, like the flute and the oboe of the same period, was more capricious and temperamental than its modern equivalent. But it was also more sprightly and plump, and the contrast between its different registers was greater than it is on the sophisticated, bland Heckel bassoons used in most orchestras today.[4]

Yet no one who has heard Schubert's songs accompanied on a good Viennese-style fortepiano, or Beethoven's sonatas played on an early nineteenth-century Broadwood, can deny that historical instruments bring out qualities in the music that are obscured or lost altogether in performances on a modern concert grand. In the hands of a skilful player, the fortepiano's crisp articulation, evenness of registers and overtone-rich sound seem as 'right' for the music of Mozart and Schubert as the harpsichord's brittle brilliance does for Bach and Couperin.[5]

Opponents of this view, who resist the rigidity and backward-looking tendencies of the purists, esteem the composer as the creator of the work they perform. They seek to enable Beethoven to speak today, through an accessible medium, but to do so in what they take to be complete fidelity to the spirit of his 'message'. To them the product of authentic performance is often stale, dry, and out of tune. The musical texture is different, and seems to emphasise everything except the themes that they have come to know and love. There is a view (which may now itself be historical!) that modern instruments are 'better' – because technologically more advanced than those which they effectively replaced. Ralph Vaughan Williams was as good an advocate of this view as anyone:

Opinions may differ as to the intrinsic beauty or otherwise of the harpsichord, but there can be no doubt that the pianoforte, with its infinite gradations of tone, from an almost orchestral fortissimo to an almost inaudible pianissimo, performs the function of a continuo much better than the harpsichord, with its hard unweilding tone.

The same applies to our oboes with their lovely tone, which no one hesitates to use instead of the coarse-sounding oboes of Bach's time: why make an exception of the harpsichord as is now fashionable? ...

It seems to me that to use the resources which we now possess reverently and with true musical insight is right; not only in the interests of the performers and hearers of our own time, but also as the highest tribute we can pay to the man many of us regard as the greatest composer the world has yet produced ... it is our privilege and our duty to use all the improved mechanisms invented by our instrument-makers to do full justice to this immortal work.[6]

Here we have the bare bones of a disagreement over the use of period instruments. I now want to suggest that this is not where the real debate lies at all – even though there are plenty of listeners and performers who want to engage at this level. The most interesting area of contention in authentic performance debate – and the one which has the greatest interest for theologians – consists in questions about the historical credentials of the attempt to re-create musical events of the past.

THE SHOCK OF THE OLD

Authentic performance is not historical at all: it is a modern way of performing old pieces. This is not a criticism, but an observation indicating that a performer who believes that he or she is 'doing what they did' stylistically is misguided. The instruments employed may be identical, but it does not follow, nor does it happen to be true, that what they are doing with or to the instrument is the same as was done in the past. Not only is this a logical point, Taruskin has highlighted quite convincingly the similarities between today's authentic style and conventional approaches to avant-garde music:

> And now we have come at last to the nub and essence of authentistic performance, as I see it. It is modern performance ... 'historical' performance today is not really historical; that a thin veneer of historicism clothes a performance style that is completely of our own time, and is in fact the most modern style around; and that the historical hardware has won its wide acceptance and commercial viability precisely in virtue of its novelty, not its antiquity.[7]

This is Taruskin's credo of authenticity – that it has grown up with modernism and shares its basic precepts. Verisimilitude, fidelity to intentions, and old instruments, have been means to an end. They have also concealed that end – to provide something new and different. Thus, concerning authentic performance, the shock of the old is one and the same as the shock of the new.

Taruskin characterises modernism as intransigently advocating precision and the negation of personality – as being 'objective, elitist, and fearful of individual freedom of expression'.[8] Its proponents took refuge in an ordered precision. They were opposed to any sense of 'subjectivity' in art and sought to preserve 'high art' at the expense of an individual freedom of expression that would lead culture and humanity over the edge into the abyss. In this respect, high modernism became intransigent, objectivist and élitist. This goal, to arrest the decay of culture, can be compared to the (futile) goal of authentistic performance – to 'arrest the decay of the music of the past by reversing the changeable vagaries of taste and restoring it to a timeless constancy'.[9] Taruskin goes on to quote Daniel Leech-Wilkinson's description of how authentic performances display certain common characteristics of dynamics, speed and timbre.[10] Earlier (non-authentic) performance style is typified by variation in these features, attempting to get at what the composer is 'saying'.[11] But authentic performance is characterised by a 'clean' sound, and the attempt to avoid what is not specifically stipulated in the score.

T. S. Eliot believed that whenever a new work appears it affects the whole canon – such that the whole music world, past and present, is changed by ongoing creativity. When a new work is created, something happens to all the works that preceded it: 'for order to persist after the supervention of novelty, the *whole* existing order must be, if ever so slightly, altered'.[12] Thus we can talk of the presence of Eliot in Shakespeare and vice versa, and of Stravinsky in Bach. What is important here is a sense of continuity, in which, as Taruskin's motto puts it, there is a 'presence of the past and a pastness of the present'. Eliot himself was encountering the demise of Romanticism, which had fostered a view of art which T. E. Hulme called 'a state of slush', by which the beauty of art is equated with its power to evoke a pleasurable empathetic response.[13] Taruskin also associates this view with Eduard Hanslick, Suzanne Langer and Roger Sessions,[14] although he suspects they would probably not admit it, since there were all 'more or less opposed' to the idea of music as a language of the emotions.[15]

So Taruskin borrows a concept of 'vitalist' performance, typified by Furtwängler's and Stokowski's Bach. Stokowski employed a harpsichord, but with significant rubato. In contrast, there is 'geometrical' performance, which tends to abstraction and immutability. Here we have a kind of retreat from the messiness of real things – an attempt to purify through regularity as characterised by a deliberate self-alienation. Taruskin is reminded of Stravinsky, and goes so far as to make that claim that:

> all truly modern musical performance (and of course that includes the authentistic variety) essentially treats the music performed as if it were composed – or at least performed – by Stravinsky.[16]

There has been a gradual change in performance style which is best understood in terms of a shift from vital to geometrical performance. The vital, or human, has been pushed out, not by a striving for verisimilitude, historical research or fidelity to intentions, but by a prior demand for 'objectivity', precision and straightforwardness.[17] Now we can see the influence of Stravinsky on Bach – from Stravinsky's geometrical style in his *Concerto for Piano and Winds* we cannot help but see Bach's harpischord concerti as potentially disposed towards geometrical performative interpretation. The idea that baroque music is strictly rhythmical has no basis in history – it is an opinion which is 'uncorroborated by any contemporary witness'.[18] This 'sewing-machine style',[19] cannot be historically associated with Bach, but it can with Stravinsky. Taruskin accuses Stravinsky of 'fundamentalism' (of which he has already accused the 'authenticists'), who maintained that 'execution ... [is] the strict putting into effect of an explicit will that contains nothing beyond what it specifically commands'.[20]

What is not permitted, is prohibited. Execution is the opposite of interpretation, which Stravinsky deplored. 'Transmission' seems to be the purpose of performance, just as Leech-Wilkinson claimed:

> an attempt to avoid interpretive gestures beyond those notated or documented as part of period performance practice. In a nutshell, the difference is that between performer as 'interpreter' and performer as 'transmitter'.[21]

In his autobiography, Stravinsky said that 'Music ... is essentially powerless to *express* anything at all.'[22] Hence, 'To the proponent of a dehumanized, geometricized art, literally no one is speaking at all.'[23] Authentic performance practice is characterised by this as much as is modern geometrical performance style. The sense of emotional detachment is highly desired by some performers, yet while it may not be difficult to achieve, it is hardly justified on historical grounds. A modern authentic performer may see the work as a construction, whereas a 'vitalist' may see it as a statement of faith or a presentation of drama. When an old piece is performed in a geometric way, it is 'concomitantly devalued, decanonized, not quite taken seriously'.[24] It is removed from its place in the tradition and played in an entirely different way – different from the way in which it had previously been done, for sure; but also fundamentally different from the way in which its creator imagined. Taruskin cannot prove that it is different; but if he is right in equating a twentieth-century geometrical style with the performers of both Stravinsky and Bach, then it seems likely that this style *cannot* be authentic if the word is to be understood as pertaining to past performance practice and/or historical verisimilitude. Thus Taruskin finds it to be an irony that some authentic performers appear to take the moral high ground, accusing their predecessors of irreverence for the canon, when they themselves (Taruskin accuses Christopher Hogwood) are less respectful.

Bach, for example, has been 'adapted with unprecedented success to suit modern taste'.[25] A hundred years ago, Glazunov and Rimsky-Korsakov were bored by the *St John Passion*. Rather than suppose that our tastes have changed, Taruskin would say that the idea of going 'back to Bach' is topsy-turvy. We did not go back to Bach, Bach was brought forward to us. This was no doubt facilitated by the adoption of a universally 'modern' performance style, and the massive distribution potential yielded by compact discs. What our modern authentic performers have done is no different from what Mendelssohn did with the *St Matthew Passion* in 1848. He reinterpreted it for his own age, and while he may be said to have resurrected it, today's performers are keeping it alive, for as soon as it becomes too familiar through repeated, geometrical performances, it will become the victim of the form of contempt through which we avoid performances and leave CDs on the shelf.

Taruskin does not see this as a negative observation. Once we have realised that authentic performance is no more than a current performance practice (rather than an old one), we are liberated to see it as modern performance, and thus be appropriately critical. Before we can judge something we have to know what it is, and Taruskin spends the majority of his words elaborating his thesis that period performance is modern performance. This being so, Hogwood and Furtwängler, Rattle and Marriner stand on equal footing – no one can claim the moral high ground.

Taruskin's view is persuasive, although it is worth remembering that while it may be true that twentieth-century approaches may be consistent with old and new music, by his own admission we cannot know what seventeenth-century performance sounded like, in which case we cannot conclude that because authentic and avant-garde approaches can be characterised equally, a non twentieth-century approach must have been different. Taruskin does offer anecdotal evidence that earlier approaches were different though, which persuades us to share his view that authentic performance style is more like modern style than the historical practice it seeks to emulate.

THE SHOCK OF THE NEW

If there is any truth in this assessment of authentic performance, then there may be an equivalent theological point. For it may seem that we have here the common debate between those who would go back to the Bible – who in 'performing' Scripture, seek to rediscover first century meanings; and those who would seek the transcendent meaning of the texts today. This question has been discussed by

Frances Young[26] and Stephen Barton,[27] and it is certainly interesting to pursue the analogical comparison of music and theology. Both have paradoxical dual natures, although it may be that this is only as far as the comparison can go. But if we bear Taruskin's point in mind, we realise that the people who we may think to be 'historically-minded' cannot claim to be – rather that their attempt to get back to basic Bible interpretation is symptomatic of a current trend, and reflects a 'modernist' theology rather than any 'historical' tradition.

Thus the recent desire to 'reclaim' Scripture from the hands of source-critics and quest-ers after the Historical Jesus amounts to a moving on, rather than a going back. Just as we cannot undo the influence of Eliot on Shakespeare, or Stravinsky on Bach, we cannot remove the effects of Harnack and Schweitzer on Jesus. Whether we agree with what has been said by critics through the ages, we cannot unsay it – we can only engage in debate, in which case the debate in which we engage becomes part of the tradition we pass on. Just as an authentic performer may seek to sidestep what Furtwängler and Karajan 'did' to Beethoven, a modern New Testament scholar may seek to undo the work of Harnack, Schweitzer, Crossan and Vermes.[28] But neither can succeed in removing a rival position – they can only engage with it.

The desire to return to a biblical picture of Christ is a modern phenomenon and is not historical at all. To *have* a biblical picture may be historical, but to *return* to one cannot be, just as a *re-creation* of performance conditions cannot be historical. The temporal location of an interpretation is determined not by the date of the object of interpretation, but by the date of the interpretation itself. Thus it is more appropriate to see any 'back to the New Testament' movement as symptomatic of modern taste and needs, rather than as a re-creation of old ones. If a reversion to Bach's style is modernism in disguise, to what extent does (modern) biblical scholarship represent a desire to put new wine into old skins?

We have seen that the distinction between 'modern' and 'historical' (or 'period') performance is a smoke screen – if either is more modern it is the so-called historical kind, which is at the cutting edge of contemporary performance practice. The real distinction is to be drawn between nineteenth-century practice, which Taruskin calls 'vitalist', and modern/historical practice, which is 'geometrical'. Modern performance is thus *modernist* performance. If there is a corollary in theology, it would be that the return to conservative biblical principles is more 'modern' than the Liberal Protestantism or Catholic Modernism with which it competes. Similarly, the more liberal historicism of Harnack and Schweitzer was, in its day, more modern than historical. Indeed it has been recognised for some time that they replaced the face of Jesus with one of their own making:

> The man is Albert Schweitzer; the drawing room is is the nineteenth-century European religious world; the old portaits are the studies of Jesus that were written, in great quantity, between the late eighteenth and late nineteenth centuries. The new picture is Schweitzer's own substitute: Jesus the apocalyptic visionary, dreaming dreams, seeing visions, daring the impossible, dying in the attempt, and becoming, by sheer force of personality, the greatest and most haunting human being who ever lived.[29]

The quest for the authentic music is characterised, like its theological precursor,[30] by a quest for novelty. Just as George Tyrrell put it:

> The Christ that Harnack sees, looking back through nineteen centuries of Catholic darkness, is only the reflection of a Liberal Protestant face, seen at the bottom of a deep well.[31]

Those who look for historical authenticity in music are in danger of seeing no more than their own reflection – the 'reflection of current taste'.[32] This current taste desires novelty predominantly, and authentistic and avant-garde performance style are of a kind such that the most ardent advocates of high modernism in music are also the ones who defend authentic performance most zealously. In theology there is still a quest for novelty: a desire to bring alive the truths of the past, in the conviction that those truths are still relevant today. Some people prefer to do that by restating the traditional formulas – which many have forgotten, or have never encountered – while others prefer to reinterpret them and redefine them. The debate over Anthony Freeman's controversial book reflects this tendency.[33] Both sides are trying to answer the question which Dietrich Bonhoeffer put so succinctly when in prison: 'What is bothering me incessantly is the question what Christianity really is, or indeed who Christ really is, for us today.'[34] His answer was that the incarnate, glorified and crucified Christ is formed, by the Holy Spirit, in every Christian, because we are all in one body, the church – the body of Christ. But his question is the one that every theologian engages with, and in attempting to answer it each draws on an understanding of history, contemporary culture, sacred text and personal experience. Each balances these differently, usually with integrity and charity, but often seeks a justification for a view as being 'authentic' to truth revealed in Scripture and sacrament. The error, it seems to me, is that, like the musical performers, the 'authenticity' appealed to is more like 'authentic performance'. But what we have seen may show that if authentic performance involves the appeal to the past, and an attempt to re-create it today, and if authenticity involves: 'knowing what you mean and whence comes that knowledge',[35] then the fact that authentic performance or historically-minded theology is new, not old, is not something for which it should be condemned. Authentic performance is the musical equivalent of any current attempt to understand and present the gospel in accessible and refreshing forms.

Indeed, a theology which seeks to make the old new is not 'historical theology' at all, it is *theology,* just as historical performance is no more or less than *performance.* A theology that looks over its shoulder, aware of its contemporary stance, truly honours the Christ who is the same yesterday and today, and can claim to be *authentic* in the proper sense. Whether that theology emphasises the Bible, the Christian community, historical research or the sacraments does not matter in terms of its status. For 'as long as we know what we do want and what we do not want, and act upon that knowledge, we have values and not dirt. We have authenticity.'[36]

NOTES

[1] Richard Taruskin, 'The Authenticity Movement can Become a Positivistic Purgatory, Literalistic and Dehumanizing', in 'The Limits of Authenticity: A Discussion', *Early Music*, February 1984, pp. 3–12 (p. 3).

[2] Richard Taruskin, 'The Pastness of the Present and the Presence of the Past', in Nicholas Kenyon (ed.), *Authenticity and Early Music*, Oxford: Oxford University Press, 1988, pp. 137–211.

[3] This kind of theory has been put forward by Nelson Goodman, who argues that for performance P to be of work X, perfect pitch compliance must be achieved. A single wrong note renders P not to be of X. See Nelson Goodman, *Languages of Art*, Indianapolis: Hackett, 1976.

[4] Thurston Dart, *The Interpretation of Music*, 4th edn, London: Hutchinson, 1967, p. 36.

[5] Harry Haskill, *The Early Music Revival: A History*, London: Thames and Hudson, 1988, p. 190.

[6] Ralph Vaughan Williams, *National Music and Other Essays*, Oxford: Oxford University Press, 1987, p. 303–304. He is referring to Bach and the *St John Passion*.

[7] Taruskin, 'The Pastness of the Present and the Presence of the Past', p. 152.

[8] *ibid.*, p. 154.

[9] *ibid.*, p. 155.

[10] In my own experience I have found that many people are no longer able (if they ever were) to distinguish performances on old instruments from performances on modern ones. When asked to decide between performances, they often get it wrong – not because of the *sound* of the instruments but in virtue of the features

just described. Thus a brisk rendition of Bach – whether on period instruments or not – will be classed as authentic (by which the speaker means 'period performance'), and a slow or ponderous recording will be deemed modern whether it employs period instruments or not.

11 Taruskin, 'The Pastness of the Present and the Presence of the Past', p. 154, quoting Daniel Leech-Wilkinson, 'What we are Doing with Early Music is Genuinely Authentic to such a Small Degree that the Word Loses Most of its Meaning' in 'The Limits of Authenticity: A Discussion', *Early Music*, February 1984, pp. 13–16 (p. 14).

12 T. S. Eliot, 'Tradition and the Individual Talent' (1917), in Frank Kermode (ed.), *Selected Prose of T. S. Eliot*, London: Faber, 1975.

13 Taruskin, 'The Pastness of the Present and the Presence of the Past', p. 159.

14 See Eduard Hanslick, *On the Musically Beautiful*, trans. Geoffrey Payzant, Indianapolis: Hackett, 1986, and *Hanslick's Musical Criticism*, ed. and trans. Henry Pleasants, New York: Dover, 1988; Susanne K. Langer, *Philosophy in a New Key*, 3rd edn, Cambridge, Mass.: Harvard University Press, 1957; Roger Sessions, *The Musical Experience of Composer, Performer, Listener*, Princeton, N.J.: Princeton University Press, 1971.

15 Taruskin, 'The Pastness of the Present and the Presence of the Past', p. 160, see also Malcolm Budd, *Music and the Emotions*, London: Routledge & Kegan Paul, 1985, for extensive and incisive coverage of this issue.

16 Taruskin, 'The Pastness of the Present and the Presence of the Past', p. 166.

17 *ibid.*, p. 164.

18 *ibid.*, p. 167.

19 *ibid.*, p. 169.

20 Igor Stravinsky, *Poetics of Music*, (bilingual), Cambridge, Mass.: Harvard University Press, 1970, p. 163.

21 Leech-Wilkinson, *op. cit.*, p. 14.

22 Igor Stravinsky, *An Autobiography*, London, Faber, 1962, p. 54.

23 Taruskin, 'The Pastness of the Present and the Presence of the Past', p. 189.

24 *ibid.*, p. 191.

25 *ibid.*, p. 197.

26 Frances Young, *The Art of Performance: Towards a Theology of Holy Scripture*, London: Darton, Longman and Todd, 1990.

27 Stephen Barton, 'New Testament Interpretation as Performance', *Scottish Journal of Theology*, 52, 2, 1999, pp. 179–208.

28 Adolf Harnack, *What is Christianity?*, trans. T. B. Saunders, London: Williams & Norgate, 1901; Albert Schweitzer, *The Quest of the Historical Jesus*, 3rd edn, trans. J. R. Coates, London: A. & C. Black, 1954; J. D. Crossan, *The Historical Jesus: The Life of a Mediterranean Jewish Peasant*, Edinburgh: T. & T. Clark, 1991; Geza Vermes, *Jesus the Jew*, London: Collins, 1973.

29 N. T. Wright, *Who Was Jesus?*, London: SPCK, 1992, p. 1.

30 See Schweitzer, and Harnack, *op. cit.* Both writers attempted to argue for the existence of an 'authentic' Christ-figure, who could be re-discovered by 'removing' the dirt of doctrine and human error. For an overview, see John Macquarrie, *Jesus Christ in Modern Thought*, London: SCM, 1990, pp. 251–268.

31 George Tyrrell, *Christianity at the Cross-roads*, London: Allen & Unwin, 1963, p. 49.

32 Leech-Wilkinson, *op. cit.*, p. 14.

33 Anthony Freeman, *God in Us: A Case for Christian Humanism*, London: SCM, 1993 and Richard Harries, *The Real God*, London: Mowbray, 1994. Also see

Gordon J. Giles, 'The Real God', *Philosophy Now*, 12 June 1995, pp. 35-39.

[34] Dietrich Bonhoeffer, *Letters and Papers from Prison*, ed. E. Bethge, London: SCM, 1971, p. 279.

[35] Taruskin, 'The Authenticity Movement can Become a Positivistic Purgatory ....', p. 3.

[36] Taruskin, 'The Pastness of the Present and the Presence of the Past', p. 207.

Editors' Note:

Many of the Taruskin essays have been republished as Richard Taruskin, *Text and Act: Essays on Music and Performance*, New York and Oxford: Oxford University Press, 1995.

6

Must We Mean What We Play?

Ian Ground

INTRODUCTION

It was Sir Thomas Beecham who said, 'The English do not care for music – but they love the noise it makes.' Sir Thomas was, of course, given to making acerbic swipes but this one has always seemed to me to have real philosophical class. Indeed, I believe it captures an insight which is often missing from the philosophical literature on music, and it contains an idea that I want to develop and reflect upon in my contribution to this book.

In art, no other medium seems quite to baffle the understanding so much as music. Depending upon one's point of view, it is either a symptom of the fact, or its explanation, that of all the media of the arts, music is the medium most likely to provoke claims concerning the reality of the transcendental. We may feel that while, for example, painting and literature in certain hands can *serve* the religious impulse, music is capable of something far more. We may feel that in our experience of particular musical works we are acquainted not with our feelings about God, or about our relation to the world as a whole, but rather, that we are being initiated into an experience of the very objects of such feelings. We can feel that music can deliver to us another world. Or perhaps, that it delivers *this* world but as it really is, behind its everyday appearance.

Sometimes this thought is regarded as explanatory of another claim about music common to the religious *and* the secular mind: the thought that, where it really matters, where we really want to say something about our musical experience, somehow we are forced to go silent; that in attempting to convey our musical experience one to another, our experience of music and our language fail to engage. It is at such moments that we have recourse to some notion of the inexpressible, the indescribable, the ineffable, giving voice to our sense that here our words and our experience or our knowledge glide idly past one another. It is because of music's relation to what is beyond everyday experience, we may feel, that there is something being said in music which, without it, we lack the means to say.

For those for whom these kinds of remark about music come most naturally, the triumph of the composer is to succeed in an impossible, because godlike task: the creation, or at least the revelation, of a world. It will be admitted that there are perhaps only a few works which do succeed in this but it may be felt that such works, by showing us what music is at its best, show us what the true nature of music is.

It is our tendency to make such claims about music that has been one factor in its ambivalent relationship with the religious impulse. Of course, there have been many other factors at work in the history of institutionalised religion's relation with the creation and enjoyment of music. By their very nature, institutions tend to be Apollonian in nature and so not the least of official religion's concern about music has been its suspicion of music's alliance with the Dionysian temperament. But I believe that the thought that somehow the making of music involves not just sensual indulgence, but also a peculiarly tempting form of hubris, has also been an important element. And so, while the religious have celebrated music as a route to the holy, they have also, in more cautious moods, attacked music for its transcendental ambitions.

The attempt to describe music in terms of its transcendental power is something common to different religious cultures and epochs and deserves the greatest respect. Fortunately, it has been a long time since talk of the transcendental made philosophers reach for their positivist guns. Still, a danger (of which philosophers have always been and, I hope, will always be, wary) is that of mislocating the transcendental. In this case, of locating it too early, or too late, or in the wrong place, in our reflections on the nature of music. This is certainly an intellectual danger. If we transpose all our perplexities into mysteries, there will certainly be melodies we can no longer hear. It is perhaps also a moral danger. To display too easy a familiarity with the transcendental is bound to make others suspicious that the everyday world is not being taken seriously enough. This is not to say that talk about the transcendental in music should be regarded as betraying a lack of intellectual sophistication, only that it should more often be the last thing we say about music and perhaps more rarely the first thing. This paper concerns what I regard as some of the first things we should say about music.

Not Knowing Our Way About

When we ask such questions as 'How does music mean what it does?', or 'How does music have the power to possess us and move us as it does?', or 'How can music speak to us without, in any usual sense, *saying* something?', we may feel that the problem is not simply that we do not know the answers to these questions and would like to Rather, we may feel, we do not know where to start looking for an answer. We are not sure what would count as an answer that would satisfy us. Will a technical study of the particular structure of a piece of music answer such questions? Would listening in on the discussions of musicians about to perform it? Would a biography, or autobiography, of a composer? Is it a psychological account we need? Or a neurophysiological account of the effect of these sounds on our nervous systems? Perhaps, we think, we need something of all these, and we put our faith in inter-disciplinary accounts. Sometimes, when we encounter questions where we don't know where to start looking for an answer, we are dealing with questions which are not entirely empirical nor entirely conceptual. Such questions, usually, are philosophical questions. For, as Wittgenstein remarked, philosophical questions have the logical form 'I don't know my way about.'[1]

Of course, it may turn out that what looks like a philosophical question about music can be reformulated in such a way that it becomes amenable to empirical solution. The history of western science is partly the history of a continual process of this kind, and it is certainly true that current empirical research into the psychology of music can be very revealing. However, despite such success, I still feel that when it comes to the questions about music which really perplex us, we do well to remember that there is a difference between answering a question and making a question answerable. We need to remove those obstacles which stand in the way of acquiring a clear view of the object of our perplexity, and this empirical research cannot do on its own.

THE CONCEPT OF ART: A POPULAR VIEW

In my view, one of the most fundamental obstacles to getting a clear view about the nature of music is a popular view about what works of art, in general, are. The popular conception runs something like this.

There are fundamentally two sorts of objects which are aesthetically interesting (see Figure 1). There are natural objects and there are artefacts. Amongst natural objects of aesthetic interest we might mention landscapes, flora and fauna, perhaps birdsong and so on. Amongst

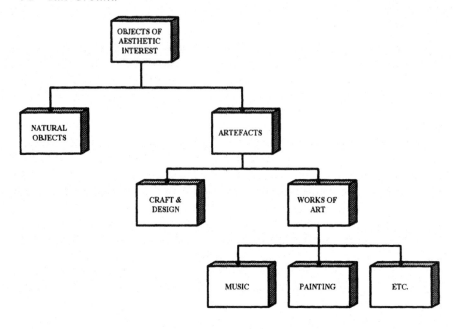

Figure 1

aesthetically interesting artefacts we might mention, on the one hand, objects of craft and design of various kinds and, on the other, works of art in all the different artistic media.

Perhaps a more sophisticated analysis of this kind would recognise that in both categories, it would be a mistake to include only certain kinds of material object. We can be misled into doing this because we too easily think that we are only engaged aesthetically with the world around us when we are deliberately attending to the Very Beautiful Object or the Very Beautiful View of some object. This makes us think of the aesthetic as the *rare* or the *unique*. And this, in turn, means that we then forget just how much of the ordinary details of life are taken up with making aesthetic decisions and how many of these decisions do not involve responding to more or less straightforward physical objects. We forget, for example, just how much of our lives that has little to do with direct first order perceptual experience involves aesthetic concerns and preferences: the way we tell stories, being bored, enjoying sport, economic activity, the ways in which we get on or don't get on with our fellows. Very important to the way in which aesthetic interests are enmeshed in social life is the idea of 'fit', of what we think of as appropriate or inappropriate congruence between, for example, a person's character and the sort of thing that happens to them in their lives. The sort of 'fit' which we describe, crudely, as 'ironic' or 'tragic'. Or the sort of fit between different aspects of someone's life so that we describe their life as being 'all of a piece'. Or the relationships between facets of different people's characters. And so on. In philosophical aesthetics we do well to remember that much of the ordinary stuff of life is ordinary *aesthetic* stuff.

This aside, what, on the view under discussion, is the difference between common or garden artefacts of aesthetic interest and works of art? Works of art are a special class of artefacts. They are special in that, unlike many other artefacts which have been made to be useful or fulfil some function, works of art have been made especially or, in some refinements of this view, *exclusively* to provoke and engage our aesthetic interest. Works of art are therefore *definable* as artefacts which have been deliberately made by people to provoke and engage the aesthetic interests of their fellows. It is an important corollary of this view that different mediums in art are definable in terms of their raw material. Thus literature can be regarded as the creation of aesthetically arresting linguistic objects, dance takes human movement as its raw material, painters colour and shape. And the musical artist creates artefacts out of sounds.

There are many theories of art which share the thought that this is the true definition of works of art. Some accounts – called 'Formalist' accounts[2] – stress that nothing more than this definition is needed: that the point of producing such objects is exclusively to provoke such an interest. If there is more philosophical work to be done, then the task is to give, not a further account of the nature of works of art in different mediums, but rather an account of the kind of interest that aesthetic interest is.

In many other theories of art (summarised in Figure 2), however, the fundamental idea that works of art are artefacts deliberately made to provoke aesthetic interest is supplemented with ideas about what this provocation and engagement of aesthetic interest must be made to do, what value it must have, what *function* it must have. The range of these supplementary ideas is extremely varied. The very general ideas that works of art exist in some way to 'enrich human experience', or 'express the artist's emotions', or even in some way to 'make known the ways of God to man', are claims familiar to most of us.

In response to these further claims, some species of Formalist are likely to take a Relativist turn. They will retort that while works of art often do have other functions, these vary over different times and cultures. Sometimes, for example, music is regarded as having a political, social or religious function; but not everywhere and certainly not

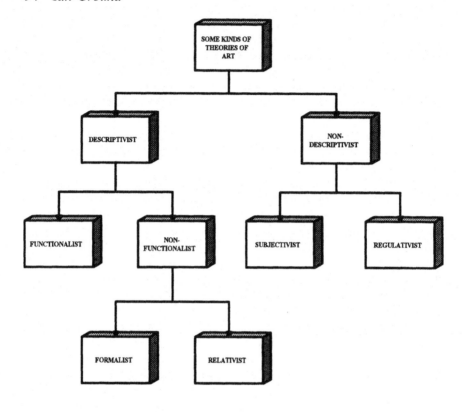

Figure 2

always. So, from the point of view of philosophical aesthetics as opposed to cultural criticism or anthropology, works of art must be defined as objects created to provoke our aesthetic interest because this is the only thing we can say of works of art that is always and everywhere true.

Naturally, there is a great deal of disagreement about all this and this tends to lend a further, though spurious, credence to the claim that what counts as a work of art at all is something relative to a particular period in history and a particular culture, that even the Formalist accounts present not transcultural truths about art but highly culture- and even class-specific truths. These broadly Subjectivist accounts reject any attempt to define or describe the nature of art because they hold that there is *nothing that we can say*, in general, about their nature. They may even hold that since there is nothing that is always and everywhere true of art, there really is not a coherent concept of art to do philosophical aesthetics about. There are just the products of different cultures and it is a mistake to think that there is some special class of these products, called art, which is deserving of special interest and respect. This, is roughly the direction that some recent post-modern thought has taken.[3]

Interestingly, however, despite their mutual and sometimes quite ferocious animosities, all these theories of art have something in common. They all agree that the original description is correct: that works of art are simply artefacts deliberately made to provoke and engage aesthetic interest. They disagree about whether anything in fact falls under this description, and if so how this description needs to be filled out to include the function or value of this provocation and engagement. If this could only be agreed, then the concept of art will have been described. These theories then think of the notion of art as one which succeeds or, for post-moderns, fails, simply to *describe a certain sort of object*.

The Musical Work of Art

What does this mean for music? A great deal of the philosophy of music has consisted of the battles between these different kinds of account. In particular, there has been a great deal of debate between various flavours of Formalist accounts of music and various flavours of Functionalist accounts. Such were the great nineteenth-century debates between Absolutists such as Hanslick and defenders of the representational and expressive powers of music such as Liszt and Wagner. So too the battles over twelve-note and serial composition in the early twentieth century. Increasingly, at least until the early seventies, these debates became sublimated into a discussion about the extent to which music can be regarded as a kind of language; both sides claiming that the success of the analogy supports their own view and both sides labouring under the erroneous impression that the concepts of language being employed in this debate are less problematic than the musical concepts which they were supposed to illuminate.

But in these debates too there is the same agreement about fundamentals. What is agreed is that the concept of a musical work of art *describes* an artefact, made out of sounds, deliberately created to engage aesthetic interest. What this means is that the concept of a musical work of art is simply a kind of label which we stick on particular sonic artefacts which exhibit particular properties. Now it seems obvious to many that the labels that we use to categorise different kinds of music, in particular music that we do and do not count as works of art, are culturally constructed. And this can tempt us to think that the concept of a musical work of art is merely a second order term used to organise our musical experience. It is essentially *post hoc*. All that really exists are sounds, organised in particular ways. Thus what has to be explained is why such patterns of sound have the interest they do: how sounds can be, for Absolutists, aesthetically interesting; for Functionalists, uplifting, exciting, integrative, and so on; for everyone in the traditional debate, how it is that, in virtue of being arranged in certain ways, sounds can become the subject of true normative descriptions. The concept of a musical work of art is put to one side. Even those who eschew these debates as misleading ways of describing empirical questions may share this view that the concept of art is irrelevant to the real questions. This is because it can seem obvious that such culturally constructed *post hoc* descriptions must be invisible to our neurophysiology. So, as far as empirical research into the nature of music goes, the concept of a musical work of art can be safely put away as an idle wheel. In all these accounts, the rôle of the concept of a musical work of art is at best a place holder for real explanatory concepts and at worst a distraction from getting to grips with the real mysteries, empirical or otherwise, of why music has the power that it does.

While this view is very widespread, in my view it involves a fundamental mistake that distorts our attempts to get a clear view of the nature of music. The reason it is mistaken to think of music in this way is that it fails to take account of a crucial difference. This difference concerns not the fact of whether or not some particular set of sounds was made by someone, but the rôle that knowing this fact plays in how we understand those sounds. The difference is between structures of sound which have been made to provoke aesthetic interest, and about which it is important to know that they were made for this reason, and structures of sound which have been made to provoke aesthetic interest and about which we do not need to know that they were made at all. Once we appreciate this distinction, we see the need for a very different approach to the concept of a work of art, and hence to the concept of a musical work of art, and the questions which puzzle us about the nature of music.

THE CONCEPT OF ART: THE REGULATIVIST VIEW

One way to develop this approach is to follow through one theme in the great classic of philosophical aesthetics – Kant's *Critique of Judgement*.[4] Now, as is well known, for all his philosophical genius Kant had rather crude taste in the arts and, in particular, it is fairly clear that he never cared much for music. Still, I believe that his work contains ideas about the nature of art, and hence about the nature of musical works of art, which have yet to be taken sufficiently seriously by those interested in the aesthetics of music.

The relevant theme in the *Critique of Judgement* concerns the nature of the distinction to be drawn between our aesthetic appreciation of nature, of landscape, skies, oceans, animal life and so on, together with other sorts of aesthetic objects, and our appreciation of works of art, of music, paintings, sculpture, literature, drama, and so on. Kant's discussion of this distinction has two stages.

The first stage is perhaps the most straightforward. As is well known, early on in the *Critique* Kant draws a distinction between two kinds of beauty: 'pure' or 'free' beauty and 'impure' or 'dependent' beauty. Now, despite recent attempts to revive philosophical interest in the concept of beauty, this is still a concept apt to create difficulties for the late twentieth-century mind. Rather than worry about these difficulties, one can if one wishes merely substitute 'object of aesthetic interest' whenever Kant mentions beauty, without substantially affecting the argument.

According to Kant, where the object of my aesthetic appreciation has 'pure' or 'free' beauty, my finding the object beautiful does not depend upon my thinking of the object as of a particular kind, or as having some function or purpose which explains its character, as therefore falling under some description. Kant claims that, in the case of an object of 'free' beauty:

> no concept is here presupposed for which the manifold should serve the given object and which the latter should therefore represent.[5]

Thus, to take Kant's famous example, a seashell may be found beautiful apart from all thought of it as a seashell; as something which has the form it has because this best enables the creature who inhabits it, to ensure its own survival. No matter how beautifully adapted the seashell may be, such considerations are irrelevant to my aesthetic interest in the beauty of its form. Such thoughts are irrelevant because, far from these thoughts playing any important rôle in my experience of the object, it would not matter to me even if there were no such things as real seashells at all. My experience would be just as aesthetically valuable even if it were not the experience of how something real appears, but only a curious illusion. Weston's photographs on this subject are a perfect illustration of this point. It is, argues Kant, only the appearance of the object in experience, the 'manifold', which is found beautiful. In these cases, since there is not presupposed any concept under which we must experience the object, we are free to experience the object more or less as we wish. We can, if we wish, attend to the inside of the seashell, or to its texture, rather than how it looks, or to how the object looks under certain, perhaps very artificial lighting conditions. Or perhaps what engages our interest is not, say, the actual pattern of sounds produced by the thrush but the way the wind makes its song fade in and out of audibility. Again, insofar as we find humpback whale song aesthetically engaging as free beauty, the fact that in reality these songs have been greatly changed in pitch so that we can actually hear them is quite irrelevant. In such cases, no description such as 'song of the thrush' or 'songs produced by the world's largest highly endangered creatures' is guiding our perceptual exploration of the songs and so we are free to take aesthetic interest in any aspect of the experience we wish.

Other examples of such 'free' beauty given by Kant include flowers, foliage-like patterns on wallpaper and other abstract patterns, creatures such as the bird of paradise, and, importantly for our purposes, certain kinds of music.[6]

In the case of 'impure' or 'dependent' beauty, my experience of the beauty of an object depends upon an *a priori* conception of the kind of object it is: the kind of object of which it may happen to be a perfect example. Without the use of such a concept, I may not find the object beautiful at all. Thus, to find a particular man, woman or child beautiful, is to find him or her beautiful as a man, woman or child. If it were possible to regard a child's face simply as a visual appearance, it might well be more aesthetically pleasing if only its features were not quite so fine but were, say, a little more weathered. But in the absence of such a possibility, more rugged features would spoil its appearance as a beautiful child.

Conversely, in a case where a concept is employed, I may properly find something ugly which might, without the necessity of applying the concept, have been beautiful. Thus, lines and traceries which might have been quite charming on their own, could appear positively loathsome if tatooed on the human body. Other examples of such dependent beauty given by Kant include buildings, which (despite the views of some architects) have to be lived, worked or worshipped in, and the beauty of a horse.[7]

Comparing this last example with that of the 'free' beauty of a bird of paradise gives a good grasp of Kant's distinction. Horses have been invested by us with all manner of tasks and functions which, to some degree, differ from culture to culture and thus our aesthetic interest in them is almost always under some description. Thus, while we might well hold that *all* horses are beautiful, judgements of the beauty of a particular horse are appropriately expressed as '*What* a beautiful horse!' Whereas it would seem distinctly odd to say, 'Gosh! What a beautiful bird of paradise!', unless this were followed by something like, 'I've seen a great many of them, you know.' Rather, we are inclined to say, 'The bird of paradise, what a beautiful *thing!*'

For the moment then, the first stage of Kant's distinction between natural objects and works of art as objects of aesthetic appreciation is clear enough. He draws a contrast between dependent and free beauty, the apprehension of one depending upon the employment of determinate concepts, the other not. The important thing to note about this distinction is that it cuts across that between natural objects and created objects of aesthetic interest. On the one side are such things as flowers, abstract patterns on wallpaper and certain kinds of music; on the other such things as horses and buildings.

The second stage of Kant's elucidation of the distinction occurs towards the end of the *Critique* but depends upon the earlier contrast. We can now ask this crucial question: does the aesthetic apprehension of a work of art depend upon the employment of any determinate concept? Kant writes, 'A product of fine art must be recognised to be art and not nature.'[8] That is, the aesthetic apprehension of works of art does depend upon the use of some determinate concept. In the case of works of art there is a concept 'presupposed for which the manifold should serve the given object and which the latter should therefore represent'. The determinate concept applied is, minimally, *that of a work of art.*

This is far from being an empty truism, and so it is worth spelling out the implications of Kant's position in more detail. For Kant, this is the important essential difference between, on the one hand, works of art and, on the other, natural and some created objects of aesthetic appreciation. Unlike natural and some created objects of aesthetic appreciation, in the case of works of art it matters that we know what kind of thing the object is. It matters that we know that it was made. And it matters not just as a matter of empirical information. It matters *aesthetically*. It is true that Kant believes that 'fine art must be *clothed with the aspect* of nature',[9] and not exhibit the labour of its creation on its face, but still we must 'recognise it to be art'. Kant is quick to point out that it does not follow from this that we can identify a comprehensive set of rules which governed the production of a work of art – he claims that fine art is producible only through 'genius' – 'an innate mental aptitude (*ingenium*) through which nature gives the rule to art'.[10]

Nor is this to say that in the case of works of art the object of our aesthetic interest is something other than perceptual appearance. Appearances are the objects of our aesthetic interest in the case of works of art just as much as in the case of natural aesthetic objects and created aesthetic objects other than works of art. But it is the perceptual appearance of the work of art, the made object, in which we are aesthetically interested; not the appearance of the object which, purely contingently, happens to have been made by someone.

What this suggests is that unless the distinction between works of art and natural aesthetic objects, together with created aesthetic objects differing from works of art, is to play no rôle at all, then the concept of a work of art must come to bear on my experience of the object. If the concept of an object as made by someone, in some characteristic sorts of ways, as the product of certain sorts of intention, played no rôle in my response to a work of art, then whether or not an object was natural or created would be, aesthetically speaking, quite irrelevant. We could happily assimilate musical works of art to such things as the sound of the wind or birdsong. So, unless we are to regard the distinction between natural objects together with created aesthetic objects, and works of art, as irrelevant, we must recognise that the application of the concept of a work of art in aesthetic experience cannot be simply founded on a discovery made in the course of the perceptual exploration of an object. Otherwise, we would not be interested in the appearance of the work, the made object, and so would not be responding to the work. Because of this, given that an object is a work of art, the application of such a concept is a condition of such a perceptual exploration counting as an aesthetic exploration. The claim then is that something is a work of art, if and only if, the recognition of it as such is internal to its aesthetic appreciation.

So far as aesthetic experience of works of art is concerned then, I cannot overhear some set of sounds and then by attending to its appearance conclude that it is a work of art. Rather, if I am to be able to attend to the relevant appearance, then the application of the concept of a work of art must guide and direct, and not merely follow from, my perceptual experience. Thus thinking of something as a musical work of art is not the expression of a judgement about the aesthetic worth of an object. It is rather a condition of hearing the object in such a way that it could come to be something which could have certain sorts of aesthetic worth – the kinds of aesthetic worth which are appropriate to works of art rather than to natural objects or created objects that are not works of art. The concept applied guides or regulates the perceptual exploration of the relevant appearances.

Without competence in such concepts, there is no reason why we should not find that loci of 'free' beauty very often coincide with, say, the noises produced in my living room when I happen to slip small silver discs into a particular machine: a fact we would rightly regard as a remarkable coincidence, even a miracle. Going to a concert or listening to Radio 3 would then be as extraordinary as walking through a forest in which every tree was aesthetically arresting and each in a quite different way. While it is unfortunately the case that this might enliven our experience of some concerts and some programmes on Radio 3, the absurdity of this as an account of our experience of works of art is apparent.

Kant goes on to develop this point further. He writes:

> every art presupposes rules which are laid down as the foundation which first enables a product, if it is to be called one of art, to be represented as possible.[11]

This is presented as just the corollary of the thesis that a concept of art must be active in our aesthetic interest in works of art. The point is perhaps similar to that made by Wittgenstein about rules: that they cannot carry their own application along with them. Kant is claiming that, for example, a set of sounds cannot carry its possibility as a work on its face. It is put forward as a condition of recognising something as a work of art that the production of the object was regulated by rules which render the object possible as a work. So, to be able to recognise a particular object as a work of art depends upon being able to claim that, in general, objects of this kind are producible according to rules. And this must hold for composers as well as for audiences. What this means is that the fact that artistic mediums have histories, traditions, is not an accidental but an essential feature of their being artistic mediums. Hence Kant's claim that the primary property of artistic genius, and so of its products, is originality.

Though in fact incompatible with a number of theories about music produced by philosophers, critics and composers, the point is an obvious one. The distinction between the aesthetic apprehension of natural and created aesthetic objects and that of works of art is not something, as it were, laying around in some intelligible heaven, waiting for aestheticians to discover and articulate it. Rather, the concept of a work of art as something distinct from either natural aesthetic interesting sounds or patterns of sound which just happen to have been made by someone plays an active rôle in determining both the creation and the appreciation of such objects. The composer interested in producing works of art must, as a necessary, though not a sufficient, condition of success, produce something which is capable of being heard as meant. And, moreover, produce it in such a way that it is the intended appearance which is the heard object of aesthetic interest. And the audience must strive to attend to the relevant appearance; in short, to care about the music rather than about the noise the music makes.

What does this Mean for Music?

Perplexingly, though he thought this account true all the fine arts, and therefore neutral as to their relative worth, Kant goes on to say that what he calls the 'art of tone'[12] is by far the poorest. He has two reasons for this. One I shall mention later. Another, trivial though somewhat amusing, is what he calls music's 'lack of urbanity'. He writes:

> For owing chiefly to the character of its instruments, [the art of tone] scatters its influence abroad to an uncalled-for extent (through the neighbourhood), and thus, as it were, becomes obtrusive and deprives others, outside the musical circle, of their freedom. This is a thing that the arts that address themselves to the eye do not do, for if one is not disposed to give admittance to their impression, one has only to look the other way.[13]

(Kant goes on in a footnote to complain about the amount of annoyance given to the public by those who recommend the singing of hymns at family prayers. Such 'noisy ... worship [compelling] their neighbours either to join in the singing or else abandon their meditations'.[14] Obviously, Kant had some trouble with his neighbours and I sometimes wonder if Kant would have felt obliged to deny, on moral grounds, that music was one of the fine arts at all had he lived in the age of modern ghetto-blasters and cheap tinny Walkmans. He would no doubt have produced a transcendental deduction of exorbitant CD prices!)

Now, the concept of a musical work of art as a regulative concept, as one which guides our perceptual explorations, has a number of important implications. Some of these implications should make us less ambitious in our efforts in philosophical aesthetics. Others should make us more so.

In the first place, we should be less ambitious because adopting a regulative account of the concept of a musical work of art means abandoning, as a philosophical task, the view that the concept of art is simply a label which we attach to certain objects once we have discovered that they possess certain properties. What is important, philosophically speaking, is not the content of the concept of a musical work of art but the rôle that it plays. And the rôle that it plays is to guide both composers and audiences to attend to the intended appearance of what, respectively, they create and what they take aesthetic interest in.

If this is what really matters, then we must abandon the attempt theoretically to describe the function or value of musical works of art. Or at least we must abandon attempts to do this other than by describing what the function or value of being able to hear music as work involves.

Thus, we should be happy to recognise that in different cultures and in different times, the content of the concept of musical art will be filled out in different ways, with different values and functions coming to the fore whilst others recede into the background. It is a moot point whether the task of uncovering the meaning of a concept of musical art for a particular culture is a task for philosophical aesthetics. I do believe that one of the important rôles for philosophy is to act as a cultural critique, of offering a deconstruction of the assumptions and values that make our particular culture. Thus it is a philosophical task to understand how, for example, the aesthetic sensibility in our own culture has been gradually transformed into a species of consumerism. But I think this a different task from trying to understand the conceptual tangles that surround the general human experience of music. Certainly it is vital that we do not confuse the two tasks. Otherwise we risk a twin danger. On the one hand, we will import the particular values of our times into what it is in our culture to be a work of art at all. So that something cannot be attended to as a work of art unless it expresses those values. And this is to fossilise what art can mean for us. On the other hand, we run the risk of importing what, in fact, it is to be a musical work in our culture into supposedly transcultural investigations into how, quite generally, music works.

Thus, we should remind ourselves that the fact that the talk of the transcendental comes quite naturally to us when we begin to talk about music, insofar as it presents a genuine philosophical problem, may be one about *us* and *our* culture and the things we make, rather than one about a particular kind of artefact which human beings everywhere are capable of making.

But if our ambitions are limited in this direction, they can expand in others. First of all, the claim that it must be possible for us to attend to the intended appearance of a musical work of art has substantial implications for our judgements about particular works of art. Thus, it will still be possible for philosophical aesthetics about music to act as the foundation for critical and musicological judgements. Second, further reflection on what it is to hear a musical work of art as a work may yet restore that connection with the transcendental which would otherwise remain merely a contingent feature of our culture's particular way of filling out the concept of a musical work of art. Let me take these in turn.

First of all, what are the implications of a regulative concept of art for our critical judgement of particular pieces of music? Clearly, we cannot lay down in advance what kinds of value or function musical works of art may come to possess. For, as Kant is happy to admit about dependent beauty in general, the concept under which such a pattern of sounds is brought, may, to a greater or lesser degree, be culturally variant. This is to say that such a concept may be historically conditioned. Hence, with one crucial exception, there is no *a priori* limit on the content of the concept regulating the production and appreciation of musical works of art. The exception is only that the content of the concept being employed is compatible with its being capable of regulating the production and appreciation of such objects and so of directing our aesthetic interest to the intended heard appearance of the work.

What this means is that if the content of a concept of art in his medium, under which a composer labours, is such as to finally frustrate the best efforts of the audience to hear the object as a work, as meant, then the object thereby fails to be a musical work of art. It is irrelevant that the sounds produced may, nevertheless, be beautiful, charming or intriguing. Natural sounds may also be beautiful, charming or intriguing. It is equally irrelevant that the sounds were, as a matter of fact, made by someone. This is true even if everyone is acquainted with this fact. What is relevant is that the sounds are such that the knowledge that they were made can serve as the starting point for finding them aesthetically intelligible, that we can be aesthetically interested in the appearance of the created sounds. And this possibility is a consequence of, *inter alia*, the particular aesthetic qualities of the work.

In the context of music this seems to me to raise serious doubts about those particular works and those traditions which seek actively to undermine the coherence of any distinction between musical works of art and collections of natural sounds. Thus the late John Cage often remarked that the reason he was so fond of his piece *4'33"* was that he could listen to it all the time. But we now have a reason for saying that it is one thing for a piece of music to direct our attention to natural sounds, it is another to produce 'works' which consist only of natural sounds.

It is because the concept of a musical work of art guides our experience of particular pieces of music that there is all the difference in the world between the use of natural sounds in Cage and in some of the works of Charles Ives, and, say, Messian's use of birdsong or Janácek's imitations of forest animal sounds in *The Cunning Little Vixen,* or the sound of the clocks gradually winding down in *Der*

Rosenkavalier. In the former cases, the use of natural sounds collapses into simple reproduction, undermining our willingness to hear the sounds as intended, whilst in the latter cases we hear the representations of the sounds, not instead of the music but through the music. In between are, I suppose, cases like the call of the cuckoo and some of the meteorological effects in Beethoven's *Pastoral* symphony, which strike me at least sometimes as part of the fabric of the symphony, but at other times as an annoying demonstration of imitative virtuosity for its own sake. It is noteworthy that in *The Ring* meteorological effects, even closer to the actual natural sounds, and indeed even the actual (if still highly wrought) sound of anvils,[15] can be heard as part of the intended appearance of the work. But here we are able to hear the sounds as part of the intended work because of the extensions to the governing regulative concept introduced by the conventions of the Wagnerian operatic form, conventions expressly disallowed by Cage.

Why is it that some artists can be so tempted to present an audience with works which may as well be aesthetically interesting natural objects? I think there is a standing temptation to composers and indeed all artists here. I think it happens often that in the course of artistic creation and composition, an artist may suddenly find herself in the grip of that frame of mind or attitude in which we find ourselves somehow attuned to the specialness or the sacredness of the ordinary and commonplace. In such frames of mind we can find ourselves attending aesthetically to the 'particularity' of an object or a sonic quality in such a way as, to put the feeling at its most baldly paradoxical, we feel that every object or sound is unique.

For some, this feeling of the uniqueness of the familiar constitutes a too rare realisation that the real, and for the poet and priest Gerard Manley Hopkins as for others, the divine, is given in the particularity of the commonplace. Indeed, for many such thinkers the value of art lies precisely in its power to redirect our attention to the holy which, on this view, can only lie in what is always close at hand.

But though there are deep connections between this sense of 'particularity' and that pervasive sense of 'fit' mentioned earlier, the extent to which a composer presents us with sounds which can be found aesthetically interesting solely through such a state of mind is the extent to which she fails to produce anything which it makes sense to call a work of art. This must be accepted even by those who hold this state of mind to be at the heart of artistic endeavour. For this purpose is not achieved merely by the provision of a stream of examples of the commonplace and the familiar. In the case of literature, Gerard Manley Hopkins did not worship the divinity in the ordinary by writing ordinary verse. He wrestled with language until its words sparked and the ordinary could be newly seen by their light. Composers, as much as other artists then, must avoid the temptation of presenting the objects of such states of attunement to the ordinary as if they automatically supplied the state of attunement themselves.

At this point, it might be objected that the account offered goes no way to explaining the sheer enjoyment of sound. Surely sounds can give intense aesthetic pleasure. Surely there are pieces of music which are immensely aesthetically enjoyable and yet the enjoyment consists solely in attending to the pleasing patterns of sound produced. Why should this not too be art?

There is here the tendency to use 'art' in neither a descriptive nor a regulative sense, but instead to think of the term as simply honorific. We think that the artefacts we admire most should be respected by the use of the term 'art'. In fact, this is the other reason why Kant thought that music was the poorest of the fine arts. He thought it too easy to enjoy music simply for its sensuous pleasure. But nothing in what I have said should be taken to imply that musical works of art must be superior to other uses to which music can be put. As if, since some piece of music isn't art, we might as well as not bother with it. Clearly most musical works are not works of art. This does not of course mean that they are in some way intrinsically inferior to musical works which are works of art. We might agree that some popular song or even some particular piece by Mozart is very enjoyable, fun to listen to, good to dance to, etc. Yet just as it would be a species of aesthetic colonialism to argue that because it did not meet the standards of some favourite sonata or symphony, it somehow failed, it would also be wrong to argue that just because it was aesthetically enjoyable, perhaps immensely so, it must therefore be a work of art. Indeed, it may be that there is a great deal more aesthetic pleasure to be had from music, *simpliciter*, than from musical works of art. Certainly something can go wrong with the way in which we regard the place of works of art in our lives. Witness a recent reviewer who called some new recording an 'everyday' Beethoven's ninth symphony. By this he meant not that it was a rather lacklustre performance, but that it was the sort of performance he could happily listen to every day since he did not, every day, want to be completely overwhelmed by the experience. He did not seem to be at all struck by the inappropriateness of listening to this music every day. So the point is not that there is something wrong with only enjoying the noise that music makes. The point is that we must distinguish between what it is that we are enjoying in music and what it is we are enjoying in musical works of art.

What we have to recognise is that (*pace* very many accounts of musical art) the job of the musical artist is not to make music out of his raw material, sounds. It is to make art, out of his medium, *music*.

CONCLUSION

The second way in which the notion of musical art as a regulative concept might make us more ambitious in our philosophical aesthetics is this. I have argued that if we are to get a clear view of the nature of musical experience, then we must at least begin by distinguishing between music, *simpliciter*, and musical works of art. I have suggested that the difference between these lies in the fact that in the case of musical works of art the object of our aesthetic attention is the intended appearance of music. That is, it is internal to the aesthetic enjoyment of music as art that we recognise it as having being made, that we can ask ourselves *why* it sounds as it does and expect to receive an answer which is aesthetically satisfying. Thus to hear music in this way is to hear it not as erupting *ex nihilo* into the sonic world, but as being produced from, and it being intended that we recognise it as being produced from, a (at least in principle) locatable point of view on the world. This is to hear music as the locus of an indefinite number of intentional descriptions; as not merely aesthetically interesting, but as aesthetically intelligible.

This, I believe, is what is true in the attempts to draw an analogy between music and language. What is important about this analogy is not that (*pace* Deryck Cooke[16]) musical phrases, harmonies and tonal modulations have semantic connections with psychological states. As if music were something we had to decode in order to understand. Of course, C major is appropriate to some feelings and not to others. But why does this connection have to be understood as a linguistic connection? Nor (*pace* Formalists) is it that music has a rule-governed grammar. As if it made sense to say that music could be ungrammatical. Though of course music does have formal substructures without which it could not be what it is. But why does this structure have to be understood in terms of rules? What is important about the analogy with language is that to understand something as a linguistic expression is to understand it as proceeding from a point of view on the world, as being something essentially spoken.

But to understand some set of sounds as something spoken by another is not to make some further empirical discovery about those sounds, namely that they mean something. For no empirical evidence could be deeper than the fact of taking what someone says as being just that: what *someone* says. Whether what is said is something that will turn out to be something we can understand is, as yet, not determined. But if we have to wait to see if the words make sense before we can regard them as spoken by someone, we are already treating them as mere noise.

Perhaps another analogy, with theology, is appropriate here. Despite the recent murmerings of some physicists,[17] to come to think of the world as something created or as something not created is not to add something to the list of interesting facts we know about the world. For whether the world is or isn't created could not be something written on its face. We have to acknowledge the world as created or uncreated and then see what, for us, flows from that acknowledgement. To treat the possibility of the world being a creation as some further, discoverable, fact about it is already to have ruled out the possibility of its having been, in any significant sense, created.

So too, I believe, for our experience of musical works of art. To come to see the art in a piece of music is not to make a further empirical discovery about it. It is to take everything about the music as meant and then to wait and hear what, if any, discoveries lay in store: discoveries that can serve as the focus of our aesthetic interest and which we can share with one another.

So it is that sometimes our appreciation of music is like this. Someone says, 'Try hearing it like this' and he makes a certain gesture with his arm, perhaps waves it in a certain way. And we hear some music playing and see a man waving his arm about. Then he says, 'Listen, can't you hear?' And we listen and we can't.

And we know what it is like to be on the other side of this too. One can feel as if the other must be deaf – 'Why does he not want to hear this!' As the theme is about to return, we look at them, smiling, encouraging them, telling them that, 'Yes, you'll hear it now, here it comes ... here it is ... now! ...', and then perhaps we swing our arms forward. Then ... 'Well, yes, I suppose I see what you mean', and then quickly, 'Who did you say it was by?' And we are heartbroken. They didn't see that our gesture was *inside* the music. They didn't see that our gesture was a reason for hearing the notes in that way. And so perhaps we shake our heads and play something we like less.

But sometimes too it is like this. I say, 'No – hear it like this ...', and I play the unfamiliar music. And now I make a certain gesture. This time you say, 'Yes – I hear it now.' In seeing how my gesture was a reason for hearing the music in that way, in seeing that my gesture *was on the inside of the music*, perhaps it is that we are mutually appraised of something it makes sense to speak of as the reality of appearances. If this is how it is then the triumph of the composer is not to succeed in that impossible, godlike task: the creation or revelation of worlds. Rather, on this view, the triumph of the artist is to succeed in an appallingly difficult, but still human-scaled, task: the embodiment of life and thought and feeling in objects; the embodiment of *the reality of points of view*.

And perhaps it is here that there lies music's essential connection with the transcendental. However, making the precise nature of this connection clearer is a task for a more ambitious philosophical aesthetic of music than mine. Since, for myself, I think this is something of which one is fully convinced, if at all, not by the presentation of philosophical arguments but by the understanding of particular musical works.[18]

NOTES

[1] Ludwig Wittgenstein, *Philosophical Investigations*, trans. G. E. M. Anscombe, Oxford: Basil Blackwell, 1963, § 123.
[2] The classic Formalist theory of art is the doctrine of 'significant form' found in Clive Bell, *Art*, London: Chatto and Windus, 1914.
[3] Terry Eagleton, *The Ideology of the Aesthetic*, Oxford: Basil Blackwell, 1990 is representative.
[4] Immanuel Kant, *Critique of Judgement*, Oxford: Oxford University Press, 1980 (first edition 1790), especially Part I, First Book, First Movement, § 16 and § 45.
[5] *op. cit.*, 230. This, and the following references, are to the standard marginal pagination.
[6] *ibid.*, 229.
[7] *ibid.*, 230.
[8] *ibid.*, 306.
[9] *loc. cit.*
[10] *ibid.*, 307.
[11] *ibid.*, 168.
[12] *ibid.*, 329.
[13] *ibid.*, 331.
[14] *ibid.*, 330 n.1.
[15] Wagner wrote for nine small anvils, six larger anvils and three very large ones, and indicated precisely how he wanted them placed.
[16] Deryck Cooke, *The Language of Music*, New York: Oxford University Press, 1989.
[17] Paul Davies, *God and the New Physics*, London: Dent, 1983 is representative.
[18] Some of the material for this essay is taken from my *Art or Bunk?*, Bristol: Bristol Classical Press, 1989.

7

Music and Worship: A Psychologist's Perspective

John Sloboda

INTRODUCTION

The rôle of music in worship is not a topic that has greatly exercised psychologists. Both the psychology of music and the psychology of religion are very much 'fringe' topics in contemporary psychology. The number of psychologists interested in both must be tiny. Accordingly, the most a paper like this can hope to do is ask some of the right questions, and speculate about possible directions in which answers may be sought.

It seems that the particular sequence of questions that a psychologist might hope to elucidate would be something like the following:

1. What goes on in people's minds when they are engaging with music? Or, more formally, what are the mental processes specific to the domain of music?
2. What goes on in people's minds when they are engaging in worship? What are the mental processes specific to the domain of worship?
3. In what way do the mental processes involved in music and in worship overlap? In other words, are there particular aspects of worshipping which are enhanced, reinforced, or afforded, by acts of 'musicking'?
4. How can we account for, or explain, these overlapping mental processes in terms of our broader understanding of human mental functioning?

These are, of course, weighty questions, requiring the input of musicians, theologians, liturgists and philosophers, as well as psychologists. This paper can hardly do more that make some preliminary comments in the direction of these questions.

In what follows I have tried to take a phenomenological approach to worship. That is to say, I concentrate on what I understand people to be doing or feeling in worship, and try to describe this in theologically neutral language. Where it has seemed necessary, for ease of expression to use terms like 'God', I am neither claiming to be theologically precise nor attempting to use any particular set of dogmatic assumptions, whether Christian or otherwise, to support the arguments.

THE BASIS OF HUMAN RESPONSE TO MUSIC: FREE OR CONSTRAINED?

Can we choose what mental processes to engage during some musical activity? If we cannot, then there is the possibility of a rather simple approach to the psychology of music. Each type of music will have a particular mental effect on a person, just as a particular drug will have a reliable effect on human physiology. In an earlier article I have called this model of musical response the 'pharmaceutical' one (Sloboda, 1989).

It should not take too much reflection to reject the pharmaceutical model as hopelessly inadequate. When confronted with the same musical situation I have many options that I can exercise. Here are just a few:

1. I can pay no attention to the music at all, and pursue my own thoughts, memories, and fantasies.
2. I can derive personal associations from listening to the music. When have I heard this music before? How was I feeling at the time I experienced this music? What personal events, feelings, reactions am I reminded of by this music?
3. I can exercise an analytic or critical faculty with respect to some aspect of the music. Is the soprano soloist singing in tune? What was that interesting harmony? Could this be Mozart? Is this a better performance of this piece than the one I heard last week?
4. I can engage with the music in a non-analytic, contemplative mode in which, whilst being attentive to it, I am not focussing on any particular event, or making specific judgements. I am 'letting the music wash over me'.
5. I can engage with the music by attending to the relationship between myself and others also engaged in the music. Am I

following the conductor? Does my voice blend with that of my neighbour? Is my neighbour experiencing what I am experiencing?

This list, which is not necessarily complete, shows that we have choices about the mental processes we engage in a musical context. Is there, in that case, anything we can usefully say about such processes that has any generality, or is it simply a case of 'you do your thing and I'll do mine'?

I believe we can go beyond total individualism by use of the notion of *affordances*. The term was introduced to psychology by the perceptual psychologist James J. Gibson (Gibson, 1966). In Gibson's eyes, human response can often be explained not so much by reference to inner states, but by reference to characteristics of the environment that constrain and direct that response. So, for instance, a chair *affords* sitting. It has the necessary physical characteristics to allow someone to sit on it. If well designed it almost, by its very nature, *invites* you to sit on it. No one has to explain to you that it is for sitting. Even a very small child with no understanding of the concept of a chair would still naturally end up sitting on it in the course of physical exploration. This is because the object fits to a set of human characteristics. Chairs have to be a particular way because humans are the way they are.

By affording some kinds of activities, environments discourage or even preclude others. It is rarely the case that the same object will afford both sitting and eating, for instance. On the other hand, most objects have multiple affordances. The same object that affords sitting can also afford throwing (you could pick up a light chair and throw it at an assailant).

Designers of everyday objects are beginning to understand how they can make life simpler by building in the right sorts of affordances (Norman, 1988). No one should ever have to struggle with a door, not sure whether to push or pull it, not sure whether the handle goes up or down. Appropriately designed handles will afford only a single movement, the correct one. A correctly designed concourse will naturally draw people in the intended direction.

When objects are used in social contexts, culture can shape the normative affordances of those objects, and these can change over time. Objects (e.g. Roman vessels) that were once used for cooking are now used as collector's items or objects of historical research. But there is a cultural inertia. Uses of objects change relatively slowly.

And so it is with music. We can choose what to do with music, but for most of us the choices are limited by culture, background, social context, and the way the music itself has been designed (in Gibsonian terminology, the affordances it possesses). A key context for music has always been worship. It must be the case that (at least some) music affords worship. Our task is to demonstrate how.

Rather than attempt a formal definition of worship, I shall assume for the moment a shared intuitive understanding of the concept, and sweep back over the five 'ways of responding' to music that I outlined above.

MUSIC AS UNATTENDED BACKGROUND

It is tempting to say that if one is not attending to music then it cannot be said to be affording anything, let alone worship. But there are different ways of not attending to music. On the one hand, one can simply ignore the music and get on with what one was doing as if it wasn't there. This tends to be my response to subdued canned music in supermarkets, restaurants, and other public places. I can also be at work deeply involved with a piece of writing and be almost totally unaware of concurrent recorded music. On the other hand, in some contexts the mere presence of the music may limit my responses and direct them in certain ways. For instance, music in a worship setting *may* define a period of time in which participants neither speak nor move about. So, although I may not be listening to the anthem, I am, perforce, sitting still, in the presence of others, with the memories of particular acts or words that have preceded the music. Worship may certainly happen in such contexts. But if I am truly ignoring the music, then the most that the music can be contributing to my worship is to signal a beginning and end to the time period within which particular sorts of mental activity may take place. Such signals can be provided in many ways, and are not in any sense special to music.

MUSIC AS A SOURCE OF PERSONAL ASSOCIATIONS

There has now accumulated a significant body of data that confirms that music is a particularly powerful evoker of other times and other places. It is no accident that almost every single guest who has ever appeared on 'Desert Island Discs' has been able to use music to illustrate appropriately his or her life story. The majority of western adults seem to remember particularly well the popular tunes of their adolescent years, and retain a strong emotional response to them. In one of the earliest contemporary texts on the psychology of music (Davies, 1978), this aspect of music psychology was wittily characterised as the 'darling, they're playing our tune' theory of musical response.

There is considerable psychological evidence to show that we remember highly emotionally charged events in a unique way. Brown and Kulik (1977) coined the term 'flashbulb memory' to identify this type of memory, which seems to be characterised by a vivid literal memory of all the incidental details surrounding the emotion-provoking incident. In the earliest study on flashbulb memories individuals were asked whether they could remember exactly what they were doing when they first heard the news that President J. F. Kennedy had been assassinated. Most people recalled exactly where they were, what time it was, who they were with, what was said. If music was playing at the time, then the music would also be remembered.

The situation is complicated for music, however, in that the past musical event may, in itself, have been a source of strong emotion. I will discuss the nature of such strong emotion and the evidence for it in a later section. It is sufficient for now to say that the association of a present musical experience may be self-referring; the present experience retrieves the thoughts and feelings of an earlier experience of that music, rather than of the other events which accompanied the music. Such experiences are often positive, sometimes profoundly so.

The associationistic function of music may be tight or loose. A tight association is the association generated by a specific piece of music (e.g. Bach's *Prelude and Fugue in G* [BWV 541] for organ). A loose association is to a type or genre of music (e.g. baroque organ music). Many people operate with loose associations which determine their willingness to engage with music in certain circumstances. Individuals whose strong personal associations with popular music are to situations of alienation and degeneracy are unlikely to be spurred to worship by such music. Such associations can be self-reinforcing. Because many people in our culture associate organ music with worship settings (as a result of experiencing many previous worship settings involving organ music), but do not so associate pop music, organ music can in itself appear 'sacred' and pop music 'profane', leading to cultural practices which reinforce the rôle of some types of music in worship and exclude others. Appearances generated through such associations alone are, however, arbitrary and culturally contingent. The issue of whether some kinds of music have intrinsic features which better afford worship than others is a separate question, and one to which we will return.

The consequences of musical associations for worship are, I think, rather clear. Music has a particular power to remind us of important past events in our life and the profound feelings which accompanied them. This can lead to celebration, joyful remembrance, or the revisiting of pain and suffering. It can lift us out of our current pre-occupations and re-focus our attention on the wider landscape of our lives. By bringing together in our consciousness events which may be distant in time, it can help us to get a better sense of the cradle-to-grave continuity and unity of ourselves as persons.

Music is by no means the only source of powerful reminders of times past. But because of its inherent capacity to evoke strong emotion, it is likely to be a particularly powerful route to personal associations.

MUSIC AS A VEHICLE FOR THE EXERCISE OF JUDGEMENT

The preceding section glossed over a crucial problem, the problem of representation and equivalence. How does a person recognise a piece of music experienced in the present as an instance of something they have heard before in the past? It can rarely be the case that the physical stimulus is identical in all respects. Only repeated hearings of the same recording in exactly the same acoustic conditions would guarantee that. What is it, then, that we use to make judgements of equivalence?

This is not a problem unique to music. It relates to any experience that we classify and categorise. How do we identify different instances of the letter 'a' as such, given that they may be written in different handwritings, orientations, sizes, etc.? Simplifying in a few sentences thirty years of intense scientific work is not easy, but the essence of mainstream theorising about the matter is that humans make progress by forming representations of objects which are less like 'photographs' and more like 'lists'. In other words, a letter 'a' might be represented as:

- a bounded circular space;
- a vertically oriented line attached to the right edge of that space.

In the process of representing objects in this way, some detailed information from the original is lost, but a more useful level of underlying structure is gained, because the representation is more abstract than the stimulus from which it is derived. Several physically different objects can be captured under the same description in a way that identifies their common function.

Psychologists are not claiming that individuals always have conscious verbal access to the nature of their representations. In many cases, the existence of the representations can only be inferred on the basis of how people actually classify objects, i.e. which objects are perceived by people as similar or identical to one another.

In music, for instance, we know that, by and large, people do not represent music in terms of its absolute pitches or frequencies. Unless a person has an acutely developed sense of absolute pitch, he or she will judge as 'identical' the sequences C-D-E-F-G and D-E-F#-G-A, so long as they are not played consecutively. This judgement will be made by anyone with sufficient exposure to tonal music. It does not require formal training. Formal training will simply allow someone to verbalise what it is about these two sequences that make them sound the same. (They are both ascending major scales starting on their respective tonics and ending on the fifth degree.)

To summarise a very large amount of research, it appears that in listening to music humans are normally representing what they hear, at least in part, as a (non-verbal, intuitive) structural description of that music (in terms of pitch classes, tonality, metre, tension and resolution, continuities and discontinuities, repetitions and transformations, etc.). What it means to recognise a piece of music is to discover a match between the structural description of the current experience and a previously stored structural description.

In a very important sense then, the mere fact of being able to recognise a piece of music means that (intuitive and subconscious) judgements were exercised on both previous and current hearing. These were the judgements that assigned *this* event to *this* pitch class rather than the neighbouring one, and so on. Of course, there are different levels of judgement. It does not require detailed note-by-note judgement to identify two pieces of music as 'organ music' or 'pop music'. It requires much detailed judgement to recognise two events as performances of the same piece, and even more judgement reliably to differentiate the two performances.

INEFFABILITY AND JUDGEMENT

What the preceding discussion highlights for us is the fact that there is a great deal of 'knowing' of one sort or another going on in engagement in music that is not necessarily translated into 'saying'. I have a sense that this gap between knowing and saying is one that offers particular affordances for worship. At the heart of much worship is the sense of being in the presence of that which is beyond capture by human concepts. In approaching the object of worship we are approaching that which is at the limits of our apprehension. And yet, neither the object of worship nor the activity of worship is alien to us. In worship, there is fulfilment. We discover in the object of our worship intimate knowledge and understanding but cannot adequately say what it is we know or understand. The adjective which describes those things which we can know but not say is 'ineffable'. Human experience of God has always possessed an ineffable core.

One recent project in the philosophy of music which seems to have crucial implications for our understanding of the rôle of music in worship is the attempt to clarify in what ways, if at all, musical knowledge is ineffable. This project has been undertaken by Diana Raffman in her book *Language, Music, and Mind* (1993), and what I have to say here draws very deeply on her thinking.

Raffman identifies three distinct ways in which individuals may know more than they can say about a musical experience. She has a particular concern to determine whether any of these types of ineffability are logically necessary for all listeners at all times, but this concern need not be ours. If ineffability can be experienced at all, then it may be relevant to worship.

Structural Ineffability

The first type of ineffability identified by Raffman is *structural ineffability*, and it relates to limitations in the ability to verbalise high-level structural features which affect the way that music is represented. She provides some examples of experiences falling into this category which will be recognisable to many experienced musicians:

> Having easily reported the pitches, rhythms and time-signature of a heard piece, along perhaps with some of its local grouping, time-span, and prolongational structures, a listener (perhaps even a highly expert one) finds himself at a loss: 'I am feeling that E-natural in a certain distinctive way, but I can't say just how. I know it's the leading tone, and that it's preparing the return to the tonic, and I know it's a weak prolongation of the E-natural in the previous bar . . . but somehow I feel there is more going on.' Or a performer feels himself compelled to play a certain passage in a certain way (e.g., to slow down, or to get louder, or to increase the vibrato speed) – consciously feels, knows, that it must be played thus, and yet cannot say why. . . . What I want to suggest is that unconscious structural representations – in particular, relatively global levels of representation – are 'making themselves felt' in our conscious experience, yet their contents elude our verbal grasp. (Raffman, 1993, pp. 31–32)

Another way of experiencing this kind of ineffability is the sense of 'rightness' about a particular musical event. We feel that 'it had to be like that', even though we have no conscious access to explicit reasons for the judgement. It seems to me that this maps rather straightforwardly onto an aspect of worship which concerns our apprehension of 'the larger design of things'. We can marvel or wonder at the rightness and beauty of aspects of creation at the same time as being unable to do more than catch hints of the underlying nature of the phenomenon. There is a kind of inexhaustibility to this level of ineffability, which spurs scientific and other intellectual endeavours. Our efforts to understand can be likened to peeling an infinitely large onion from the inside. There is always another higher level of explanation beyond the one that has been discovered. The permanent gap between intuitive contemplation and intellectual understanding is a central feature of the worshipping experience.

Feeling Ineffability

The second type of musical ineffability is characterised by Raffman as *feeling ineffability*. This comes about because of the essential sensory-perceptual or experiential nature of music. Knowing a piece of music involves, along with other things, *knowing what it sounds like*. 'A person deaf from birth cannot know a piece of music' (p. 40). This does not mean that a trained musician has to hear a particular new piece of music to know it. It is possible to compute what it sounds like (at least to some degree of specification) by examining a score, provided that one has a rich enough base of prior musical experience to fall back on. But without this sensory underpinning there is no possibility of full knowledge.

This type of ineffability is by no means unique to music. All sensory experiences, from sunsets to 'the taste of last night's chicken curry' have the same ineffability. They require 'actual occurrent sense-perception of the relevant stimuli at some point' (p. 4). Yet, according to Raffman, there seems to be a special quality to the feeling ineffability of musical knowledge that commands our particular attention in the way that last night's curry does not. Her thought is that it is the grammatical structure of music that (mis)leads us to expect something effable as an end result of 'following' a piece of music. 'Music's grammatical structure may mislead us into semantic temptation' (p. 41) in a unique way not brought about when we observe a sunset, or even a painting. This comes about because of music's formal similarity to language.

I will try and put this another way. Music's formal structure and its similarities to speech (sequential, unfolding over time) suggests to us that it is saying something to us, or pointing our attention to something. What it is pointing to, among other things, is the actual sensual experience itself, which by definition cannot be fully described in words. Unlike a sunset, therefore, music *announces itself to us*. This power of music to draw our attention to our own sensations and encourage us to consider them as significant seems also to me to have an obvious purpose in worship. Many traditions of worship encourage the development of an attentiveness and a readiness to be 'spoken to'. Yet few traditions encourage worshippers to expect that the 'word of God' will always come directly through language, spoken or imagined. Rather, the message may come through images, experiences, sensations, memories. And so worshippers are encouraged to be still and pay attention to everything. Music may smooth our path towards such attentiveness by in some way simulating a situation in which we sense we are being spoken to, thus sharpening our attentiveness accordingly. Since the music is not literally saying anything (in the strict linguistic sense), our attentiveness is available for other purposes. We are made ready to 'hear God's voice'.

Nuance Ineffability

Raffman proposes that the third and final type of musical ineffability is *nuance ineffability*. This type of ineffability comes about because we do not have verbal categorisations or schemas as fine-grained as the stimuli we can discriminate. For instance, we may be able to characterise a pitch as 'middle-C'. If we are particularly acute, we may be able to label it as 'a slightly sharp middle-C', but none of us would be able to operate at the level of cycles-per-second. Although most of us could detect that there was some difference between two pitches of 250 Hz and 255 Hz respectively, we would not be able to name the difference at that level.

The reasons for nuance ineffability are inherently psychological. Raffman cites a number of such reasons, of which I think two are compelling. First, as Raffman argues, 'it is hard to see what point there would be to a schema whose "grain" was as fine as perception'. The fact that we describe musical stimuli in broad categories (such as C, D, etc.) is arguably a result of our need to reduce the intolerable information load that would be placed on our cognitive system by representing every nuance. In other words, human processing limitations make total effability nuances a psychological impossibility. Second, she argues that the just-noticeable-difference (JND) for perceptual properties varies with stimulus and observer characteristics (including alertness, health, etc.).

If these arguments are correct, there will always be a residual ineffable component in any conceivable representation of music. As Raffman poetically describes it, musical experience will always be characterised by 'an evanescent corona shimmering around the structural frame of the piece' (p. 96).

This ineffability is a kind of opposite to structural ineffability. Structural ineffability occurs because, however powerful our mental telescopes, we can never quite get a fix on the biggest picture. Nuance ineffability occurs because our mental microscopes can never reach the smallest level of magnification. Blake's invocation 'To see a world in a grain of sand' (*Auguries of Innocence*) describes exactly the inexhaustible detail within a musical performance. Such detail is, of course, present in any sensory experience, but again, as was the case with feeling ineffability, we can suppose that the quasi-linguistic nature of music points us towards the 'shimmering corona' and encourages us to endow it with significance. In worship there are contemplative states in which tiny, usually ignored, details of experience are perceived in great clarity, as if for the first time. Musical experience may encourage such states.

To conclude this rather lengthy analysis of musical ineffability, we can see that there are strong arguments for supposing that much musical experience challenges us to go to the limits of our ability to pass easy judgements. We are constantly getting tripped up over one or another form of ineffability. It doesn't seem to me that the act of making well-practised verbal judgements (about music or anything else) has any particularly special relevance for worship. Where worship seems to be afforded a particularly strong foothold is precisely at the boundaries of what can be said. Music brings us particularly effectively into an awareness of the ineffable, and thus into a core attribute of worship.

MUSIC AS A VEHICLE FOR NON-JUDGEMENTAL CONTEMPLATION

The preceding section has suggested what I now need to say explicitly. There may be a sense in which, while listening to music, we cannot help but make judgements about it. These are not so much verbal judgements, as those subconscious and automatic acts of assigning notes to the basic categories of representation. There is much research literature that shows that when we are very familiar with particular structures and codes our cognitive system performs these routine analyses whether we like it or not. Therefore, when I refer to non-judgemental contemplation, I really mean an attitude of mind in which a listener does not engage in specific verbally based activities leading to verbal judgements (e.g. 'what key is this in?', 'is the trumpet playing in tune?', etc.).

In a restricted sense, therefore, the 'pharmaceutical' model rejected earlier may have some merit. Within a given musical culture, and among individuals who have had comparable prior musical experience, there may be some automatic and subconscious mental processes which are indeed determined primarily by the nature of the particular piece of music being heard. However, if these processes are predominantly inaccessible to consciousness, what is it that a listener may be aware of that derive directly from these processes but are neither associations, nor verbal judgements? One major category of such objects of awareness is the category of affective experiences: feelings, moods and emotions. It seems clear that there are at least some musically generated affective states that are not simply triggered through association to previously experienced instances of the same or similar music. Music has some inherent characteristics which promote affective responses.

Two lines of evidence (more extensively reported elsewhere: Sloboda, 1991) support this assertion. First, music is reported by a wide range of individuals as evoking, often on first hearing, emotions and feelings of an unprecedented intensity and unique character. If someone has feelings she never had before to music she never heard before, then specific associations cannot be playing a major rôle in the generation of that state. Secondly, the nature of the affective response to music is sometimes determined by very precise structural characteristics of the music, such as a particular harmonic structure, and seems to be shared by members of a culture. In general these structures are rather abstract, and can be realised in a wide range of specific sequences. It is not the case that there is any simple one-to-one mapping between a key, melody, interval, or chord, and a specific emotion.

There are two main structural determinants of affective response to music. The first, which we could call 'global', relates to overall characteristics of a piece or a section. For instance, smooth, quiet, slow music tends to evoke moods of repose or resignation. Fast, jagged, loud music tends to evoke agitated moods, whether of happiness or anger. There seems often to be some rather straightforward analogy being drawn to the characteristics of a human being's behaviour when in such moods. So, for instance, a sad person tends to behave slowly and quietly.

The second determinant, which we could call 'local', relates to the moment to moment changes in affect which are experienced as the music unfolds. So, although we may experience a whole piece as 'sad', we find that sadness reaches a peak of intensity at a particular moment. It appears that many of these moments are determined by the precise confirmations and violations of expectations that are built up in the course of listening. Of course, two people listening to the same piece of music may not always experience the same emotion, any more than the same person may do so on different hearings. But what the available data do strongly suggest is that if these moment-specific emotions are felt at all, then they are felt at the same points in the music by all listeners. Variations in emotional experience are not caused so much by idiosyncratic ways of representing the music, as by contextual factors (e.g. the prevailing degree of emotional arousal in the individual, the importance of the event of which the music forms a part, etc.) and by the individual's own construal of the emotional response (e.g. one individual may find it wholly therapeutic to be moved to tears by a musical passage, another individual might find it excruciatingly embarrassing).

An example of a musical feature that appears to provoke emotional responses associated with crying (e.g. tears, lump in the throat) is the repeated suspension or appogiatura. Many composers and commentators have explicitly recognised this characteristic as indicative of pathos, and this does not seem to be an arbitrary feature to serve the same effect. The emotional response has something to do with the repeated harmonic tension and relaxation that such structures produce within a tonal context.

It is particularly relevant to the discussion of the rôle of genre in worship to note that these structural features are not the province of narrow genres. One can find exactly the same use of appogiaturas in baroque orchestral music as in 1980s pop ballads, yielding exactly the same kind of emotional effect. What can differ, but not in a simple way that is mapped onto genres, is the complexity, subtlety or 'disguisedness' of the way in which a basic structure is deployed by the composer. It is such subtlety which distracts us from noticing too readily that the same underlying structure is present in two pieces of music that affect us in similar ways, and adds a sense of wonder or newness to what might otherwise seem manipulative and overly sentimental.

History has a refining effect. By and large, what survives from ages past is the interesting and unusual rather than the trite. Contemporary music, on the other hand, contains much which is of little value, precisely because history has not yet been able to weed out that which people do not value. I am convinced that many of the value judgements about genres suitable for worship are based on average 'trite-ness' ratings on the pieces of each genre known to an individual. On these grounds, the average pop track is bound to be more trite than the average sixteenth-century anthem in press. The average piece of music especially written for church use in the twentieth century is also likely to be more trite than the historical canon.

Here, then, is where individual differences will 'get in the way' of the contemplative response. Many people will resist the emotional effect of some music, simply because the effect is too blatant or obvious. Such resistance is not unique to music. I have heard people complain that they find themselves resisting being moved to tears by the crude manipulative dramas of soap operas. Several musicians I know complain that they find tears coming to their eyes during the performance of 'Land of Hope and Glory' at the Last Night of the Proms, even though they claim to loath both the music and the shallow sentimentality of the occasion. They almost feel ashamed of their response and try to suppress it.

For true contemplation it is necessary mentally to instruct oneself to forget where the music comes from, to forget one's associations to it, to forget whether one likes it or not, and simply let it work its effect. There is a strong element in worship of quieting one's own inner voices to 'let God speak'. This is often expressed as a subjuga-tion of one's own will and inclinations to God's. Precisely because music does have such strong personal associations, but also *of its own nature* evokes emotional responses which may be quite at variance with one's personal predispositions towards it, there is a clear sense in which the contemplation of music embodies the particular challenge to 'self' that marks out contemplative worship.

MUSIC AS A VEHICLE FOR EXPERIENCING PERSONAL RELATIONSHIPS

Engaging with music can bring the participant into particular kinds of relationship with others. I have already alluded in the previous section to the fact that music has a tendency to co-ordinate at least the shape of the rise and fall of emotional response to music in a body of people. We are all likely to feel most strongly at the same point, even if the precise colour of our feelings differ from one to another.

Such co-ordination becomes even more focussed when we are engaged together in making music. In music-making we are contribut-ing to a larger whole, so that our small individual contribution becomes more significant. This happens in two ways. First, and more simply, our effort is amplified (as when a large body of people are all singing the same tune). Secondly, and more profoundly, new things are achieved through co-ordination of different activities. New aspects of a melody emerge when it is put in counterpoint with another one, because added to the individual characteristics of each melody is now the harmonic and rhythmic structure that is created by the relationship of the two melodies.

Music is thus a very good analogy for certain key aspects of worship. In almost every religious tradition there is the notion of a worshipping community, that in some way the co-ordinated worshipping of a body of people united by common activity is somehow more powerful and effective than individual prayer. Worship reflects human solidarity. And secondly, worship is expressive of relationships between one individual and another. Any relationship is more than the sum of the two individuals. Something new and valuable is realised in the meeting of persons; and in many traditions, including the Christian one, some of the profoundest theological concepts are attempts to grasp just what the newness consists in.

There is, of course, a major problem about communality. A sense of solidarity is not, in and of itself, a guarantee of goodness. Music and other forms of communal activity can inspire people to unite for evil as well as good ends. Sometimes, the 'godly' act is to refuse to be caught up in communality, and stand alone. It seems to me, therefore, that music can only be used for effective communal worship where there is already an existing community, bound by common understandings and commitments, where trust and 'good works' underpin relationships. In this context, music in worship deepens and strengthens mutual commitments. Music cannot, in and of itself, create community.

CONCLUSION

I hope that this paper has demonstrated that there are several characteristics of human response to music which are particularly effective 'affordances' for worship. Many of the mental processes encouraged by music are also present in worship. What I have not done is to show, in any very systematic way, that activities other than music do not have the same auspicious set of affordances, thus demonstrating music's unique rôle. We really need a comprehensive psychological analysis of all human activities that might impinge on worship, comparing and contrasting the affordances of each. But that is a task for a different time and place.

REFERENCES

Brown, R. and Kulik, J. (1977), 'Flashbulb Memories', *Cognition,* 5, pp. 73–99.

Davies, J. B. (1978), *The Psychology of Music,* London: Hutchinson.

Gibson, J. J. (1966), *The Senses Considered as Perceptual System,* Boston: Houghton Miffin.

Norman, D. A. (1988), *The Psychology of Everyday Things,* New York: Basic Books.

Raffman, D. (1993), *Language, Music, and Mind,* Cambridge, Mass.: MIT Press.

Sloboda, J. A. (1989), 'Music, Psychology and the Composer', in S. Nielzen and O. Olsson (eds), *Structure and Perception of Electroacoustic Sound and Music,* Amsterdam: Elsevier, pp. 3–12.

Sloboda, J. A. (1991), 'Empirical Studies of Emotional Response to Music, in M. Riess-Jones (ed.), *Cognitive Bases of Musical Communication,* Washington D.C.: American Psychological Association, pp. 33–46.

8

Music and Spirituality:
Are Musicians More Religious?

Rosamund Bourke

This chapter consists of three sections. The first briefly reviews studies of aesthetic experience in music that may be relevant to religion. The second describes my own research on the religiosity of musicians. The third attempts to draw some conclusions.

AESTHETIC EXPERIENCES IN MUSIC AND RELIGION

Aesthetic response to music would seem to have much in common with religious experiences. Crickmore (1968) sought to devise a quantitative measure of aesthetic listening. He assumed that if a musical composition has been assimilated aesthetically it will leave the listener feeling interested, happier, more relaxed, with a desire to remain quiet, satisfied, and without any particular mental pictures. Listeners were asked to rate themselves at the end of each piece of music on these points; the scores provided a six-point syndrome. He found evidence of growth in appreciation on a second hearing of the music. Appreciation appeared to be independent of the personality characteristics of extraversion and neuroticism, suggesting that music may be enjoyed by a variety of temperaments. Although music students produced more of the syndrome, technical students could also become absorbed in the music. One commented, 'I was not listening to the music, it was *me* inside.' When he analysed his results with student groups, one of the factors found was described as 'a desire for silence'. Crickmore notes that if the experience of listening to music is to have depth, internal silence – cessation of inner speech – is necessary. While welcoming the changes brought about by Vatican II in encouraging lay people to sing, Crickmore (1967) emphasised the value of active listening to the traditional music of the church as a means of reaching a state of deep contemplation.

Madsen believes that aesthetic experiences depend on the focussing of attention. For his experiments the listeners manipulated a Continuous Response Digital Interface (CRDI) designed to record ongoing responses to music without requiring a verbal response. In one experiment musicians listened to the last twenty minutes of Act I of *La Bohème* and manipulated the CRDI dial to indicate their perceived aesthetic response. 'Aesthetic experience' was purposely left undefined. After the experiment, all the listeners reported that they had had at least one aesthetic experience and that the graph produced by the dial roughly corresponded to their experience. The 'peak experience' might be very short – 15 seconds or less, but seemed to require several minutes in highly concentrated focus of attention, especially during the previous 30–45 seconds (Madsen, Brittin and Capperella-Sheldon, 1993). Almost identical graphs were produced by the same musicians who took part in a second trial. A later investigation found that musicians and non-musicians (i.e. college students not majoring in music) had very similar aesthetic responses to five different western art-music selections (Madsen, Brynes, Capperella-Sheldon and Brittin, 1993). One of the pieces was 'Laudate Dominum' from Mozart's *Vesperae Solennes de Confessore*. This produced one or more aesthetic experiences in 93% of the non-musicians and in 90% of the musicians. The average rating of the magnitude of the experience was 6.80 for the non-musicians and 6.17 for the musicians, compared with 6.27 for non-musicians and 7.13 for musicians with *La Bohème*. Madsen's experiments are very interesting, but do they tell us much about these moments of heightened insight – moments whose impact is perhaps long remembered?

Gabrielsson asked for descriptions of the most intense experience of music a person had ever had. Of the total of some 800 participants in the project, about 62% were women. Ages ranged from thirteen to ninety-one years, and musical preferences spread across most musical genres. Analysis of the rich data collected still continues, but initial results from 149 respondents produced seven basic categories. One category, 'transcendental and existential' included various religious experiences that appeared to transcend reality (Gabrielsson and Lindstrom, 1993). In one report the individual was so moved by hearing Sibelius's second symphony that he wrote to thank the composer, then walked in the woods thanking God for something so incredibly beautiful created by a human mind. In this instance the aesthetic experience certainly led to a religious one. However, many experiences that appear to be religious are not necessarily interpreted as such by those who report them (Beit-Hallahmi and Argyle, 1997). Beit-Hallahmi and Argyle recognise that music and religion are closely linked and that music is used in worship in all religions. They cite Greeley's (1975) research which found that 'listening to music' was the most frequently reported trigger for religious experiences. However, they believe that some peak experiences, for example those brought on by music or the beauty of nature, may be experienced purely as aesthetic. A study by Hills and Argyle (1998) has thrown some light on the relationship between musical and religious experiences. They asked adults who were members of musical groups or churches or both to complete scales to describe the intensity of their emotional feelings for musical and church activities. They concluded that musical and religious experiences are basically similar; musical experiences were more intense for most items, even items such as 'glimpsing another world' and 'loss of sense of self', which had previously been used only to assess mystical aspects of religious experience. Differences were also found: while social and mystical factors appeared in both analyses, the religious items also produced a transcendental factor and the musical items produced a factor related to challenge and performance.

Perhaps both music and religion have their origin in what William James in his classic work *The Varieties of Religious Experience* (1902) called the 'unconscious'. Inspiration from the unconscious plays an importance part in composition and in the performance of music (Shuter-Dyson, 1988). This accords well with the concept of God as creator continuing to work through human agents.

Music has unique power to help silence our preoccupations and make us ready to hear the voice of God. As we have seen, non-musicians as well as musicians can enjoy a deep aesthetic appreciation of music. All humans *qua* human are capable of response to music. Indeed much evidence is available about the earliest development of music in the newly born. For example, very young infants are able to perceive a musical passage as a coherent pattern (Trehub, Schellenberg and Hill, 1997), although for high achievement in music a long path of practice in a supportive environment is required. The importance of earliest influences of parents and social environment is as well recognised for religion as for music. However, rather less research seems to have been carried out to investigate childhood spirituality (Nye, 1996).

Empirical studies of school music-making led June Boyce-Tillman (1996) to represent musical development in the form of a helix. She has now extended her model to include a level she calls

'Transcendence'. One side she describes as 'Spiritual', for it represents an acute awareness of the Divine. The other side she entitles 'Mystical', representing an integration of these elements into a personal belief-system that influences all the person's musical activity. Her concept of musical development is not intended as a stage-by-stage model. The experienced musician may revisit the lower levels in all musical activity, and even in the youngest children there will be indications of the upper levels. The look of wonder in the eyes of children exploring the magic of the sound of a drum is like the wonder in the eyes of Messiaen talking of his choice of gongs in one of his symphonies.

While it seems that music has the power to induce a state of contemplation, a quieting of one's inner voices to 'let God speak' (cf. Sloboda, chapter 7 above), we need to recognise both that many intense experiences of music may be wholly secular and that the presence of God may often be found in noisy surroundings.

ARE MUSICIANS MORE RELIGIOUS?

Introduction

My own research was inspired by Kemp's (1996) finding that sensitivity was an important factor in the personality of musicians, and by Francis who reported a stable relationship between low scores on Eysenck's psychoticism (tough-minded) factor and religiosity on his Attitude toward Christianity Scale (see, e.g., Francis, 1992 and Francis, Lewis, Brown, Philipchalk and Lester, 1995). This suggested to me that musicians might be more positively inclined towards religiosity.

The Attitude toward Christianity Scale has enjoyed considerable use in the United Kingdom and abroad. It consists of 24 items concerned with affective response to God, Jesus, the Bible, prayer and church, each scored on a five-point scale ranging from 'agree strongly' through 'uncertain' to 'disagree strongly' (Francis, 1989; Kay and Francis, 1996). To assess personality Francis mainly uses the various forms of the Eysenck Personality Questionnaire. The four personality dimensions covered by Eysenck are extraversion, neuroticism, psychoticism and whatever is being measured by the Lie Scale. Francis has consistently found that psychoticism is negatively related to religiosity, confirming Eysenck's view that tender-minded social attitudes are concerned with ethical and religious ideas which act as barriers to the immediate gratification of aggressive and social impulses; such attitudes are formed by social conditioning (Francis, 1992). The other notable relationship that Francis has reported is between his Attitude Scale and the Lie Scale. This can be interpreted in a variety of ways depending on whether the Lie Scale is considered to measure actual lying, lack of insight or social conformity. Pearson and Francis (1989) identified two different types of 'lying' that were measured by the scale. Only one seemed to be related to religiosity, the items being concerned with good behaviour possibly functioning as an index of the kind of behaviour promoted by Christian teaching. Francis has generally found neither the extraversion-introversion dimension nor the neurotic-stable dimension to be particularly associated with religiosity.

In his book *The Musical Temperament* (1996), Kemp provides a comprehensive account of research on the personality traits of musicians. For his own research he used the Cattell Personality Questionnaire, testing 496 school musicians, 688 full-time music students and 202 professional musicians, as well as students who showed no overt musical interests. These large numbers enabled him to attempt to identify a core of personality traits which remain constant and are of central importance for the performing musician across the whole age-span. He was also able to make separate analyses according to age, gender and instruments played. For example, he found that string players tend to be introverted compared with brass players, whose reputation for extraversion and relative tough-mindedness he confirmed.

Cattell believes that sixteen personality traits are required to give a comprehensive picture of human personality. However, certain of these intercorrelate to produce broad factors comparable to those of Eysenck. Thus anxiety as assessed by Cattell is similar to neuroticism as measured by Eysenck. There are some differences: Cattell's extraversion seems to emphasise outgoingness and group dependency, Eysenck's emphasises sociability and liveliness; Cattell's pathemia includes both sensitivity and imaginativeness and seems to resemble Eysenck's tender-mindedness. From his own research on the personality profile of Anglican clergy, as well as from the American studies he cites, Musson (1989) found evidence of the importance of Cattell's emotional sensitivity and imaginative factors. What Cattell terms 'good upbringing' (conscientiousness and high self-esteem) would seem to correspond to the Eysenck Lie Scale, in that these are factors most likely to betray 'faking good'. I am at present engaged on a study of the Cattell personality factors and the Francis Attitude toward Christianity Scale which may throw some light on how different measures of personality and religiosity are related.

The picture Kemp draws is a complex one. Of special importance are introversion and pathemia. The musician can be seen as a 'bold introvert' who possesses the capacity for long solitary hours of practice but also the personal internal strength required for performance. Besides the Cattell Personality Questionnaires, Kemp also used the Myers-Briggs Type Indicator for some of his research. The results particularly confirmed the importance of 'feeling' and 'intuition', which are closely related to Cattell's pathemia. As for anxiety, Kemp concludes that musicians' anxiety manifests itself particularly in emotional instability and a form of frustrated tension; these forms of behaviour are revealed during higher education, particularly among talented musicians attending special music schools, and continue to be apparent in professional life. Anxiety in more experienced players may help them to reach a higher standard of performance.

The hypothesis of my research was that musical persons, being tender-minded, would be more religiously inclined than unselected students. I looked for participants among (i) children who were attending specialist music schools, and (ii) students who were following a course leading to a music degree or who had successfully passed a music degree course and were training to qualify as music teachers.

Child Musicians

With the co-operation of two specialist schools of music, 47 children completed the Francis Attitude toward Christianity Scale along with the Junior Eysenck Personality Questionnaire. 33 were girls and 14 were boys. 4 girls from the junior department of a conservatory also volunteered to take part. Only 14 of the 51 children were under fifteen years of age. (It would of course be desirable to include more younger children and equal numbers of both sexes.) The children also answered questions about the instruments they were currently playing, those they had played in the past and the instruments they most enjoyed listening to.

As far as personality is concerned, the average scores on psychoticism were low: 1.93 for the boys and 1.46 for girls. (Females usually do score lower on psychoticism than males.) The difference between these figures and those reported by Corulla (1990) for unselected fifteen-year-olds would, statistically speaking, reach a level likely to be found by chance less than 1 in 1000 times ($p < 0.001$). In so far as Eysenck's tender-mindedness resembles Cattell's pathemia, this confirms Kemp's findings. All the students at one school and many from the second school were string players, hence likely to be highly sensitive according to Kemp's research. 43 of the children played the piano. There were only two who played a brass instrument, but both scored low on psychoticism (contrary to what might be expected). Only a few of the children were highly introverted, the averages for the group being close to those reported by Corulla. Only the Lie Scale scores among the girls were much different from Corulla's. The relatively high score here may reflect the conscientiousness and high self-esteem likely to be found among string players and pianists at this stage in their development.

There was a wide range of scores on the Attitude toward Christianity Scale: all the way from 24 (the lowest possible) to 119 (the highest possible is 120). The scores averaged 74 for boys and 76 for girls, both higher than those reported by Francis (1989) and Gibson (1989) for children aged sixteen. The girls were, as is generally found, more religious than the boys. Attitude to Christianity correlated strongly with church attendance (0.64) and with private prayer (0.81). Only 3 of the boys and 16 of the girls attended church at least once a month, only 14 prayed by themselves at least once a week. Only 14 out of the 51 had ever belonged to a church choir. Singing in a church choir seemed to improve the likelihood of private prayer more than it did attendance at church.

When the personality scores were correlated with attitude to Christianity, the correlation with psychoticism was negative (–0.13). This is a lower degree of negative correlation than the –0.20 to –0.30 that Francis reports between the attitude scale and tender-mindedness. However, the rather small number of musicians I was able to include is sensitive to atypical scores. One boy scored 107 on the Attitude to Christianity Scale and claimed to pray twice a day, yet his psychoticism score was 6. He played the piano and cello. The instruments he most enjoyed listening to included saxophone, drums and double bass, as well as 'modern piano music'. If he meant by this phrase music that is discordant, this would tie up with the research finding that subjects who score high on psychoticism tend to prefer dissonant triads and hard rock (see Kemp, 1996, chapter 10). (It would of course be unwise to put too much weight on one case.) Most of the discrepant scores occurred in the nine cases where the children scored below 55 on attitude to religion but had psychoticism scores of 0, 1 or 2.

The only correlation to reach a statistically significant level (p < 0.05) is the inverse one between attitude to Christianity and extraversion. Evidently, the introverted musicians were more inclined to be religious. The Lie Scale correlates positively with attitude to Christianity at about the level that Francis has reported.

In a piece of American research the Junior Eysenck Personality Questionnaire was used in eight different schools to investigate whether children who were learning to play a musical instrument differed in personality from Eysenck's norms. The instrumentalists did not differ from Eysenck's norms for middle school children, nor did personality appear to affect whether or not children would continue to play in high school (Cutietta and McAllister, 1997). No measure of musical aptitude is mentioned, but the children were unlikely to possess the high level of talent of those who participated in my research.

The item 'I often "lose myself" in music' was added to the 24 items on Christianity. This statement was enthusiastically endorsed, only two students disagreed and only five were 'uncertain'. This might suggest that there may be truth in the remark of a headmaster that for these adolescents music may take the place of religion (or at least of Christianity and church) in their lives. The correlations of this question with the other variables were very low.

Adult Musicians

Three groups of adult musicians have been surveyed.

English Students

77 postgraduate music students who were studying for a qualification to teach music, 7 who were already music teachers and were seeking an M.A., 6 students of a college music course and 16 other adults who were involved in music education completed the Attitude toward Christianity Scale along with the short form of Eysenck's Personality Questionnaire. 73 of the participants were female, 33 were male. Apart from a few more mature persons – who lectured in music or who were involved in research – most of the participants were aged twenty-five or under. They too answered questions about the instruments they played.

The average scores for psychoticism, 3.24 for the males and 2.18 for females, are not far from those reported by Eysenck, Eysenck and Barrett (1985) for groups aged between twenty-one and thirty (3.57 for males and 2.56 for females). Francis *et al.* (1995) obtained even lower scores with UK students: 3.18 (males) and 1.90 (females). Thus the participants in my research were not particularly low in psychoticism. According to Kemp's findings on the personality of music teachers, musicians who decide to become teachers and are accepted for training need to be more extravert and less sensitive than performing musicians in general. As for the other personality characteristics, the males and females did not differ on extraversion, which was quite close to average; their neuroticism rating was rather more than, and their Lie Scale scores notably more than, the averages reported by Eysenck. However, compared with Francis's results, the women were lower in extraversion to a statistically significant degree. Table 1 presents the mean scores for the English students and the other two groups who took part in my research, along with those obtained by Francis *et al.* (1995) with 106 male and 272 female undergraduates (these students were unselected as regards music). More recently Robbins and Francis (1996) have obtained very similar figures for a further 360 students.

Table 1: Means of Personality Variables and of Attitude toward Christianity Scale
(Averages found by Francis *et al.*, 1995 in parentheses.)

	Male			
	English	*Scottish*	*British*	
Psychoticism	3.24	3.26	3.33	(3.18)
Extraversion	7.79	9.33*	8.84	(8.09)
Neuroticism	6.00	5.10*	5.33*	(6.58)
Lie	3.70	2.32	2.98	3.05)
Christianity	83.91	80.00	86.05**	(76.63)

	Female			
	English	*Scottish*	*British*	
Psychoticism	2.18	2.23	2.18	(1.90)
Extraversion	7.79*	8.73	8.80	(8.83)
Neuroticism	6.88	6.96	6.77	(6.75)
Lie	4.49	3.65	3.62	(3.91)
Christianity	89.19	77.53	83.52	(84.29)

* $p < 0.05$ (i.e. difference from Francis likely to be found by chance less than 5 in 100 times)
** $p < 0.02$ (i.e. difference from Francis likely to be found by chance less than 2 in 100 times)

Table 1 also shows the women in the English group to be on average more religious than the men: 89.19 compared with 83.91. Looking at the extremes of the distribution, 4 men but 9 women had religiosity scores of over 115. At the other end of the distribution, 4 men had scores lower than 55, as did 7 of the women. All the high scorers attended church or another place of worship weekly and prayed daily. We may ask what distinguishes these highly religious males from the low scorers. The male high scorers had an average score of 1.25 on psychoticism, of 6.25 on neuroticism, of 9.25 on extraversion and of 2.00 on lie. The lowest had psychoticism scores averaging 4.00, neuroticism 8.00, extraversion 7.75 and a lie score of 3.00. Two of the highest scorers played the piano, one played the organ, the other played violin, piano, drums and guitar. One of the lowest played oboe, three played the guitar, one of these also played the piano. (Which kind of guitar was not stated, but it may well have been the electric guitar since teachers in training are encouraged to learn about the pop music which so many of their pupils enjoy.) All the women high scorers played the piano, their score on psychoticism averaged 1.89, on neuroticism 4.89, on extraversion 6.22, and on lie 4.56. The lowest scorers averaged 2.71 on psychoticism, 6.28 on neuroticism, 7.57 on extraversion and 2.71 on lie. Three played the piano, one sang, two were woodwind players. None played the guitar. Certainly there is a marked contrast on psychoticism, particularly in the case of the men, between the highest and lowest scorers on religion.

Church attendance among the whole group correlated strongly with attitude to Christianity (0.70), as did private prayer (0.68). 33% stated that they attended church once a week and 32% that they prayed daily. 17% disclaimed belonging to any denomination.

When the personality scores were correlated with attitude to Christianity, the correlation with psychoticism (-0. 33) was close to that so often obtained by Francis (see Table 2). The other variables correlated with attitude to Christianity at about the same level as Francis *et al.* (1995) reported with their UK student group.

Scottish Students

82 Scottish students, 31 males and 51 females, completed the Francis Attitude toward Christianity Scale and the short form of the adult Eysenck Personality Questionnaire. 45 were following a university course leading to a B.A. in Applied Music. During the first two years

Table 2: Correlations between Personality Variables and Attitude toward Christianity
(The values reported by Francis *et al.*, 1995 in parentheses.)

	English	*Scottish*	*British*	
Psychoticism	−0.3260	−0.2486	−0.1683	(−0.3084)
Extraversion	−0.0474	−0.2121	−0.0320	(0.0420)
Neuroticism	−0.0871	0.1247	−0.1614	(0.0070)
Lie	0.2007	−0.1165	−0.0092	(0.1340)

Note: Partial correlations controlling for gender were calculated for all the above correlations. However, the differences were small and therefore are not reported here.

of their course they concentrate on their music studies. In the third and fourth years the B.A. students can follow a strand that includes business studies, or one that provides training for the work of fostering music within the community. Only a few seem to be choosing the latter course. 37 students were enrolled in an Ed.B. course, majoring in music. These students were younger than the English groups, 60% of them being under twenty years of age.

As can be seen from Table 1, there was little difference between their average scores on psychoticism compared with the English groups, but they were more extravert, the males were less emotionally labile, and both sexes scored lower on the Lie Scale. The higher extraversion may be explained by a different type of student being attracted to the Applied Music course and by the instruments they chose to play. As many as 82% played the piano, compared with 57% of the English groups. The numbers for strings and woodwind were very similar. There were far more brass, percussion and guitar players than among the English.

Both males and females scored lower on the Attitude toward Christianity Scale than did the English groups. What is unusual is the low score of the women, lower than their male counterparts. The difference from the students in Francis's group is statistically significant at the 0.05 level. A possible explanation may lie in the numbers who chose to play trumpet, percussion and guitars – instruments traditionally viewed as 'male' (see Kemp, 1996, ch. 8). This might suggest that they hold a more modern ('macho') approach to music and perhaps also to religion. (This is not meant to imply that all female players of these instruments are less likely to be religious!)

Compared with the English group, more of the Scots disclaimed membership of a religious group (29% compared with 17%). However, 32% claimed to attend church weekly and 18% to pray daily. (See Gibson, 1989 for a discussion of the attitudes to Christianity among adolescent Scots.)

When their personality scores were correlated with attitude to Christianity, the correlation with psychoticism was –0.25 (see Table 2). This is statistically significant and within the range of the correlations consistently found by Francis. The correlation with extraversion was also negative, almost to a statistically significant level ($p <$ 0.056); like the child musicians the introverts were apparently more likely to be religious. Unlike the English groups, the neuroticism correlation was positive, although still near zero; conversely the Lie Scale was negative.

The numbers so far tested are too small to make any meaningful comparisons between the B.A. students who choose the business strand and those who decide to train for work promoting musical activities in the community. It might be supposed that the latter might be more positive in their attitude to religion.

'British' Students

The third group to be included in my study consisted of 162 students; 43 men and 119 women. Of those 33 (9 men and 24 women) were attending a university in Northern Ireland and 19 (6 men and 13 women) a Welsh university. The rest were at universities in England. All were either studying for a music degree or were music graduates seeking a qualification to teach. 20% were under age twenty.

Their scores on psychoticism were very similar to those found in the other two groups. Both men and women were fairly high in extraversion. As 44% played woodwind instruments higher scores on introversion might have been expected (see Kemp, 1996). The proportions who played piano, strings and brass instruments fell between those of the other two groups. Like the Scots, the men were low in neuroticism to a statistically significant degree.

30% claimed to attend church weekly and 29% to pray daily; 21% did not acknowledge belonging to any religious group. The students in Northern Ireland tended to be highly religious, 4 of the men and 14 of the women reported that they prayed daily, while 6 of the men and 17 of the women attended church at least once a month. 5 of the Welsh men prayed daily as did 10 of the Welsh women; 4 of the men and 14 of the women attended church at least once a month. Taken as a group, the score of the 'British' women students on the Attitude toward Christianity Scale was only slightly lower than Francis's women students. The men scored on average nearly ten points higher than the comparison males. This was significant at the 0.02 level. Their scores clustered rather closely around the mean (standard deviation 19.11) while those of the women were more widely scattered (standard deviation 26.22). The correlations between psychoticism and attitude to Christianity was –0.17, weaker than Francis's but still statistically significant. The other significant correlation was a negative one with neuroticism – apparently the religious students were more emotionally stable.

CONCLUDING COMMENTS

The present evidence shows considerable variation in religiosity among the musicians that I have so far been able to test. Many are highly religious, others are not. All three groups of male musicians were above average in attitude to Christianity, while only the first group of women were above average. It would seem that male musicians who choose to follow university courses, many with a view to becoming teachers, are indeed more inclined to religiosity.

That women are in general more religious than men is a well-established finding (see, e.g., Beit-Hallahmi and Argyle, 1997). The total number of men who took part in my research was only 107, so caution is needed in interpreting the result. It is perhaps tempting to wonder whether the relatively low scores of the women is due to some gender reversal influence. With musicians over fifteen years of age Kemp (1996, chapter 6) found some effect of androgyny – the men had more 'feminine' characteristics, the women more masculine. Musson (1998) suggested that some of the personality differences he found might be attributable to male clergy being closer to the female norm of the general population. However, the personality characteristics of the musicians in my research do not seem to support any such speculation. In particular, the psychoticism scores are not far from the averages cited by Eysenck *et al.* (1985), by Francis *et al.* (1995) and by Robbins and Francis (1996).

The children at least do appear to be more tender-minded when compared with norms for the general population. In the case of the child musicians the low correlations between religiosity and psychoticism is partly due to a few who were both tough-minded and religious, but there were more who scored low both on psychoticism and religion. The correlation found among the adults conforms to the -0.30 which Francis has so consistently found. Even a correlation of 0.30 does allow for many 'atypical' cases. Nowadays social conditioning may tend to influence young people towards caring activities not connected with the church.

Sloboda (this volume) stresses the ineffable quality of music. Active musicians who are especially sensitive to its ineffable quality may feel that a verbal questionnaire specifically on Christianity and church does not do justice to their feelings of spirituality. A questionnaire such as that used by Hills and Argyle (1998), which included 'spiritual' items, might receive more positive responses. Musicians often complain about the limitations of tests of musical aptitude and appreciation in leaving the essence of musicianship unassessed. Perhaps a research study in cathedral schools where the students are exposed to both musical and religious influences might be illuminating.

We cannot, of course, expect musicians to be immune to the social pressures of secular values. From their survey of 13,000 young people between the ages of thirteen and fifteen, Francis and Kay (1995) concluded that by school year ten only 37% of pupils believe in God. If for many musicians music *is* their God, it is surely true that many others have just as strong obsessions – with making money, football, surfing the net, etc. Indeed we all need salvation from our own selfish pursuits.

Religion and music should be mutually supportive. For example, the aid offered by Christian belief in coping with the anxiety that is likely to be encountered during professional life might well be a source of strength for the musician. Salvation and grace are in the Christian view freely available to all persons – including the tough-minded, even if they are more reluctant to hear the Christian message. Christian educators and RE teachers might care to ponder the words of an American music educator speaking about memorable musical experiences: 'It is by allowing ourselves to be ... exposed to extra-ordinary and thrilling performances that we are ... reminded of what makes our work with children so vitally important.'

REFERENCES

Beit-Hallahmi, B. and Argyle, M. (1997), *The Psychology of Religious Behaviour, Belief and Experience*, London: Routledge.

Boyce-Tillman, J. (1996), 'A Framework for Intercultural Dialogue in Music', in M. Floyd (ed.), *World Musics in Education,* Aldershot: Scolar Press, pp. 43–94.

Corulla, W. J. (1990), 'A Revised Version of the Psychoticism Scale for Children', *Personality and Individual Differences*, 11, pp. 65–76.

Crickmore L. (1967), 'Music, Liturgy and Contemplation', *The Clergy Review*, LII, pp. 705–712.

Crickmore, L. (1968), 'An Approach to the Measurement of Music Appreciation, I and II', *Journal of Research in Music Education*, 16, pp. 239–253 and 291–301.

Cutietta, R. A. and McAllister, P. A. (1997), 'Student Personality and Instrumental Participation, Continuation and Choice', *Journal of Research in Music Education*, 45, pp. 282–294.

Eysenck, S. B. G., Eysenck, H. J. and Barrett, P. (1985), 'A Revised Version of the Psychoticism Scale', *Personality and Individual Differences*, 6, pp. 21–29.

Francis, L. J. (1989), 'Measuring Attitude towards Christianity during Childhood and Adolescence', *Personality and Individual Differences*, 10, pp. 695–698.

Francis, L. J. (1992), 'Is Psychoticism really a Dimension of Personality Fundamental to Religiosity?', *Personality and Individual Differences*, 13, pp. 645–652.

Francis, L. J. and Kay, W. K. (1995), *Teenage Religion and Values,* Leominster: Gracewing Fowler Wright.

Francis, L. J., Lewis, J. M., Brown, L. B., Philipchalk, R. and Lester, D. (1995), 'Personality and Religion among Undergraduate Students in the United Kingdom, United States, Australia and Canada', *Journal of Psychology and Christianity*, 14, 3, pp. 250–262.

Gabrielsson, A. and Lindstrom, S. (1993), 'On Strong Experiences of Music', *Musik*

Psychologie, Jahrbuch der Deutschen Gesellschaft für Musikpsychologie, 10, pp. 118–139.

Gibson, H. M. (1989), 'Measuring Attitudes towards Christianity among 11- to 16-year-old Pupils in Non-denominational Schools in Scotland', *Educational Research*, 31, 3, pp. 221–227.

Greeley, A. M. (1975), *The Sociology of the Paranormal*, London: Sage.

Hills, P. R. and Argyle, M. (1998), 'Musical and Religious Experiences and their Relationship to Happiness', *Personality and Individual Differences*, 25, pp. 91–102.

Kay, W. K. and Francis, L. J. (1996), *Drift from the Churches: Attitude toward Christianity during Childhood and Adolescence*, Cardiff: University of Wales Press.

Kemp, A. E. (1996), *The Musical Temperament: Psychology and Personality of Musicians*, Oxford: Oxford University Press.

Madsen, C. K., Brittin, R. V., and Capperella-Sheldon, D. A. (1993), 'An Empirical Investigation of the Aesthetic Response to Music', *Journal of Research in Music Education*, 41, pp. 57–69.

Madsen, C. K., Byrnes, S. R., Capperella-Sheldon, D. A., and Brittin, R. V. (1993), 'Aesthetic Responses to Music: Musicians vs. Non-musicians', *Journal of Music Therapy*, 30, pp. 174–191.

Musson, D. J. (1998), 'The Personality Profile of Male Anglican Clergy in England: the 16PF', *Personality and Individual Differences*, 25, pp. 689–698.

Nye, R. (1996), 'Childhood Spirituality and Contemporary Developmental Psychology', in R. Best (ed.), *Education, Spirituality and the Whole Child*, London: Cassell, pp. 108–120.

Pearson, P. R. and Francis, L. J. (1989), 'The Dual Nature of the Eysenckian Lie Scales: Are Religious Adolescents more Truthful?', *Personality and Individual Differences*, 10, pp. 1041–1048.

Robbins, M. and Francis, L. J. (1996), 'Are Religious People Happier? A Study Among Undergraduates', in L. J. Francis, W. K. Kay and W. Campbell (eds), *Research in Religious Education*, Leominster: Gracewing Fowler Wright, pp. 207–217.

Shuter-Dyson, R. (1988), 'Creating, Performing and Listening to Music', in A. Kemp (ed.), *Research in Music Education: A Festschrift for Arnold Bentley*, International Society for Music Education, Edition Number Two, pp. 81–87.

Trehub, A., Schellenberg, G., and Hill, D. (1997), 'The Origins of Music Perception and Cognition: A Developmental Perspective', in I. Deliege and J. Sloboda (eds), *Perception and Cognition of Music*, Hove: Psychology Press, pp. 103–128.

PART THREE:
REFLECTIONS

on Music in the Contexts of
Worship and Education

9

When in Our Music God is Glorified

Timothy Hone

INTRODUCTION: ARMCHAIR SPIRITUALITY

During the last ten years the charts of best-selling recordings have included a number of surprises. Discs of plainsong, music by composers as diverse as Hildegard of Bingen or John Tavener, Górecki's third symphony – all these have enjoyed cult status. Recordings have also provided listeners with the opportunity to become familiar with a variety of fifteenth and sixteenth-century liturgical music: repertoire which, in its day, was heard only by the wealthy patrons who employed the composers and performers who created it. Music by Christóbal de Morales from the early sixteenth century has appeared with a twentieth century gloss in the form of a saxophone commentary by the great jazz player Jan Garbarek,[1] while in 1997 the best-selling classical recording was a disc of sacred music.[2] Barriers of taste and categorisation have been eroded, so that music which had become the esoteric preserve of scholars now attracts wide interest. Many listeners seem to find in this music a spiritual dimension which fulfils their need for something which transcends everyday experience.

People who are pursuing a private spiritual search, perhaps by listening to a compact disc of plainsong in an armchair at home, seem to be seeking something few churches provide. This presents a challenge for those responsible for music in worship: might it be possible to use music as a bridge, reaching out to those seeking some religious dimension as they struggle to cope with the pressures and insecurities of life at the end of the twentieth century?

Ironically, these developments have occurred during a period in which most churches have rejected the very aspects of their musical heritage which are now enjoying a revival of interest elsewhere. I am confident that the great musical inheritance of the church has *not* become irrelevant and that it can still speak to our fundamental uncertainties and doubts, as well as celebrating faith and belief. For this reason, I maintain that there is an urgent and vital need to preserve it in a living context wherever the resources are available. Music of real intellectual and spiritual power belongs within the belief-system which provided the stimulus for its creation. The church needs both to value its heritage and to nurture a living tradition of excellence. If it simply reduces its musical activity to disposable, accessible musical products which reflect an instant-access 'fast food' culture, then it risks alienating those with creative sensitivity and intellectual curiosity.

This serves to remind us that the rôle played by music in church is merely part of the way in which music is used in society as a whole. Clearly, it is important to try to identify some of the factors which lie behind this situation.

THE DEVELOPMENT OF MUSICAL STYLES

Many of the styles of music used in church have been shaped by external forces. In particular, the changing nature of musical patronage has been a decisive factor. Through the centuries, the church's musical repertoire has been influenced by the bodies which nurtured it: monastic communities, cathedral chapters, university collegiate structures and courtly establishments. Intellectual ideas have also had a profound influence. Major forces, such as religious reformation and counter-reformation, changes in political ideology, the impact of humanism, absolutism (enlightened or otherwise), secularism and mass culture, have transformed the music which has been produced and the ways in which it has been used. In the church, as in the secular world, music has frequently been an offshoot or display of power and wealth, however subtly disguised.

On this basis, one might argue that church musicians should now seek a new point of departure as they search for musical values, in order to create music for worship purified from past error. However, to proceed in this way risks destroying the roots of past experience which are the best source of growth and development:

> Only a fool will build in defiance of the past. What is new and significant always must be grafted to old roots, the truly vital roots that are chosen with great care from the ones that merely survive. And what a slow and delicate process it is to distinguish radical vitality from the

wastes of mere survival, but that is the only way to achieve progress instead of disaster.[3]

From the church's rich musical inheritance, today's musical practitioners are free to find new values in all music, as they re-create it afresh in their own time and place, unfettered by the conditions which led to its creation.

However, in order to make sense of this diversity of musical expression, and to provide a practical framework within which to exercise the musical choices which help to shape the environment within which people worship, we need a proper understanding of how music itself functions. As that awareness deepens it may be possible to develop a more theologically informed perspective of the ways in which music is used in worship and in human society as a whole.

MUSIC AND CREATIVITY

The use of music in Christian worship is an affirmation of human creativity as a gift of God. This is a supreme gift, since in our own creativity we can know for ourselves something of the essence of God's primary motivation and purpose.

All musical activity is a form of involvement with the raw materials of creation.[4] Shaping these materials involves selection and craftsmanship. Even basic paradigms, such as musical scales, involve the identification of discrete pitches from the infinity of available notes. The making of a musical instrument requires skills in shaping, adapting and combining materials. At a number of levels, therefore, music helps to bring order out of chaos through the choices we make. These choices reveal what we regard as beautiful, striking, meaningful and interesting about the world of sound.

In learning to understand our own creativity we can come to respect that of others. We can deepen our response to God's own creation – the world itself in all its richness and variety. Conversely, we can learn to grieve for its poverty and suffering. Our heightened awareness of the gap between potentiality and actuality might even challenge us to take responsibility for reducing its distress.

If music is to open our minds in this way it needs to reflect more than our own narrow concerns and enthusiasms. All music deserves consideration for inclusion. By being open to the sound world of societies other than our own, we may learn to be more respectful of their culture and more aware of the feelings and aspirations of those who created it.

USE OF MUSIC: PERFORMERS AND COMPOSERS

Our use of music in church needs to be more creative. Irrespective of period or style, a piece can be chosen because it is felt to have something to offer to our own community. Music has the potential to be heard afresh, to speak in a new way, each time it is re-created. However, this will happen only if we bring to each performance some of the creative imagination and insight which resulted in its initial composition. For the successful presentation of some of the more flexible styles of music now common in worship this is particularly important: the way in which we arrange and present items for the instrumental and vocal resources at our disposal adds an additional layer to the creative process, realising the potential of a written score which may only define the basic melodic and harmonic content.[5] Music is an incarnational art. We need to engage creatively with a piece in order to make it our own.

The contribution of performers can be undervalued or regarded with suspicion in church circles. A view is sometimes expressed that church musicians should fulfil their service in humility, in a manner which is as self-effacing as possible. Such an attitude shows a lack of insight. Music ministry at its best has a sacrificial nature which makes great demands on its practitioners. It is important to recognise and affirm both their gift and the discipline with which it is exercised.[6]

MUSIC: OBJECT OR PROCESS?

Before taking the discussion further, we must guard against a potential confusion which often obscures discussions of music: namely, the failure to distinguish between *music as object* and *music as process*. A thorough philosophical exploration of this distinction is not possible here, nor is it necessary.[7] However, the practical consequences of the distinction are far-reaching.

For those reflecting on musical experience, the musical *object* is the most common starting point. This objective approach became possible only as a result of the invention of musical notation, which created the conditions for the identification, repetition and study of an individual musical work.

We need to recognise that the relationship between music and its notation is symbiotic. In the development of western Christian music the invention of notation was a decisive act. Before its appearance, the preservation of the plainsong repertoire depended solely on oral transmission and on the ability of skilled performers to retain vast amounts of music in the memory (facilitated, to a certain extent, by its monodic nature). As a result, the chant underwent a slow process of continuous but organic change: there was no possibility of preserving a particular stage in its evolution or codifying a single performance. The composer had no separate identity and the preservation of the repertory was the responsibility of trained performers. At the same time, each community had the opportunity to develop and vary the musical *corpus* according to its own collective needs and instincts, resulting in a correspondingly strong ownership of a particular version of a musical 'work' by an individual group.

The invention of notation made it possible to fix the details of a musical composition. Early plainsong notation merely signified relative pitch as an *aide-mémoire*. It was only in the later stages of development that rhythmic patterns were fixed with sufficient precision to make possible the basic synchronisation essential for structured *polyphonic* music-making. Around the same time, in the twelfth century *organa* of Léonin, the *composer* appears for the first time as a named artificer, bringing order out of a world of infinite possibilities by the process of selection. From this point, the development of composition and of notation follow parallel paths in which new possibilities stretch the capabilities of the art to its limits. Much of the contrapuntal music of the fourteenth to sixteenth centuries is a response to new notational possibilities: the development of the isorhythmic motet; the use of canon, augmentation, diminution and inversion; the adoption of various mensural tricks – all this pyrotechnical display is a kind of *jeu d'esprit* on the part of the composer, who seems to have aimed to make music in spite of, not as a result of, the extra (self-imposed) challenges.

The appearance of notation also brings about the illusion that *the score is the music itself*. In fact, the score merely allows the composer to fix certain parameters in order to enable performers to re-create a formal sonic pattern. Performing musicians need to allow their creative imagination full play if the notation is not to become a barrier between them and the intensity of inspiration it conveys. Part of their task is to reveal the essence of the musical ideas they discern behind the notes.

The listener, on the other hand, forms a relationship with the music *through the sound it makes*, rather than through the conventional signs of a manuscript or printed score. Only a highly skilled listener could claim to be able to hold all the details and formal development of even a short piece clearly in the memory, in such a way that the musical object can exist in remembered time complete in its essentials. It is only the existence of a score which makes it possible to consider a musical work as an abstract *object*, in the same way as a painting, a piece of sculpture, or an everyday item such as a chair.

One of the consequences of the objective approach is that it provides a foundation for the suspicion with which music has sometimes been regarded by influential thinkers within the church. Emphasis on *music as object* readily leads to a charge of idolatry. A musical object can easily be thought of as a diversion from the main purpose of liturgy, a mere decoration, a non-essential whose very attractiveness makes it threatening. However, I suggest that, while the aesthetic contemplation of a musical object holds many attractions for philosophers,[8] most people do not respond to a musical experience in this way. More commonly, music is *a process with which we engage*. A process (unlike an object) is not easily isolated and defined, and for that reason is less vulnerable to attack. If music is understood as process, it can enjoy a much more symbiotic relationship with liturgy, without which a truly creative partnership of the two is rarely achieved.

It is also my hope that if we can uncover the basic principles on which music, *understood as process*, operates, these may be applicable outside the specific style preferences of a particular group. In order to achieve this, we need some understanding of the musical art in action[9] by examining the situations and ways in which human beings use music, and asking the basic question of musical anthropology: are human beings inherently musical?[10]

HOW MUSICAL ARE WE? MUSICAL LITERACY AND ITS EFFECT ON PARTICIPATION

I believe that people should be regarded as innately musical *because of their capacity to hear structured sound and to interpret it as musical experience*. In contrast, the general tendency is to regard as musical only those (relatively few) people who develop their creative gifts as composers, or those who discipline themselves to acquire instrumental or vocal skills.

Furthermore, since it is unusual to acquire anything other than the most rudimentary knowledge of musical notation except as part of the process of learning a musical instrument, many people in western society are inclined to dismiss themselves as 'not really musical' because they lack the skills to play an instrument well, and because they 'cannot read music'. As a society, we take the demands of belonging to a literate culture seriously, but we are not committed to acquiring a corresponding musical literacy.

Literacy, verbal *and* musical, has particular consequences when new material is introduced into worship. The process of radical liturgical revision since the 1960s has forced Anglican churchgoers to become reliant on the text of a book and on the cues of a service sheet to guide them through services which were once familiar. Most people have the necessary skills to cope with this, yet it is inevitable that their experience of worship will differ in subtle but significant ways from that which obtained when many of the standard texts were known by heart. However, relatively few people are familiar with musical notation in a way which allows them to deal confidently with a corresponding proliferation of musical items. They cannot read a new musical setting with the same ease as a text consisting only of words. This situation is perpetuated by an attitude which assumes that, since most people do not read music, it is not necessary to provide musical notation for congregational use.

Further reflection suggests that there is a tension in church between a *process-based aural-oral culture* and one which is *object-focussed* and *literate*. This tension seems to me to be at the root of many fundamental misunderstandings and shortcomings in the discussion of liturgy and worship. When we worship, we may return in part to more primitive and instinctive thought patterns. In any case, a lack of musical literacy can force members of a congregation to function (in terms of their musical ability) as oral-aural people. However, the skills of memory essential to an oral-aural culture have largely disappeared. As a result, the challenge of learning new music of any degree of complexity becomes formidable, and most people simply give up. In order to get an assembly to sing at all, it becomes necessary to offer a musical diet limited in scope and size. This soon becomes stultifying, both for them and for those engaged in music ministry.

At a deeper level, this insight may offer an explanation of the unwillingness of many within the church (as elsewhere in society) to accept change, even when it may be necessary for survival. Intransigence can be a symptom of a more primitive fear, characteristic of a pre-literate, less rational age:

> Oral-aural man does not like the non-traditional because, beyond his limited means of control, it advertises the tenuousness of his hold on rationality.[11]

As a counter-measure, we need to give people the skills of musical literacy which will enable them to use new musical material as readily as they do revised spoken texts, thus retaining their hold on rationality. At the same time, we must allow for the fact that in worship we

seek to meet deeper needs which our rational minds cannot always de-
mystify. For this reason, we could encourage a more primitive
response to both words and music to surface by developing both the
quality and quantity of memorised material which members of a
community hold in common.

The transformation of this situation has profound implications for
music education, which are too far-reaching for the church to under-
take alone. A number of elements are necessary:

- people need to be taught that it is the ability to relate to music
  which is the vital part of being musical; few people do not respond
  in any way to a musical experience;
- the mystique surrounding musical notation needs to be swept away
  by an educational provision which makes elementary musical literacy as fundamental as basic verbal and numerical skills;
- the range of response to musical creativity needs to be expanded in
  all its forms, so that people are encouraged to find it natural to
  compose, to sing and play, and to listen to music of many styles
  and periods.

These key changes in educational policy need to become priorities for
society as a whole. There are conflicting indications as to the extent
to which current educational trends are likely to prove beneficial. At
the same time that National Curriculum guidelines seem to offer a
greater breadth of musical experience and more opportunity for
creative composition, there is a decline in the opportunities for singing
and instrumental experience except in those schools which can afford
to buy in expertise.[12]

IMPROVISATION

Our own society still retains one link with the immediacy of music
in a pre-literate culture through the use of improvisation, a skill
still exercised by organists and jazz musicians (among others).[13]
Here the music is truly evanescent, there is no second chance. Since
the event cannot be repeated, the listener is likely to give more
vital attention to the music as it evolves. Through listening atten-
tively to an improvisation, it is possible to experience instantaneous
creative activity (since composer and performer are one). It is an
opportunity to share in the musical process in the most immediate
way and is the closest many people will get to understanding what
it is to compose. Improvisation is the most striking example of
musical art in action.

One of the greatest exponents of this art was Pierre Cochereau, *organiste titulaire* at the Cathedral of Notre Dame, Paris from 1955–1984. Monsignor Emile Berrar has written:

> He drew us into his joyous celebration, which helped make a prayer become, easily and imperiously, a kind of jubilation, an exaltation before God. After his final improvisation that fixed most of the congregation to their seats in a devotional silence, we often heard of people, on the verge of tears, who had experienced what Saint Augustine wrote about the rôle of music as the ultimate form of prayer and how, beyond the spoken word, it can swell the heart and soul with immense joy.
>
> Those final improvisations were not a conclusion, not a closing act. They opened doors: those of the cathedral on to the illuminated square, and those of the celestial City of Jerusalem on to the light that will always shine.[14]

Used in the liturgy, fine improvisation can capture the particular spiritual aspirations of the present moment in a unique way, lifting the hearts and minds of the gathered community through a shared activity of the imagination.

PARTICIPATION IN THE MUSICAL EXPERIENCE

The idea of 'a shared activity of the imagination' offers a much needed corrective to a commonly held understanding of the nature of liturgical participation. The current trend in liturgical practice is to stress the contribution of the whole gathered community to the celebration. Specifically, this emphasis has dominated Roman Catholic thinking about the Eucharist since the Second Vatican Council's call for 'full, active participation on the part of the whole people of God' in the 1963 *Constitution on the Sacred Liturgy*.[15] While the Conciliar documents[16] provide necessary correctives to an earlier emphasis on the ritual offering by the priest alone, assisted to a greater or lesser extent by ministers skilled in specific tasks (not least professional musicians), such a requirement carries its own dangers and limitations. Most problematic is the assumption that to participate fully in the eucharistic assembly each member should be active musically. This has had the unfortunate effect in many places of reducing the musical content to items which can be attempted by all members of the congregation.

I believe that this shows a fundamental misunderstanding of the nature of participation. Consider other human activities in which people gather in great numbers. We do not assume that a football match would be more entertaining if the entire crowd joined the players in chasing the ball around the pitch. Audiences at the theatre do not speak lines of the text, nor take the parts of characters within the play. Instead, people can participate in a social experience by giving their collective attention to a stimulus and allowing themselves to become vulnerable to it. Perhaps to an even greater extent this is true of the experience of listening to music.

Where does the musical event take place? In the imagination of the composer? In the performance by the musicians? In the mind of the attentive listener? An affirmative answer is surely equally valid in each situation.[17] For many people who are instinctively receptive *listeners*, the requirement to make a vocal contribution themselves can at times lessen their musical response. Musicians who offer their services in a liturgical context must never forget the whole assembly, but they should not feel guilty when they encourage people to listen rather than expect them to sing. To bring an attentive imagination to bear on well wrought music, sung or played by those with appropriate skills, can be a liberating experience, freeing the mind for prayer and contemplation. Listening to music in this way reminds us that we are perceptual beings, and that it is of our essence to respond to outside stimuli. When we affirm the value of the musical experience we are taking the same pleasure in creativity displayed by a God who observed everything he had made and found it very good.[18]

If we regard listening to music as a process which we enter through the power of the imagination, rather than a critical encounter with a sonic object, we discover more creative possibilities for the use of music in a liturgical context. If we encourage worshippers to engage with it in an imaginative way, music has the potential to build a bridge from an individual response to a shared collective experience. For this reason, wherever people have gathered in groups for a common purpose, music has often been used as a powerful unifying tool.

MUSIC HELPS TO CREATE COMMUNITY

When music is used in worship it helps to turn the assembly into a community. In his study of the Venda tribe, John Blacking observes:

> Venda music ... is also political in the sense that it may involve people in a powerful shared experience within the framework of their cultural experience and thereby make them more aware of themselves and of their responsibilities toward each other.... Venda music is not an escape from reality: it is an adventure into reality, the reality of the world of the spirit. It is an experience of becoming, in which individual

consciousness is nurtured within the collective consciousness of the community and hence becomes the source of richer cultural forms.[19]

In a similar way, the Gathering Rite of the modern Roman Mass tries to bring together a group of individuals into a new collective reality – the church. Most simply, it involves the gathered people of God in a combined act of praise, through the use of a well-known hymn or song. This unity might be most clearly expressed in unaccompanied unison singing, while harmonised music and polyphony may present other views of the body of Christ, reflecting (according to their relative complexity) a balance between unity and diversity, a reminder that 'we, though many, are one body'. An act of shared listening could serve a similar purpose, and in some circumstances might be more powerful, since individuals are not distracted from the common purpose by 'trying to get it right'.

All music-making co-ordinates random energy into a structured, coherent whole. A similar process is a pre-requisite if a group of people is to function as a Christian community.[20] Music-making provides both a paradigm of community and the means whereby community can be brought into being.

Communities define themselves by the practices they adopt when they meet together. However, there is a danger that the chosen musical elements of the celebration which help to weld together those who are initiates, may by the same token cause those on the outside to feel excluded or even repelled.

Differences in cultural values ... flow ... from the existence of socially constructed and different cultural criteria which not infrequently display a mutual incompatibility.[21]

On this basis, no church can hope to cater for every taste. Those which try to do so frequently opt for a musical blandness which simply fails to function at any profound level, and dismays those of any musical sensitivity. Individuals with a strong commitment to the diversity to be found within the body of Christ need rather to learn to respect the strongly held personal preferences of other Christians, and to value them for the sake of the people concerned. Conviction is a vital element of all music-making and may persuade even those whose natural tastes lie in other directions.

In any case, certain factors are a fundamental part of the musical process in action and underpin compositions of diverse styles and textures. If we concentrate on these elements it may be possible to isolate principles which are valid for the use of a variety of styles of music, and to find ways of approaching music with which we may be less familiar. As part of this inquiry, we might consider a fundamental aspect of the 'musical art in action' by exploring the ancient ritual inter-connection between music and life and asking to what extent the use of music in our own culture reveals a severing of that connection.

MUSIC AND RITUAL

> Without music no discipline can be perfect, for there is nothing without it. For the very universe ... is held together by a certain harmony of sounds, and the heavens themselves are made to revolve by the modulation of harmony. Music moves the feelings and changes the emotions. In battles ... the sound of the trumpet rouses the combatants, and the more furious the trumpeting, the more valorous their spirit. Song likewise encourages the rowers, music soothes the mind to endure toil, and the modulation of the voice consoles the weariness of each labour. Music also composes distraught minds, as may be read of David, who freed Saul from the unclean spirit by the art of melody ... every work we speak, every pulsation of our veins, is related by musical rhythms to the powers of harmony.

Thus wrote Isidore of Seville in the seventh century.[22] In contrast to his holistic approach, in which music, life and ritual are integrated and inter-dependent, let us examine a more recent phenomenon, the public concert, an event in which music is the main focus, detached from everyday functions. Such events have acquired rituals of their own, which seem to be born out of a deep human need for formalised functioning, but without providing a real substitute for a more ancient symbiotic ritual correspondence between art and life. If we attend a classical concert we expect that the audience will arrive before the music starts and leave only when it has finished; that people will listen with stillness and attention before offering polite applause in recognition of the efforts of the musicians. The performers, in their turn, will behave in an equally conventional way, even to the point of wearing clothes now rarely otherwise seen outside the most formal social occasions. Although the expectations of a pop concert are somewhat different, and are typified by a greater informality, which encourages greater interaction between performer and audience and a more demonstrative response to the music, nevertheless, the music is still set apart for attention, and the implicit ritual expectations are just as well understood by those who attend.

There are striking correspondences between the arrangements for presenting music in the concert hall and worship in church. The physical arrangements are often markedly similar (audience = congregation; auditorium = nave; stage = sanctuary; musicians = ministers; concert clothes = vestments). Moreover, the behaviour of a middle-of-the-road congregation corresponds largely to that adopted by an audience at a classical concert, while more charismatic assemblies often adopt characteristics found on more overt display at a popular music event.

Nevertheless, such rituals are, in a sense, artificial. Only when we recover a more primitive understanding of the way music operates in conjunction with ritual will it become possible to achieve a more comprehensive awareness of the contribution it can make to worship.

MUSIC AS BEARER OF THE WORD

Christianity is a religion of a divine Word made flesh. It is not therefore surprising that most music used in Christian worship is closely associated with text. In practice, it is important to distinguish between different levels of association:

(a) formulaic intonations and chant patterns which can be adapted to many different texts (e.g. plainsong intonations for prayers and readings, psalm tones in various styles);

(b) the repetitive mantra-like use of a musical phrase based on a single word or group of words, in which the sound of the word becomes as important as its meaning;

(c) strophic settings in which the same music serves for a number of different verses within a single verse composition; furthermore, the same music may be used for a number of different texts so long as their metrical structure is the same; the music is not neutral, but nor is it so strongly reflective of a single text that appropriate interchange is impossible (hymns are the most obvious example of this type);

(d) strophic settings where it is assumed the musical setting belongs to one text only (most songs and choruses are of this type);

(e) through-composed settings of existing texts (most anthems are of this type; the complexity of the setting can vary enormously);

(f) the addition of a text to pre-existing music (perhaps most common in popular musical culture since about the 1920s, where this is a frequent mode of collaboration between musician and lyricist);

(g) a composition where words and music are the product of the

same creative mind; there are numerous examples in a diversity
of styles: the sequences of Hildegard of Bingen; the music
dramas of Richard Wagner; the Christmas music of John Rutter;
the worship songs of Graham Kendrick.

The relative contribution of words and music will obviously affect
the way in which the combination of text and music is perceived. A
sung gospel is heightened speech: the music is serving the function of
helping to project the text in a large building, as well as lending
solemnity by creating a sound world which differs from casual speech.
By contrast, the Sanctus of Bach's *B Minor Mass* expands beyond
normal liturgical decorum, transforming and intensifying the text and
providing the sympathetic listener with a vision of heavenly splendour. It does this by the devices of repetition and prolongation; by the
creation of counterpoint which occupies a large acoustical space over
many octaves; by the use of a rich choral sound divided into many
vocal parts; through the use of instrumental colours (in particular,
trumpets and drums) which are associated with earthly occasions of
pomp and ceremony. In a sense, the statement it makes is justified
theologically rather than liturgically. The work as a whole creates its
own ritual, a kind of para-liturgy. As a result, it is difficult to envis-
age an earthly liturgical celebration which could adequately frame this
music. The same is true of other large-scale settings: Beethoven's
Missa Solemnis, Verdi's *Requiem*, the *Grande Messe des Morts* of
Berlioz, Britten's *War Requiem*. These works transfer liturgical ritual
out of the private confines of the gathered congregation of believers
into more public arenas. There they have the potential to challenge
and confront those who may otherwise be indifferent to the Christian
message. Even stripped of their liturgical context and action, they
may, for some, be 'converting ordinances'.[23]
At a more mundane level, the power of music to colour a text, as
well as the strength of certain associations between words and musical
settings, can be illustrated simply, if naïvely, by interchanging the
words and music of two well-known hymns, such as 'My song is love
unknown' and 'Ye holy angels bright'. Although the tunes normally
associated with each (*Love Unknown* and *Darwall's 148th*) provide a
satisfactory metrical framework for either hymn, the effect of the
interchange is distinctly strange. Darwall's tune is tonally unambigu-
ous, with strong harmony deriving mostly from primary triads.
Melodically, it is characterised by scales and by trumpet-like phrases
constructed of notes of tonic chords. As such, it is a fine match for
the joyful optimism of the hymn text with which it is normally associated. John Ireland's tune *Love Unknown* is tonally much more

complex, particularly in the un-nerving shift of harmony from E flat to D flat, which sounds questioning at 'O who am I?', threatening for 'Then "Crucify!" is all their breath', and finally reassuring for 'This is my Friend'. The alchemy is complex, and more readily experienced than described. If words and music are inter-changed, Darwall's tune seems too positive for the words of 'My song is love unknown', making the crucifixion appear too easily achieved. In its turn *Love Unknown* produces a complexity of response which is too inhibited and reflective for 'Ye holy angels'.

Of more creative significance is the effect of different musical settings of frequently used texts, particularly those of the Ordinary of the Mass and the Canticles of Morning and Evening Prayer. Here a change of musical setting (or even the use of a chant of contrasting character) can cause the text to be heard afresh, evoking new associations and enabling new meanings to be found. In this way music can assist the incarnation of the word in a creative encounter which allows us to recognise its truth as it enters our understanding.

Music also helps to make the text more memorable, and to fix it in our minds for future meditation. In these exegetical and didactic rôles music is functioning in much the same way as preaching, although it uses very different means to achieve its effect. This may suggest that extended scriptural exegesis and long or elaborate musical settings belong to different occasions. To combine both in one service can make heavy demands on the attention and mental participation of the congregation, which may result in neither preaching nor music making its full effect.

At its most profound, music is capable of giving new meaning to the incarnate word. It provides a limitless range of possibilities with which to flesh out either that word itself, or our human response to it. This is a creative, incarnational task, one which Christian musicians must carry out with sensitivity and insight. In order to do so, it is necessary to consider the nature of sound itself and the effect of the environment within which it is heard.

THE MUSICAL ENVIRONMENT

Musical sound is not different in *kind* from other sounds within the environment. That is to say, it is transmitted by vibrations in the air with which we are surrounded, and the processes by which we hear it and respond to it are the same as those employed for other sounds. Indeed we listen to 'silence' in exactly the same way. Cage's *4'33"* (in which the pianist goes through all the preparations for a musical performance but then sits still for the duration so that members of the audience begin to turn their attention to the sounds of the room in which they are listening) is but the most obvious example of a piece which interrogates the process of listening. Musical instruments rely on natural functions for the creation of sound, despite the fact that their fundamental characteristics may be artificially adapted in order that they can fulfil a musical function more easily. Similarly, the processes of transmission (even in our electronically-enhanced age) ultimately depend on vibrating air and the receptivity of ear and brain to interpret these vibrations as music. Musical sounds differ only in *quality* and *intent*, in the sense that they are specifically set apart for our attention.

In this sense, music is a defined encounter with the surrounding environment. It leads us outside ourselves since, although we interpret what we hear within our brains, we are aware (as sentient beings) that its source is elsewhere. Music thus offers a striking example of something which is both immanent and transcendent.

It might be thought that the act of giving attention to the sounds of music would lead to an increased awareness of the sounds of the environment. However, on the whole, history reveals a tendency for people to use music as a way of obliterating other man-made sounds, leading to an increased alienation from the sounds of the natural world. As industrial processes and increasing mechanisation filled the world with noise, individual musical instruments became more powerful and the orchestra grew in size in order to create an artistic experience of comparable power, capable of blotting out the noise of the industrial soundscape. The contribution of our own age to this process has been the widespread adoption of electronic amplification and synthetic sound.

Excessive amplification can threaten the basic principles on which musical communication depends: ultimately it blunts the response of hearing (in particular the ability to discern differences of pitch, rhythm, intensity and timbre) as the body begins its own defence against the onslaught of excessive sound invasion. It may even reduce music to undifferentiated chaos – noise. One may also feel concerned that the creation of an increasingly synthetic sound world, rather than creating new sonic possibilities, has frequently produced timbres which are less sharply differentiated than those available from traditional instruments.

Christian musicians need to react to this situation with wisdom. Without simply turning aside from new developments, they might offer other musical possibilities which show a more harmonious relationship between people and the environment.

> Music, as sound, cannot help but stress the integrative and relational in human life, that is, the way in which we are all in constant and dynamic touch with the world. Music thus enables people . . . to feel the world as well as knowing it.[24]

Music for the unaccompanied human voice offers the most striking alternative to the synthesised complexity which has become ubiquitous.

Unfortunately, dependence on electronically derived and transmitted sound is central to much contemporary culture. At a practical level it is easy to understand this, since it is easier to acquire a certain level of facility on an electronic keyboard or bass guitar than to play their acoustic prototypes well. Ultimately, such developments seem bound to lead to an impoverishment of music-making. At the same time, Christians who believe in a God who has intervened decisively in his world on behalf of the whole creation, should not be afraid to allow the potentially life-transforming power of any part of that creation to play its full and appropriate part in worship. One of the most difficult tasks for those working in music ministry is to find an appropriate balance between the possibilities of either embracing contemporary culture wholeheartedly or standing critically apart from it. In order to do this, it is necessary to concentrate on the essential processes which are common to all music-making, which provide a context within which to work out that challenge.

MUSIC STRUCTURING TIME

One of the primary functions of music is to structure time. Since this is one of the deepest human needs, it is not surprising that almost all cultures have given music so central a place. In addition, the transitory nature of sound itself offers a striking paradigm for the condition of our own precarious existence: its only certain destiny is ultimate extinction. Music serves to fill time with meaning, and in doing so offers a structured alternative to the ultimate loneliness of silence on the one hand, and the chaos of noise on the other:

> music becomes that unique aesthetic form which arises spontaneously in every culture from the action of an autonomous, deeply intuitive sense of time (implanted in man's mental makeup) on a fundamental reality of the physical universe. Man creates in music a palpable, perceptual metaphor of the universe in a passionately coloured succession of expressive events which become a transformation of the raw data of physical reality in and of themselves. Man's rhythmic energies, rooted

in his physiological and neural constitution, are inextricably bound up
with his ability to create time in music.[25]

When we listen to music it is as though we can hear time passing.
Both composer and performer play a part in this process. They control
the extent to which the music seems to be made up of motion or stasis,
with events which are precisely structured or apparently free, utilis-
ing a sound-world which may be more or less complex in its
presentation of the musical idea. Musical time can even seem to move
as a series of layers, each with its own internal pattern of movement,
co-ordinated yet independent.

However, because music is instantaneous, and the individual point
of musical time evanescent, we are forced to attend to it in the present
moment. We can know the past only through the memory, and the
future is hidden (though, in music as in life, events in the past may
lead us, rightly or wrongly, to expect that things will turn out in a
certain way). Music occupies time, and fills it with controlled events,
in a way which is ultimately life-affirming and life-enhancing.

> Music is not only the creation and concretization of time, it is also the
> creation and concretization of memorable temporal events ... In its own
> way, music provides a durational model of past, present and future
> through the experience of events which not only return but whose return
> is anticipated.[26]

A very telling comparison of the way in which music can structure
time differently at the most basic level, may be made between two
works of Haydn, both conceived for use in church. At the one extreme
stands the Introduction, seven slow movements and Earthquake which
make up his *Seven Last Words of Our Saviour from the Cross*. Each
of the seven main movements lasts a substantial time, some as much
as ten minutes, providing a structured space in which the worshipper
can reflect on each word after it has been pronounced. The cumula-
tive effect of the whole sequence concentrates the listener in
meditation on Christ's passion, for a time which seems as drawn out
as death itself. Contrast this with the Gloria of his *Missa Brevis S
Joannis de Deo* in which the telescoped setting (simultaneous singing
by each voice of a different portion of the text) results in a piece
which last less than a minute, sweeping up the listeners and propelling
the liturgical action forward in an intensity of joyous celebration.

The consideration of length is fundamental if music is to be used
well in a liturgical situation. Much will depend on the expectations
and usual practice of a congregation. However, there are spaces
within normal worship situations where extended periods of time

already exist which could be given deeper meaning through the use of appropriate music (live or recorded): the communion of the people is an obvious one, but there are also opportunities within the simple structures of Morning and Evening Prayer. Music can also be combined with an appropriate liturgical action: the lighting of candles or the offering of incense. In this way it is possible to set aside time for reflection in which people can begin to restructure their busy-ness.

Musical works were also created at a point of historical time, and belong in some sense to their own time and place. When we recreate them they take on new meaning. Music is also potentially nostalgic, bringing into the present the resonance of other worlds (complementing what can be glimpsed in the visual and literary arts).[27] Through this experience we can be liberated from the narrow confines of our own outlook and attitudes.

MUSICAL SIGNALS

At a more prosaic level, we might consider the way in which we use sound to *punctuate* the liturgy. In everyday life sound signals are so familiar that we tend to take them for granted: bells and electronic bleeps wake and alert us to important events; audible signals indicate that it is safe to cross the road; sirens sound warnings; musical logos interrupt radio announcements; jingles reinforce advertising slogans.

We make similar use of signals in church: the sanctuary bell calling attention to the most solemn action of the service is an obvious example; fanfares and musical acclamations are not uncommon. However, I think it would be good to look afresh from time to time at the musical signals used in worship with a view to making them more comprehensive, varied and hierarchical. This hierarchy needs to be examined both within the context of a single service and across the seasons of the liturgical year. For example, the Gospel might be marked out as the most important reading by singing responses before and after its proclamation, but on the great feasts of the church it might also be preceded by a fanfare. The Eucharistic Acclamations might be said during the solemn seasons of Advent and Lent and sung during the rest of the year. The striking of all the church bells together simultaneously might proclaim anew the incarnation of Christ as the climax of the Eucharistic Prayer on Christmas Eve. These are only obvious suggestions. In addition, the Anglican Church could learn a great deal from the Roman practice by reinstating the Gospel Alleluia, by singing the Great Amen at the end of the Eucharistic Prayer, and by making a more general use of seasonal musical acclamations where the sound of the words (necessarily left untranslated) is as important to the effect as their meaning in evoking a specifically Christian ritual culture: *Hosanna in excelsis; Maranatha; Deo gratias.*

MUSIC DEFINING SPACE

Not only does music articulate the passing of time, but a musical work may be said to define a particular space.

We must begin by considering the characteristics of the room in which the music is performed. In some cases the music will simply fill the space, without taking on distinctive characteristics of the acoustic environment. More often, a balance needs to be struck between the musical forces involved and the building in which they are heard. A soloist may sound ethereal in a Gothic cathedral, but unrefined in the enclosed space of a rehearsal room. Music helps to define the acoustic space and is, in its turn, modified by it.

The way in which music shapes our environment is especially pervasive. Although we can close our eyes or turn away in order to avoid *seeing*, it is much harder to avoid *hearing*. We may not choose to listen actively, but nevertheless our hearing mechanism will vibrate sympathetically with the sound, and our brains will receive the sensory stimulus. For this reason, those who choose music for use in worship carry great responsibility. The architecture of the church building may be fixed, and the décor capable of only limited change, but the musical hangings can be varied at will, and juxtaposed endlessly. It is possible to create unadulterated musical surroundings of Gregorian chant, fourteenth-century polyphony, baroque splendour, eighteenth-century Viennese *joie de vivre,* nineteenth-century sub-operatic decadence or twentieth-century *angst.* Equally, it is possible to select elements of many styles, which interact in creative but risky tension.[28] In any case music is one of the most immediate and effective ways in which variety and new life can enrich the worshipping experience.

Just as different musical elements react with each other, the way in which music is perceived will also be affected by the structure of the building in which it is heard, the way it is furnished and decorated, the number of those gathered for worship and how they are accommodated, the experiences they bring with them, and their willingness to be open to what they hear. It is likely that certain sorts of music will seem to have an obvious propriety or decorum: they will seem 'at home'. Examples would include Gregorian chant in the great echoing spaces of a Norman cathedral or a Wesley hymn in a Methodist chapel. However, the unexpected and apparently inappropriate can also have great power to surprise people into a strong and deep-rooted response. The powerful experience of hearing the music of Duke Ellington in a liturgical context in Durham Cathedral is recounted elsewhere in this collection.[29]

A building is rarely a neutral space for music. Its acoustic properties inherently change the transmission of sound within it. The whole ambience of a service in the chapel of King's College Chapel, Cambridge is a unique blend of music, acoustics and architecture which can combine to produce an effect of almost overwhelming sublimity. Attempts to capture this atmosphere, as many try to do, in their own services of Nine Lessons and Carols are almost doomed to seem earthbound by comparison. In the same way, it may be misguided to try to sing a large-scale hymn such as 'O Jesus, I have promised' to W. H. Ferguson's great tune *Wolvercote* (very much a product of the English public-school tradition of hymnody) 'where two or three are gathered together' for Evening Prayer in a village church. By the same token, the intimacy of certain worship songs, ideal for a house group, may be completely at odds with the soaring spaces of a Gothic cathedral.

As a result of this, it is important to choose music which can work with the resources and acoustic space available. In addition, it may be necessary to consider locations for the performers which take into consideration the repertoire, the liturgical action, and the desired effect. Once we have recognised the proper contribution which musicians have to make, we may no longer wish to abandon choirs to chancels or galleries simply in order to get them out of the way. However, in other situations it may not be necessary (or even desirable) for the performers to be seen in order for the music to make its full effect.

A balance also needs to be achieved in the way in which we use music within a single liturgical celebration. The effect of contrapuntal Mass movements spaced at the high points of a service otherwise sung to plainsong is very different from their sequential performance in a concert. Hymns, responses, antiphonal psalmody, intoned readings, instrumental voluntaries and Taizé chants each have their own characteristics, which may make one more appropriate than another at any given point in the liturgical action, as well as carrying implications for how, where and by whom they should be performed, and what else might legitimately take place at the same time.

When the proper space of each item is respected and balanced within the shape of the service as a planned sequence, the worship will have a depth of meaning and a potential for transformation which goes beyond the contribution of the individual items. Planning with this kind of sensitivity, although painstaking, is vital if we are to take seriously the responsibility for ordering worship with which we have been entrusted. At its most creative, liturgical space might be likened to a large computer screen on which it is possible to juxtapose any chosen elements. Consider this description of primeval art:

> All is within the continual present, the perpetual flow of today, yesterday and tomorrow. ... Whenever possible previous lines are not destroyed, but the lines of both earlier and later works intermingle till they sometimes – but only to our eyes [substitute *ears*] – appear inextricable. It was recognised quite early that this superimposition was not due to idle chance but to a deliberate reluctance to destroy the past.[30]

We too need to bring the past into the present in a way which is creative and which provides a context for items from our own time and culture.[31]

MUSIC TRANSFORMING SPACE

A more complex concept of the way in which music may be said to structure space is to do with the technical considerations of the range of notes it uses, its textural complexity and the saturation of its harmonic and tonal language. Metaphorically, it can be said that music occupies both horizontal and vertical space. Consider a piece of fifteenth century polyphony – a movement from a Mass setting of Ockeghem, for instance.[32] Vertically, it occupies the distance between the highest and lowest sounding notes; horizontally, it reveals a complicated and fascinating connection between the first and last notes (whether within a section or the piece as a whole depends on the span of our listening). Since the structure is played out and heard in real time, the characteristics of the audible space at any one moment (frozen for an instant) will differ according to the individual's perception of it. That perception constantly changes in a way which may allow us to imagine the music as a three-dimensional yet transparent object moving freely in space. It is like a multi-faceted object slowly rotating – a mobile, perhaps. Figuratively, we might be able to comprehend more clearly multi-dimensional spatial concepts which otherwise rarely enter human understanding. There is a particular fascination here in the connection with scientific thinking at its most speculative and abstract.

Seen from an historical perspective, the space which music occupied gradually expanded until it became saturated, in the course of its development from monodic plainsong, through organum, modal counterpoint, tonal polyphony, regular periodic structures, irregular structures using expanded tonality, to the self-conscious fragmentation and complexity of the early twentieth-century crisis. (Of course, not all of these developments have found their way into church.) If we plan to introduce a greater variety of styles, it is essential to consider the musical space occupied by a particular piece when considering an appropriate place for it within a liturgical action. Music whose texture is relatively uniform makes a better companion for other liturgical events than pieces which work through dynamic developing processes to a crisis, climax or resolution. The reason why sixteenth-century modal counterpoint has often been regarded as the quintessential expression of the Christian faith may be because it does not draw too much attention to itself. As such, it is an acquiescent partner in the liturgical celebration.

The use of background music is common in everyday life. From the 'musak' of the supermarket through to the atmospheric film soundtrack this use (or abuse?) of music is ubiquitous. If we do not give music full attention, it may not engender a full, creative response, but it can still structure time or help to create a particular atmosphere. Where is this line to be drawn in church? The planned use of spoken prayer against a musical background may enhance worship, a loud exchange of the week's gossip competing with the organist's final voluntary is unlikely to do so.

Some music needs to be given its own space – its scale and vigour seem to demand that its integrity be respected. Its use in the liturgy is justified because of the intensification of experience it can offer. Such music typically operates within dynamic structures. In particular, this is true of music underpinned by the conventions of tonality (however expanded the concept may be in early twentieth-century repertoire) and developing rhythmic structures. Tension and resolution (both harmonic and rhythmic) are balanced to produce music which is expressive and cohesive. The music seems to progress towards a goal and, as listeners, we feel satisfied when it is reached. When we enter its world through the imagination, we become involved with it. We become vulnerable to the way in which it structures our hearing in new ways, which may bring delight and pleasure but may equally confront us with sounds which suggest emptiness, loneliness, despair or destruction – even madness. The funeral march, the fourth of Webern's *Six Orchestral Pieces*, presents a vision of desolation. By entering the world of this music we may reach deeper levels within our inner psyche, leading us in turn to respond to the world in ways less superficial than those which are the product of normal living. Music can provide a safe environment which allows us to look into the abyss deep within our souls, or to confront the horrors of a world which has been abused by human power. Most importantly, it also provides us with a route back to wholeness, to sanity, to *redemption*.

Despite this potential, music with such a power to disturb or confront is rarely given a place in worship. We enshrine the superficial, the tawdry, the merely functional, but marginalise the power of great art to hold up a mirror to our own society and to our own sinful nature. The Agnus Dei of Britten's *Missa Brevis* is one conspicuous exception to this criticism, but pieces which enter profoundly into the pain of human existence and respond to the agony of the cross are not regularly used in most traditions. Similarly, the church has usually been reluctant to give composers adequate opportunities to write music which questions and challenges received thinking. In part, the reason is practical: there is a lack of rehearsal time in which to prepare more complex scores. However, many commissions for new music display, in their extreme caution, a fear of the new. This does little to affirm our belief in a God who takes risks with his own creation.

If we are to take music seriously as an agent of transformation we have to be prepared to take risks about the way we use it in worship. The changing moods of the liturgical year allow striking opportunities for experimentation, both within the regular structures and at extra-liturgical gatherings. The penitential rites encourage the use of music which can act as an agent for the expression of our sorrow. On other occasions, music can help us experience the liberation and overflowing of joy which results from the knowledge of our redemption. Music is a gift of grace, but grace operates where we are in the real world, not in a kind of religious place apart, cocooned from brutal truth by the cotton wool security which much religious music provides.[33]

> Living human perceptions are geared for change, and can only function for limited periods in an unchanging environment . . . . Consciousness involves awareness of change, which means a continuous process of negotiation with the real world.[34]

In our negotiation with the real world we also have to negotiate with our own selves. Music is one of the ways through which we can hope to achieve some sense of inner reconciliation – a first step towards reconciliation with the world in which we live and to the God who brought it into being.

For many people music is profoundly revelatory. At the same time it provides a sense of structure, a safe place in which it is acceptable to yield to the revelation.

> The experience of revelation in itself is immediate, unavoidable, and by that definition disturbing. Since the most important experiences are those which touch us most profoundly, it should not be surprising that there are some for whom any intense experience is by definition offensive.[35]

> In a significant number of cultures music seems to act as a form of mediation between the known and unknown, the acceptable and unacceptable, that which is powerful and that which is dangerous.[36]

Much worship has become too safe, too cautious. It needs to provide a meeting point for God and his people, between the individual believer and the transcendent creator. Because of its structured nature, music seems particularly helpful in creating a safe space within which worshippers can risk being open to God. The security of an ordered sound-world provides a shelter within which people may find the freedom to be simply themselves. They can expose themselves to an intense experience without the necessity of preserving a public *persona*. In this way, music may help to bring into being an integrated personality, more truly revelatory of God-given potential. At the same time, when individuals gather in community to share this common activity of the imagination, they can know themselves more completely as the chosen and dedicated people of God, empowered through grace to proclaim the triumphs of the one who has called them out of darkness into his marvellous light.[37]

> How often, making music, we have found
> A new dimension in the world of sound,
> As worship moved us to a more profound
> Alleluia![38]

CONCLUSION

The previous discussion suggests a broad agenda.

- We need to develop a proper understanding of the way in which music functions and to reflect on this theologically, as the basis for a practical approach towards the use of music in all our social structures.

- Widespread, creative involvement with music through the experiences of composing, performing and listening needs to be encouraged.
- We should affirm that people are inherently musical because of their capacity to hear structured sound and interpret it as musical experience.
- The idea of participation as 'a shared activity of the imagination' should act as a corrective to other, more corporeal, interpretations of the term.
- We should affirm that all music-making is potentially an opportunity for wholeness, for the building of community, and for the experience of transcendence.
- Churches should build bridges towards those who value the inherently spiritual nature of the musical experience.
- The church as a whole should recognise the need to reclaim its own rich and diverse musical traditions.
- We should affirm the importance of giving music of many kinds a central place in worship.
- We need to take more risks about the kinds of music which we admit into church, and the way in which music is used in creative juxtaposition with other liturgical elements.
- We should learn to respect the cultural preferences of other Christians, and try to value all music-making which has conviction.
- Musicians should be valued for their contributions to worship (and to society as a whole) and they should be helped towards a more theological understanding of their activity.
- We need to recover a relationship between music and ritual in which the two elements are integrated and inter-dependent.
- The planning of worship must proceed with the complete integration of music and liturgy if each is to illuminate the other in as complete a way as possible.
- We need to recognise that music is a process with which we engage. It is 'art in action', especially in its symbiotic relationship with liturgy.
- Those who have responsibility for worship should become more aware of the ways in which music structures time and space, so that pieces can be given an appropriate placing within the liturgy.
- Musical signals (responses, fanfares, acclamations etc.) can be used to articulate and emphasise the key moments in our liturgies. More seasonal items (that is, the Proper as well as the Ordinary of the Mass) could be given musical treatment, and the Anglican Church, in particular, would do well to re-instate the Gospel Alleluia and Great Amen (as well as other acclamations) as part of the congre-

gational sung celebration of the Eucharist.

- When words and music come together, we should become more responsive to their mutual interaction, and strive to use this creatively.
- The need for excessive amplification should be challenged at the point where it threatens to dull our hearing and make us less responsive to musical communication.
- Music is a transforming medium which offers the potential for revelation. If we are to use it with confidence we must first create an environment which provides liturgical and pastoral care so that people feel sufficiently secure as they come to worship.
- We need to think carefully about the ways in which music is used to create community. What sort of community are we trying to create through our worship? Which music will help us to achieve that?
- In partnership with society as a whole, the church should make a commitment to the development of widespread musical literacy, and should help congregations to acquire a functional familiarity with notation, which can be used as an *aide-mémoire* and so facilitate access to a more eclectic repertoire.
- At the same time, the church should encourage the development of simple musical structures, refrains, responses, ostinatos etc., which can operate in liturgy at a more primeval, pre-literate level, acting as mantras to free the mind to take on a more spiritual focus.
- The spontaneous activity of improvisation should be valued for the flexible and creative way in which it can be used in worship. Training in improvisation should become a normal part of a musical education.
- We experience music as something which is both immanent and transcendent. As such, it offers us profoundly important access to these aspects of God's nature.
- Music should be valued for its potential to allow us to enter other worlds through our involvement with it.
- The church should encourage composers (especially through commissioned pieces) to be more adventurous in exploring new sound worlds using both natural and synthesised sound.
- We should question the value of synthesised sound when it seeks merely to imitate 'natural' instruments, rather than opening up new worlds of sound.
- Above all, we need to bring the best of our creative gifts to every stage of our offering of music to God. This will be a costly process, but it may serve to remind us that sacrificial giving is at the heart of Christian discipleship.

NOTES

1 The Hilliard Ensemble and Jan Garbarek, *Officium* (ECM 1525).
2 The Choir of New College, Oxford, *Agnus Dei* (Erato 0630–14634-2).
3 Bela Bartok, quoted in Basil Spence, *Phoenix at Coventry*, London: Geoffrey Bles, 1962, p. xvii.
4 See Jeremy Begbie, *Music in God's Purposes*, Edinburgh: The Handsel Press, 1989, p. 5.
5 Of course, this pragmatic approach is not unique to a particular style of late twentieth-century church music – it was common practice, for instance, in early baroque opera.
6 For a thorough discussion of the demands of music ministry, based on an evangelical exposition of biblical teaching, see Leen La Rivière, *Music in Ministry: A Biblical Perspective*, Leeds: Ears and Eyes Publishing, 1987.
7 A clear exposition is given by Patricia Carpenter, 'The Musical Object', *Current Musicology*, 5, 1967, pp. 56–87.
8 See Ian Ground's paper, 'Must We Mean What We Play?', elsewhere in this volume for a discussion of this approach as derived from Kant's *Critique of Judgement*.
9 See Nicholas Wolterstorff, *Art in Action*, Grand Rapids, Mich.: Eerdmans, 1980, in particular pp. 183–189.
10 The best introduction to musical anthropology is still to be found in the pioneering work of John Blacking, in particular, *How Musical is Man?*, Seattle: University of Washington Press, 1973. His paper 'The Study of Man as Music-Maker' in J. Blacking and J. Keali'inohomoku (eds), *The Performing Arts*, The Hague: Mouton, 1979, pp. 3–15, offers a concise introduction to his thinking. A more recent collection of papers has appeared as J. Blacking, *Music, Culture & Experience*, ed. R. Byron, Chicago: University of Chicago Press, 1995.
11 W. J. Ong, *World as View and World as Event*, quoted in John Shepherd, *Music as Social Text*, Cambridge: Polity Press, 1991, p. 22.
12 See Coral Davies, 'Music in General Education', elsewhere in this volume for an account of how creative teaching can help young children use music to express important events in their lives.
13 See Bill Hall's paper, 'Jazz – Lewd or Ludens?', elsewhere in this volume.
14 Notes to the recording *Pierre Cochereau l'organiste de Notre-Dame* (Solstice SOCD 94/96).
15 English text of the *Constitution on the Sacred Liturgy*, London: Incorporated Catholic Truth Society, 1967, p. 12. For a more detailed exploration see F. R. McManus, *Liturgical Participation: An Ongoing Assessment*, Washington, D.C.: The Pastoral Press, 1988.
16 See Jan Michael Joncas, *From Sacred Song to Ritual Music*, Collegeville, Minnesota: The Liturgical Press, 1997, for a detailed summary and critique of the relevant documents. See also Emmanuel Gribben's essay, 'Make Music for the Lord', elsewhere in this volume.
17 Roman Ingarden deals with the philosophical and aesthetic issues raised by these questions in *The Work of Music and the Problem of Its Identity*, London: The Macmillan Press, 1986. My concerns are purely practical.
18 Genesis 1:31.
19 Blacking, *How Musical is Man?*, p. 28.
20 See also Jacques Attali, *Noise: The Political Economy of Music*, Manchester: Manchester University Press, 1985, in particular p. 6.

21 John Shepherd, *Music as Social Text*, Cambridge: Polity Press, 1991, p. 58.

22 From Oliver Strunk, *Source Readings in Music History I*, London: Faber, 1981, p. 94.

23 John Wesley's phrase.

24 Shepherd, *Music as Social Text*, p. 217.

25 G. Rochberg, 'The Structure of Time in Music', in J. T. Fraser and N. Lawrence (eds), *The Study of Time II*, Berlin: Springer-Verlag, 1975, p. 136.

26 Rochberg, 'The Structure of Time in Music', p. 142.

27 See Reinhard Strohm, *Music in Late Medieval Bruges*, Oxford: Oxford University Press, 1985, pp. 1–9, for a masterly evocation of the sounds and sights of that great cultural centre.

28 The funeral service of Diana, Princess of Wales, held in Westminster Abbey on 6 September 1997, juxtaposed traditional and contemporary music with memorable effect.

29 Bill Hall, *op. cit.*

30 S. Gideon, *Space Conception in Prehistoric Art*, quoted in Shepherd, *Music as Social Text*, p. 25.

31 Current trends which allow for the juxtaposition of layers of liturgical texts, each carrying their own historical linguistic resonance, are very welcome. See Phyllis James, Michael Perham and David Stancliffe, 'Image, Memory and Text', in Michael Perham (ed.), *The Renewal of Common Prayer*, London: SPCK, 1993, pp. 27–36.

32 I was thinking, in particular, of movements such as the Kyrie, Sanctus, Benedictus and Agnus Dei of his *Missa Ecce ancilla Domini*.

33 See also the comments in my interview with James MacMillan, elsewhere in this volume.

34 Robin Maconie, *The Concept of Music*, Oxford: Oxford University Press, 1990, p. 174.

35 Maconie, *The Concept of Music*, p. 176.

36 Shepherd, *Music as Social Text*, p. 214.

37 cf. 1 Peter 2:9–10.

38 Fred Pratt Green, from his hymn *When in our Music God is Glorified*.

10

Power Praise

John Inge

> The tears flowed from me when I heard your hymns and canticles, for
> the sweet singing of your church moved me deeply. The music surged
> in my ears, truth seeped into my heart, and my feelings of devotion
> overflowed, so that the tears streamed down. But they were tears of
> gladness.[1]

So writes St Augustine in his *Confessions*, describing how deeply he
was affected by the music he heard at his baptism. Augustine reflected
deeply upon music and wrote a treatise on it, *De Musica*.[2] In
commenting on *De Musica*, William Jordan argues that part of
Augustine's motivation in writing it was to 'lead the reader to understand that music can have an anagogic function'. In other words, 'the
contemplation of music leads us to the contemplation of the eternal'.[3]
However, elsewhere he expresses concern about the emotional power
of music which, he feels, is indicative of its earthly nature – like St
John Chrysostom, who writes that music is 'sensual and pagan,
obstructing our progress toward the real world of the spirit'.[4]
Augustine and other church fathers were critical of music precisely
because of its ability to affect us so profoundly. In what follows we
shall affirm Augustine's recognition of the power of music in general,
and 'hymns and canticles' in particular, and argue that, in view of that
power, more attention should be given to them by church leaders and
theologians.

St Augustine's words above speak of the *emotional* power of music.
That power is immense. As John Sloboda points out elsewhere in this
volume, a wide range of individuals report music 'as evoking, often
on first hearing, emotions and feelings of an unprecedented intensity
and unique character',[5] and it would seem that ordinary people are not

as readily or as deeply affected by other art forms as by music. Film and television are the only other media that affect such huge numbers of people. There, too, the power of music is evidenced by the way film makers use it to heighten the emotional effect of film at crucial points, for music has great power to 'express the subtleties of human emotions'.[6] The fact that music touches people so deeply at an emotional level means that it has unrivalled power to bind people together. This is more than anything else true of singing.

COMMUNITY POWER

Those who have experienced the singing of a crowd at the Cup Final, or of the audience at the Last Night of the Proms, know of this power: those who sing at football matches do so in order to express and strengthen their feeling of unity and solidarity. Football matches and the rather more esoteric Last Night of the Proms are two remnants of community singing which was once much more widespread. It had a very large place in the life of Victorian England, and was extremely effective in binding people together. Older people will remember cinemas being hired by the local operatic society for performances of Gilbert and Sullivan's Savoy Operas: many people took part and hundreds came to enjoy these great community occasions. With bands playing regularly in the park, and choral societies attracting huge membership, music was as much part of civic and community life as it was of church life. Its power was immense and its purpose, if unstated, was clear: to cement community.

My own confirmation of the immense power of singing to bind communities in a secular context came from working as a chaplain at Harrow School. Once each term the whole school assembles to sing Harrow School Songs, of which there are many, the most famous being 'Forty Years On'. They date, mostly, from the nineteenth century and are reminiscent of Gilbert and Sullivan at their worst. Yet the power of the songs used in this setting is enormous. Churchill was a pupil at Harrow and remembered this potential to unite and encourage from his time there. He asked to come to School Songs when things were at their most difficult during the Second World War in order to find the same encouragement: the effects of such singing run deep. At these gatherings the nine hundred adolescents gathered show none of the impery which might be expected to result from such an exercise: the whole thing is taken extremely seriously. They sing with great gusto words which inculcate devotion to 'the Hill', a religion of its own. Witnessing such happenings gave me an insight into the way in which community singing was so powerful in Victorian England. It was used in all sorts of settings other than churches, and such publications as William Morris's *Chants for Socialists* (1884) linked music to causes other than religion.

A GOOD POWER?

Some of the causes to which music has been linked are not good ones. A glance at the history of Europe during the twentieth century reminds us that music is used to unite people in order to divide them from others, most notably through the inculcation of a feeling of nationalism. Nationalism, linked to the rediscovery of folk music, has inspired composers such as Grieg to produce music of quality. National anthems still have a great effect on people, which is in many ways commendable as is the love of one's country – but the love which is 'entire and whole and perfect' and 'asks no question', to which one oft-sung hymn exhorts us, is nothing less than idolatry. The appalling effects of this idolatry have been seen in two world wars. Hitler knew how to use music to encourage the love which asks no question, as have other dictators and tyrants.

Music can be a very emotive point of dissension in church life. In England, since the Reformation, only smell has had an equivalent power to evoke and to divide. People are still capable of becoming 'incensed' about incense as they are about music, but about precious little else. Smell is very evocative[7] and has an uncanny power to conjure up past situations: Sloboda makes reference to the fact that there is a significant body of data which confirms that music is also a particularly powerful evoker of other times and other places.[8] There is, as we have already noted with music, something almost mystical about these things in terms of their power to reach so deep into the human psyche. In a parish church setting controversy often surrounds the question of whether old or new music is the most appropriate for worship, as it did prior to the enthronement of George Carey as Archbishop of Canterbury. This is not a new phenomenon: an old man in a congregation to which I ministered remembered the scandal caused by a curate at a neighbouring parish church in which he sang as a boy in the choir. The curate wanted to deprive them of their much loved Moody and Sankey in favour of a new-fangled publication known as *The English Hymnal*. In some Anglican churches difficulties now surround the question of whether guitars are appropriate for church worship though, interestingly, many of those keen to use them are now in their thirties and forties and are looked upon with some amusement by some younger people. There is a sense of *déjà vu* about all these difficulties. The introduction of organs was as controversial at one time as the advent of guitars in church; the appearance of robed choirs caused as much discontent as does the formation of music groups today. What we can learn from this is that music, and all that goes with it, has immense power to divide people as well as unite them, because of all that it carries, particularly with respect to emotion. It is possible to argue, perhaps, that music is morally neutral. This applies to 'good' music as well as 'bad'. We cannot say that 'good' music is more benign than 'bad' music: it is well known that some of the worst war criminals of the Second World War were very cultured people who loved good music. It can be used to good or bad effect, and the same piece of music can be used to do very different things to people in varied settings. Even if we argue that music is morally neutral we may recognise that it can be a symbol, or sacrament, of God's presence and love. Sacramental elements can all be used to good or bad effect: water is life giving but can be used for drowning even when blessed. Consecrated wine can produce drunkenness.

Many people would want to say that music is good, despite its shadow potential, because it provides them with a lifeline, a means of emotional and spiritual escape. Music of all sorts is listened to endlessly by millions of people. Sometimes popular music is accused of being banal, with lyrics speaking of love and sex – things with which people would rather occupy their minds than the drudgery of mindless work. But we must beware of being dismissive: Shakespeare suggested that music might be 'the food of love'[9] and did not declare some of that food unclean. Music is found to be uplifting and cheering and it might be that Nietzsche is right in arguing that it serves many people by functioning as 'an alternative to religion as a way of structuring reality, giving expression to their hopes and fears in an ordered form, and enhancing life as it reconciles them to it'.[10]

BELIEVING IN MUSIC

For believers music does more than this. It provides an entrance into a different world, effecting a sacramental and symbolic connection with our deepest yearnings. George Steiner believes that 'it may well be that man is man, and that man "borders on" limitations of peculiar and open "otherness", because he can produce and be possessed by music'.[11] James MacMillan tells us that he has long 'seen music as a striking analogy for God's relationship with us', quoting the Jesuit

John McDade who, after Augustine, believes that 'music may be the closest analogue to the mystery of the direct and effective communication of grace'.[12] Steiner goes so far as to say, 'I believe the matter of music to be central to that of the meanings of man, of man's access to or abstention from metaphysical experience.'[13] In similar vein Barth writes:

> I must have been five or six years old at the time ... my father was musical and was fond of improvising on the piano .... One day, he was playing something by Mozart. I can still picture the scene. He began a couple of bars from *The Magic Flute* .... They went right through me and into me, I don't know how, and I thought, 'That's it.'[14]

Elsewhere Barth referred to the music of Mozart as a parable of the kingdom. It spoke to him in a unique fashion:

> Why is it that this man is so incomparable? ... He has heard, and causes those with ears to hear, even today, what we shall not see until the end of time – the whole context of providence. As though in the light of this end, he heard the harmony of creation to which the shadows belong but in which the shadow is not darkness, deficiency is not defeat, sadness cannot become despair, trouble cannot degenerate into tragedy and infinite melancholy is not ultimately forced to claim undisputed sway .... Mozart causes us to hear that even on the latter side, and therefore in its totality, creation praises its maker and is therefore perfect.[15]

Like Barth, believers would want to argue 'that which is made reveals something about its maker, as a book its writer or a house its occupants. Music may be seen, therefore, as telling us something not only about its composer and performers but also about the God who has given it.'[16] Paul Tortelier says that each time he plays Bach he kneels before angels, and the music critic Bryan Northcott points to Messiaen as a musician who 'views composing wholly as a matter of revealing the divine order'.[17]

The notion of kneeling before angels reminds us that there is a mystery about music. Questions about where it actually resides are difficult to answer. Is it with the composer, the performer, or the listener? Where is it to be located? Benjamin Britten referred to these three as a 'holy triangle'[18] and if the answer is a mysterious locus between them, there is a voice within us which wants to place that point half-way to heaven. Music can be sublime and has the power to lift us above ourselves: 'When we experience music as absolute, powerful, mysterious and ineffable, we single out the qualities conventionally ascribed to the sacred, the numinous, or to God. Similarly the elation and exaltation provided by music are the nearest thing to the ecstasy of mystical religion.'[19] Music expresses, with power much greater than words, 'something of the mystery, the order and the glory of creation and its creator'.[20] As John Beer recently put it:

> Those who sing their part for God are rooted, of course, in biblical habits: our Scripture is shot through with sounds of praise, the sheer delight in instrumental and vocal resonances, imitating, as it were, the music of heaven. And though all creatures were made to resound the creator's praise, it is given to human creatures to know the mystery of how the sounds of nature, people and things may be woven musically into a language, to delight both the human and the divine ear. . . . And in due time, in the trinitarian way of things, the mystery of God's being, experienced by us in diversity and unity, is set out; each new 'raid on the inarticulate', to use T. S. Eliot's phrase, is a struggle to speak of three themes of divinity distinguished only by their relationship to the undivided whole, reflecting a mutuality, a co-inherence of love, a divine economy of music making, as it were in sonata form. The loving creativity and givenness of God – from our perspective, the first expo- sition of the divine nature – issues in the development of his being in human shape, a unique 'visual aid' to the divine character, a second movement, so to speak, of God towards his creation, a free fantasia of the divine being played upon an instrument of frail flesh. But these themes are experienced afresh in a recapitulation of the divine truth, Spirit blowing in the church and world, recalling us to that unity of being in which we are to share. Three movements of a divine sonata, but movement not in God's time; for these musical sounds are the product of an eternal notation, composed by love.[21]

Is this good theology? I think it is. A cursory glance at the Scriptures will show the overwhelming importance of music and singing to the Christian scheme of things:

> The singing of heaven is only the end of a great thread which runs throughout Scripture – where music (and singing in particular) is used to heighten the key moments in the story of God's relationship with his people. There are no fewer than 166 uses of the verb to sing, 48 refer- ences to singers and 35 to singing in the Bible. The writer of the Book of Job, for example, tells us that, at the creation of the world, 'the morning stars sang for joy' (Job 38:7). At the Exodus, to mark the birth of the nation Israel, Moses sang a song to the Lord (Exodus 15:1-18) . . . . Singing also heralds the birth of Christ, in the song of the angels (Luke 2:14), and the birth of the new creation, in the songs around the throne of the Lamb (Rev 5:12ff). The psalms are, of course, full of

references to singing; and in the New Testament, the early Christians are exhorted to 'sing psalms, hymns and spiritual songs, and make melody to the Lord' (Col 3:16 etc.).[22]

Music is of profound theological importance not only because of its power to unite but because of its association with divine revelation and its articulation of the sublime. As Hans Küng puts it, 'tones, sounds can speak and in the end say something inexpressible, unspeakable: in the midst of music the "ineffable mystery".'[23] This power of music means that its evangelistic and spiritual potential cannot be overestimated. And where is it at its most potent, if not in hymns and songs? The early Methodists knew of this power and made use of it: the preface to the Methodist Hymn Book begins with the sentence 'Methodism was born in song.'[24] And the revival which Methodism brought about was greatly influenced by singing and depended upon it. The most powerful instrument of evangelism available to the early Methodists, other than the preaching of John Wesley, was hymnody – for they realised that in hymns, 'men speak to the most high and he to them.'[25]

HYMNS AND SONGS

Hymnody, which reached a peak of popularity in England in the nineteenth century, has had immense importance in England over many years. In the 1850s and 60s more than 400 collections appeared in England alone.[26] Obelkevich draws attention to the fact that hymns were taught in board schools as well as church and Sunday schools and were thus known to many working class people who rarely attended church. They were often sung at home as well as in church and the favourite time and place was Sunday evening around the piano, recalled by D. H. Lawrence:

> .... the old Sunday evenings at home, with
>   the winter outside
> And hymns in the cozy parlour, the tinkling piano our
>   Guide.[27]

Hymns 'were sung on Whit walks and (to different words) in the trenches during the Great War; "Abide with Me" was part of the festivities at the F.A. Cup Final. If there has been a "common religion" in England in the last hundred years it has been based not on doctrine but on the popular hymns.'[28]

The above claim is bold, but one in which I think there is some truth. In hymnody the revelatory, evangelistic and community-building power of music, to which we have made reference above, is combined to enormous effect but, despite all this, many have remained somewhat disdainful about it. In his magnificent book on spirituality, *Yes to God*, Alan Ecclestone makes much reference to art and poetry but precious little to music. At one point he tells us, 'To be told that we desperately need the poet to come to our aid in shaping a relevant spirituality still strikes the majority of Christians as a little odd. Hymn writers possibly, with their incredibly bad verses, but hardly poets.'[29] Such attitudes are not new. Owen Chadwick points out:

> Austere musicians accused the romantic composers of hymn-tunes like J. B. Dykes (as with his tune for *Lead kindly Light*) of weakness and sentimentality, as if taste was being debased for the sake of the common people .... Stainer warmly defended Dykes, for he saw that a hymn tune was not only a melody but an instrument of evangelism. And it was agreed that if musicians insisted on the highest music in churches, the result must be a break between the churches and musicians' art.[30]

It is, perhaps, their own inability not to be affected by music which they regard to be second rate which means some musical purists rail against it. As Steiner puts it,

> Cheap music, childish images, the vulgate in language, in its crassest sense, can penetrate to the depths of our necessities and dreams. It can assert almost irrevocable tenure there. The opening bars, the hammer beat *accelerando* of Edith Piaf's '*Je ne regrette rien*' – the text is infantile, the tune stentorious, and the politics which enlisted the song unattractive – tempt every nerve in me, touch the bone with a cold burn and draw me after into God knows what infidelities to reason, each time I hear the song, and hear it, uncalled for, recurrent inside me. Wagner raged at his inability to excise from within his remembrance and involuntary humming, the tin-pot tunes of a contemporary operetta, *The Postillion of Longjumeau*. There are rhyme, puns, jingle-effects flat as stale water, which mesmerize not only readers and listeners but the greatest of poets (Will Shakespeare on *will*, Victor Hugo in hundredfold thrall to *ombre/sombre*).[31]

The fact of the matter is that, as Steiner goes on to say that our personal canon includes 'the bad rhymester, the pedlar of facile images, the organ-grinder whose work is not only ineradicable from our memories, but continues to nourish, to quicken our innermost wants. No man or woman need justify his personal anthology, his canonic welcomes. Love does not argue its necessities.'[32] It would not normally occur to ordinary Christian communities to justify their 'personal anthology' or 'canonic welcomes', and should this appear to leave the door wide open to philistinism it is worth remembering that the Christian faith is not to be equated with good taste. The greatest saint can be the most terrible philistine, just as the most 'civilised' person, in terms of taste, can be demonic.

We should bear this in mind, perhaps, when considering criticisms of modern church choruses, often accused of being banal. Ruth Gledhill provoked considerable correspondence when she referred to 'meaningless evangelical choruses' in *The Times* a little while ago.[33] Some of them could not be thought, by any stretch of the imagination, to be good music but they do have enormous popular appeal and one is reminded of debates which took place in the nineteenth century, and of 'the abuse – "depressing", "degenerate", "hysterical", "insincere", "effeminate", etc., dealt out to Dykes and Barnby. Harmonic mannerisms such as diminished seventh chords and dominant sevenths in cadences were dismissed as "sickly sweet" and "nauseating".'[34] But these simple tunes have a power which can be harnessed for the faith. A spokesman for the Royal School of Church Music spoke eloquently on Radio 4 of the dilemma he found himself in when some choruses, which were not good music, affected him profoundly from a Christian point of view.[35] They undoubtedly have a power to convert people to the faith they proclaim. Modern choruses may be seen as expressions of love whose words, though less sophisticated than Shakespeare's sonnets or Donne's poetry, are typical of articulations of love in our age – secular love songs tend not to be much more articulate. There are writings by such people as Graham Kendrick which have more to them, as far as both words and music are concerned, than some other modern worship songs. But though some will remain, most of the rest will pass into oblivion, just as did most of the hymns of the nineteenth century. What we need to be aware of is the fact that they can have great power in the present. Moger reminds us that, 'compared with traditional hymns, worship songs become very easily embedded in the consciousness because they are short and sung repeatedly. Hence the power of a short song is considerable, and often greater than that of a reading or a sermon.'[36]

My plea here is that, if we recognise, accept and embrace the power of music in general and such songs in particular, we should pay more attention to the words. If hymns are so powerful, would it not behove us to put more resources into examination of their theology? What do hymns say to us about the nature of God? A look at one hymn book which is still widely used is instructive. *Hymns Ancient and Modern*

(1861, appendix 1868, revised edition 1875, supplement 1889), which is of 'moderate Tractarian inspiration'[37] and was dominant in the church by the end of the nineteenth century, is still used in an enormous number of Anglican churches. An examination of the social and political themes of *Hymns Ancient and Modern* has been carried out by Stephen Wilson.[38] Obelkevich uses his work to argue that:

> God is represented as a remote and sometimes martial figure: father, king, lord and judge (so that) the cardinal virtues become submissiveness and obedience. The hymns legitimate existing political authority and the social hierarchy; they recommend charity rather than justice and they defer the rewards of the righteous poor to the afterlife. Though portraying the relation between man and God in erotic terms, they reject sexuality and reveal a masochistic streak, as if to justify pain and suffering.[39]

We might want to argue in defence of these hymns that most of the imagery employed is scriptural, but the fact is that the book remains somewhat selective in its use of biblical images. Would it not be sensible for us to look more carefully at what theology is contained within the hymns and songs which are sung in our churches? It is a matter of some irony that the Church of England, in common with other churches, has strict rules about the wording to be used in liturgy whereas more or less anything can be sung as hymnody in the course of worship. This is all the more strange in view of the power of words and music combined which, as we have seen, is much greater than either of these alone. Many people learned and memorised what theology they know through the singing of hymns. Hymn singing has been rivalled only by nursery rhymes as a method for memorising words. Ordinary people who have been exposed to hymnody during their childhood and youth will be able to repeat both the words and music of hymns when most other aspects of church are beyond recall:

> Beatrice said nothing. She looked at herself in the hall mirror without affection and hummed a little tune, 'O Lord and father of mankind'. How irrational hymns were, burrowing about persistently in one's subconscious when one didn't subscribe to a word of them.[40]

Joanna Trollope's Beatrice Bachelor is a fictional atheist, but her experience of the persisting power of hymns is one that can be seen in many people, believers and non-believers alike. As we have argued, music which is sung touches people very deeply and hymns are often firmly lodged in the psyche from early childhood because they form a potent combination of words and music in which people are actually involved as participants rather than listeners. The words often form the basis which they use to understand the nature of the God in whom they believe or do not believe, as the case may be. Brian Wren writes, 'God talk in worship is of the utmost importance, because it slants and shapes our conceptions of God from early childhood. One reason it is so powerful is that worship looks for an encounter with God and therefore aims not to criticise language, but to open us to meet God through it.'[41] God talk which is sung is of paramount importance.

CONCLUSION

We are witnessing today a new flowering of hymnody within the church at large. Church leaders are bombarded with literature recommending this or that new publication. The situation is somewhat akin to that which pertained in the Church of England before *Hymns Ancient and Modern* and other standard volumes captured the market, a period during which a plethora of hymn books was in use: the five central churches of Nottingham each used a different hymn book in 1855,[42] and a survey in 1872 revealed that in one Worcestershire town thirteen hymn books were in use.[43] In the midst of this flowering my concern is that, given the immense power of music for good or ill which we have noted, we are in danger of missing opportunities and potential. Much time and energy is given by the Liturgical and Doctrine Commissions of the Church of England to liturgy and doctrine respectively, and to good effect. But more resources should be directed towards church music in general and hymnody in particular, and church leaders and theologians need to encourage poets and musicians to produce hymnody that will 'shape a relevant spirituality' and speak to us of the things of God in a profound and yet accessible manner. We need to take seriously the comment of the writers of *In Tune with Heaven* that, 'of all the new writing of texts for the church today, that of hymns and worship songs is the most common and important'.[44] The report was not well received, but the sentiment which this quote reflects is, I would argue, a very important one. If only we could identify and encourage a successor to Charles Wesley, for the importance of music and singing in the Christian scheme of things cannot be overestimated if music is 'the greatest good that mortals know. And all of heaven we have below.'[45]

Henry Purcell wrote the much loved tune *Westminster Abbey* which is sung as a hymn to J. M. Neale's translation 'Christ is Made the Sure Foundation'. 'The permanence found in this hymn is provided by Christ "the corner stone" and the Trinity who continue "while eternal ages run".' But 'we, as Christians, are living stones, moved and used by God; the thing that we will do permanently, according to Neale, is to adore God "in glad hymns eternally".'[46] Can it be that hymns have such eternal importance? Whatever the answer to that question, I believe that their significance in the here and now is often grossly underestimated.

NOTES

[1] Augustine, *Confessions*, IX, tr. E. Pine Coffin, London: Penguin, 1961, p. 190.
[2] Augustine, *De Musica*, ET New York: The Fathers of the Church, 1947, see especially book six.
[3] W. Jordan, 'Augustine on Music', in H. Meynell (ed.), *Grace, Politics and Desire: Essays on Augustine*, Calgary: University of Calgary Press, 1990, pp. 123–135.
[4] Quoted in *In Tune With Heaven: The Report of the Archbishops' Commission on Church Music*, London: Hodder and Stoughton, 1992, p. 35.
[5] See above p. 121.
[6] *In Tune With Heaven*, p. 46.
[7] The French philosopher Michel Serres reacts against the preoccupation of philosophers with language by proposing that smell has priority over language. His arguments could equally apply to music. See R. Mortley, *French Philosophers in Conversation*, London: Routledge, 1991, p. 53.
[8] See above pp. 113–114.
[9] Shakespeare, *Twelfth Night*, I.i.
[10] See Astley and Savage in this volume, referring to Nietzsche (below p. 220). Nietzsche was an accomplished pianist and composer and went so far as to say that music was 'something for the sake of which it is worthwhile to live on earth'. But, unsurprisingly, he would have repudiated any notion of its having divine significance. He became disillusioned with Wagner because of Schopenhauer's influence on him. See F. Nietzsche, *The Birth of Tragedy and the Case of Wagner*, ET New York: Vintage Books, 1967.
[11] George Steiner, *Real Presences*, London: Faber and Faber, 1989, p. 19.
[12] James MacMillan on Radio 4.
[13] Steiner, *Real Presences*, p. 19.
[14] Karl Barth, *Wolfgang Amadeus Mozart 1756/1956*, Zurich: TVZ Verlag, 1956, p. 7, quoted in Colin Gunton, 'Mozart the Theologian', *Theology*, XCIV, 761, 1991, p. 346.
[15] *ibid.*, p. 348.
[16] *In Tune With Heaven*, p. 34.
[17] B. Northcott, in *The Independent*, 25 May 1991.
[18] Benjamin Britten, on receiving the first Aspen Award, 31 July 1964, quoted in C. Campling, *The Food of Love*, London: SCM, 1997, p. 21.
[19] J. Obelkevitch, in J. Obelkevitch, L. Roper and R. Samuel (eds), *Disciplines of Faith*, London: Routledge, 1987, p. 563.
[20] *In Tune With Heaven*, p. 34.
[21] Sermon delivered in Ely Cathedral on the Feast of St Etheldreda 1997 by Canon

John Beer.

22 Peter Moger, unpublished sermon delivered in Ely Cathedral, 4 May 1997.
23 Hans Küng, *Mozart: Traces of Transcendence*, London: SCM, 1992, p. 33.
24 *The Methodist Hymn Book*, p. iii.
25 *The Methodist Hymn Book*, p. iv.
26 Obelkevitch, *Disciplines of Faith*, p. 550.
27 D. H. Lawrence, quoted by Obelkevitch in *Disciplines of Faith*, p. 554.
28 Obelkevitch, *Disciplines of Faith*, p. 554.
29 Alan Ecclestone, *Yes to God*, London: DLT, 1975, p. 59.
30 Owen Chadwick, *The Victorian Church*, Part II, London: A. & C. Black, 1970, p. 397.
31 Steiner, *Real Presences*, p. 183.
32 Steiner, *Real Presences*, pp. 184–185.
33 *The Times*, 25 February 1995.
34 Obelkevitch, *Disciplines of Faith*, p. 555.
35 Radio 4, *The Sunday Programme*, 26 February 1995.
36 Peter Moger, *Music and Worship: Principles to Practice*, Nottingham: Grove Books, 1994, p. 14.
37 Owen Chadwick, *The Victorian Church*, Part II, London: A. & C. Black, 1970, p. 398.
38 Obelkevitch, *Disciplines of Faith*, p. 554.
39 Obelkevitch, *Disciplines of Faith*, p. 554.
40 Joanna Trollope, *The Men and The Girls*, London: Bloomsbury, 1992, p. 74.
41 Brian Wren, *What Language Shall I Borrow?*, London: SCM, 1989, p. 5.
42 Owen Chadwick, *The Victorian Church*, Part II, p. 398.
43 Owen Chadwick, *The Victorian Church*, Part II, p. 397.
44 *In Tune With Heaven*, p. 55.
45 J. Addison, 'A Song for St Cecilia's Day'. See A. Gulkelch, *The Miscellaneous Works of Joseph Addison*, London: G. Bell, 1940, p. 22.
46 *News of Hymnody*, Nottingham: Grove Books, January 1995, p. 1.

11

Make Music for the Lord

Emmanuel Gribben

THE PRACTICAL CONTEXT

I have just returned from Sunday morning Mass and I feel good. Good about my priesthood, my ministry and the parish I serve in. The reason for this was the uplifting, prayerful and joyful experience of the Eucharist which has just taken place. I stood at the altar and listened to the Great Amen resounding through the church and thought to myself, 'Yes Lord, it is good to be here.' Yes of course there were screaming babies, choreographic disasters amongst the altar servers, and the tempo and tuning of some musical items was not entirely as one would have wished. But – and this is a very important *but* – we were worshipping God in spirit and in truth. We were trying to give of our best to the glory of God and in so doing we glimpsed the truth that, yes, the liturgy was the source and summit of the church's activity.[1] This was no mere theory propounded by the Council Fathers but a lived reality, and we were being sustained and uplifted by our worship.

Many factors have served to make our parish worship so positive an experience. However, one aspect in particular concerns me in this brief essay, namely the music. We have made significant changes in our approach to music in this parish and these have paid dividends. We set up a music group comprising an array of different instruments. Side benches were removed from the front of the church to accommodate this new group together with the choir, who were persuaded to come down from the organ loft at the rear of the church. The organ was retuned to enable it to play with the other instruments. New hymn books containing a selection of acclamations and Mass settings were purchased for the congregation and the ministry of cantor was expanded and developed somewhat. The result, after much hard work, patience and sensitivity, is that we rejoice in a congregation that really participates and not merely sings *at* Mass but sings *the* Mass. What has been achieved here is not unusual or extraordinary but something that, given the will and the investment of time and resources, is possible in any parish, even where resources and personnel seem scarce.

I believe that the real problem is that most of us are not yet sufficiently convinced of the importance and priority that music in our worship must be given. If we really took on board the Council Fathers' assertion that our musical tradition is a treasure of inestimable value occupying a place higher than that of any other art,[2] then we would pour the necessary resources and energy into liturgical music. In consequence, before continuing to discuss some of the practical aspects of how we should sing, it would be worthwhile asking the question: Why do we need to sing in the liturgy?

WHY SING?

When the Council documents were written there was some astonishment among members of the Second Vatican Council that the subject of music should comprise a separate chapter of the Liturgy Constitution almost equal in length to the chapter on the Eucharist.[3] This was an indication of the importance of music in the liturgy and reflects the fact that its rôle was seen by the Council members as essential to the liturgy. They state: 'As sacred song united to words, it [music] forms a necessary or an integral part of the solemn liturgy.'[4]

Music Serving the Expression of Faith

The pre–eminence afforded to music reflected an appreciation of the power and influence that music could exert upon an act of worship. One of the primary functions of music lies in its ability to enable the assembly to express their faith. Faith, like love, if never expressed lies dormant and begins to die. It is in expressing our faith that we renew and strengthen it. The American bishops, in their now classic document on church music, wrote:

> Love never expressed dies. Christians' love for Christ and for each other, Christians' faith in Christ and in one another must be expressed in the signs and symbols of celebration or it will die.[5]

Music's great powers of signification render it a powerful symbol for the expression of our faith. The scholastics reminded us that in speaking of God and the things of God we are at best *homines balbutients*, 'poor stutterers'. However, just as those who stutter in speech can often sing with ease, so we who stutter in our words about faith can take courage and sing those words with a great degree of trust and faith. All our spoken words, because of the limitations of language, are incapable of bearing the depths of meaning to which they point when dealing with the ultimate realities and mysteries at the heart of our worship. The right music can enable our faith and love of God to find as deep and complete an expression as possible. The American bishops in the same document underline how vital the effective expression of our faith is to the whole of our spiritual growth when they state: 'Faith grows when it is well expressed in celebration. Good celebrations foster and nourish faith. Poor celebrations weaken and destroy it.'[6]

In music we have a tremendous resource for the upbuilding of communities of faith. The potential is enormous, as is attested by the crucial part music has played in the growth of communities such as Taizé. However, in the American bishops' statement there lies a serious warning. To sing bad liturgical music that frustrates the expression of faith is not merely neutral. By failing to express and renew faith, it can begin to destroy it. The right music sung well in our parishes is not just a desirable extra; it has an essential part to play in the sustenance and growth of faith in our communities.

Full, active and conscious participation has virtually become the battle-cry of post-conciliar liturgists. Participation has certainly been placed at the top of the liturgical agenda by the Council. One has only to attend a football match or the Last Night of the Proms to see how powerfully music can weld a group of people into a homogeneous assembly. Music has the unique ability to resonate inside two individuals at the same time. It can almost immediately enable a whole congregation to unite as one voice singing the same rhythm and at the same pitch. Through a common song a congregation can address the Lord as one people and share the fact that God is present among them and for them. Rhythm, whether it is oral, aural or visual, locks people together to each other and to their common values.

The reality taking place goes still deeper. When a congregation sings together as one voice it is not merely a group of people united in song, but the voice of the church. By virtue of our common baptism we are grafted onto the body of Christ. When the local community gathers for worship, the gathering is not merely a chance grouping of individuals, but rather the coming together of the baptised, the people of God, who in gathering manifest and effect the church. Music plays an invaluable part in enabling us to express and experience our identity as church. In his response to the question as to why Christians sing when they are together, Dietrich Bonhoeffer wrote:

> In singing together it is possible for them to speak and pray the same word at the same time; in other words because they can unite in the Word ... it is the voice of the Church that is singing together. It is not you that sings, it is the Church that is singing, and you as a member of the Church, may share in its song.[7]

Through our song we can express our baptism. We manifest and fulfil the truth that we are 'a chosen race, a royal priesthood, a consecrated nation, a people set apart to sing the praises of God'.[8] Moreover, through our song we participate in that unceasing hymn of praise from Christ to the Father. As members of his body, the church, we are drawn into his eternal song of thanksgiving.

Music Serving Celebration

With the conciliar reform there has been a recovery of the understanding of the liturgy as a celebration. The Fathers of the Second Vatican Council, quoting St Paul, tell us that we come together giving 'thanks to God for his unspeakable gift' (2 Cor 9:15).[9] In the liturgy we are expressing our gratitude to the Father for the gift of his Son. In fact Joseph Gelineau has suggested that the Father gave us music because without it we could not begin to express our gratitude for so wondrous a gift.[10] Every liturgy is a celebration, a feast, a commemoration of the Easter victory of Christ. Profound participation in such a celebration without song is inconceivable.[11] The quality of joy and enthusiasm which music adds to community worship cannot be attained in any other way. If we are to respond to God in accordance with our human nature then that response necessarily involves song. It is the nature of the beast; at a party or festive gathering the natural thing to do is to break into song. Surely, therefore, when we gather around the Lord's table to celebrate the heavenly banquet we too must sing!

Music Serving Ritual

Anthropologists are agreed on the essential part that music must play in ritual. Combined with ceremonial choreography, music is the mode by which the liturgical act is carried out. Without music, a liturgical act loses much of the rhythmic structure that is so important in ritual

activity. Music itself is built upon the good use of repetition, the need
for rhythm and pattern. Characteristics such as these comprise the
essential ingredients for ritual. It too requires structure, rhythm,
pattern and repetition. Aidan Kavanagh points out that when the ritual
rhythms of sounds and sight disappear, what one is left with is more
a seminar or a classroom lecture.[12] That is, one is left with modes of
activity that separate more than integrate. We need music for our
rituals and these in turn are what build and shape our communities. If
we seek evidence of this we need only look to the power of ritual in
Northern Ireland. The songs, the beating of the drums and the parades
are far more than harmless gestures. It is rituals such as these that
sustain the identity and the divisions between the communities in that
land. Ritual, and music as a vital part of it, are very powerful forces
indeed.

Music Revealing Structure

Music highlights the texts of our liturgies and makes them more
prominent than if they were merely said. Hence, by singing certain
texts we can reveal the structure of our rites. For example in singing
the gospel acclamation we highlight and underline the importance of
the word and draw attention to the fact that when the Scriptures are
read in church, Christ is present and speaking to his people.[13]
Likewise, the Eucharistic Prayer is the centre and high point of the
Mass. In singing the Eucharistic Acclamations we seek to make this
evident. Music therefore has a necessary part to play in providing
balance and shape to liturgical celebrations.

HOW DO WE SING THE MASS?

Clearly music is not a peripheral aspect of the liturgy. It is an essential element to celebration, to ritual and to the adequate expression of
and upbuilding of our faith. The question remains, How do we set
about enabling our congregations to sing the Mass? How do we find
the right music which inspires, uplifts and enables our communities to
pray and praise God?

The starting-point for such a quest must be with sensitivity to the
specific parish, an awareness of the traditions of that parish, an awareness of the advantages and limitations of the particular building and
its acoustics. Often I have attended diocesan music days and summer
schools at which hundreds of musicians would enthusiastically learn
new music and then try to perform the same music in their home

parish. Sometimes this would work well, but some musicians seemed unable to appreciate that a catchy and exuberant song that worked fine with a group of enthusiastic and trained musicians would not work so well with an aged congregation. And a choir of three elderly ladies accompanied on a harmonium could not perform some very grand Gloria for massed choirs and trumpets, try as they might! Sensitive adaptation to the resources and the people available is essential.

The principle needs to be established that the primary musical resource in any parish is the *congregation itself*, and that the rôle of the choir, organist and other musicians is to carry out their ministry in the service of the assembly. They are to make their talents available for the glorification of God and the sanctification of his people. Their ministry, like all others, is one of service. They are there to enable the congregation to pray and give praise to God.

Participation Needs Cantors

In the wake of the Council, out of a concern for participation, many parishes experimented by misguidedly disbanding their choirs or distributing them among the congregation. Such an experiment was attempted in my home parish when I was a boy. The result was that the choir, scattered throughout the church, became self-conscious and they too stopped singing.

If we want the congregation to participate then we must, if possible, bring our choirs into the main body of the church and develop the ministry of cantor. No teacher would walk into a classroom, stand at the rear behind the children and attempt to teach them a new song. It would seem absurd. However, in many churches, choirs sing new music from the gallery in some vain hope that parishioners will pick it up. Basic communication principles apply here as in any other situation. There is a need to have eye contact, to speak to people, to help them to feel at ease and to offer them guidance and leadership. This is the rôle of the cantor, an ancient ministry which we must rediscover and develop. To carry out this ministry one doesn't have to have a voice like Luciano Pavarotti's; a simple clear voice, a certain degree of tact and the ability to hold a melody suffice.

Admittedly, the few minutes before Mass when the cantor rehearses new music with the congregation can be fraught with problems. However, if we set our sights low, and do not expect too much too soon, eventually we will build a repertoire of acclamations and hymns in our parishes. Of course this presumes that we resist the temptations of too much novelty and choose good quality music that is suited to the capacity of the congregation. We must avoid the all too prevalent tendency to short-termism, the seeking of instant results. The American bishops, in regard to this, stated that:

> To admit the cheap, the trite, the musical cliché often found in popular songs for the purpose of 'instant liturgy' is to cheapen the liturgy, to expose it to ridicule and to invite failure.[14]

If the purpose of music is to express and respond to the profound mysteries of our faith, then there can be no place for the sentimental or the banal. Hence musicians and clergy must exercise discernment and not blindly accept every new piece that crosses their path.

Evaluating the Liturgy

Whilst there are, especially of late, good liturgical resources being produced,[15] there is also much that is not worthy of the mysteries we celebrate. Without the restraining control of art, the sentimental and the banal can soon result. Four criteria should be applied in assessing the suitability of music for our worship. There must be a musical, a literary, a liturgical and a pastoral judgement.

The musical judgement asks whether the music is technically, aesthetically and expressively good. This is a judgement that should be made by competent musicians. Further, there is a *literary judgement* to be made. Is the text to be sung faithful to the Scriptures and to the church's liturgy? Is it poetically good? Surely we do not really want to be singing about 'breaking bread together on our knees'. (This text invariably conjures up in my mind visions of parishioners rather zealously snapping long French baguettes across their knees ...)

The liturgical judgement reminds us that music's rôle is ministerial and must serve the liturgy. It is the nature of the liturgy that determines the type of music required. The Poulenc *Gloria*, for example, is a magnificent composition but wholly inappropriate for a celebration of the Eucharist. Its scale and length would completely unbalance the rite. It would be like placing the dome of St Paul's over our local parish church. No doubt it would be very splendid, but wholly out of place. The degree to which music is faithful in its service of the liturgy and the assembly constitutes a vital part of its liturgical worth. The current approach is to search for themes and relevance, but this, while being laudable, must not be the sole operating principle.

The pastoral judgement not only asks whether a particular congregation is able to sing the music, but also whether a particular congregation should be singing a certain composition. We may find in the hymn book a song that captures perfectly what we feel the

Scriptures are saying, but the pastoral judgement may well settle for a less appropriate hymn because this congregation will be more familiar with it and will sing it much better. Participation and a rousing sing may be more desirable than thematic unity. These are the pastoral judgements and compromises that every liturgy planner must weigh.[16]

Evaluating our music and choosing the right music for a particular congregation demand careful attention. If we are prepared to do so, if we are prepared to develop the ministry of cantor and can find competent accompanists, then there is no reason why we cannot transform the quality and spirit of our worship. We are not in need of extraordinary resources. Someone with a reasonable singing voice and an adequate accompanist can dramatically improve the worship of a community. I remember for one Vigil Mass inviting a teenage lad and his friend simply to sing the psalm, lead us in some simple acclamations and sing a responsorial song at communion. In so doing they rejuvenated that evening Mass. Joseph Gelineau suggests that with regard to the music in our worship, we ought perhaps to dare to do less in order to mean more.[17] This is wise counsel.

Two Essential Principles

Whatever judgements and pastoral strategies we may decide upon, it must always be with two principles clearly in mind. First, music is the servant of the liturgy and must never be allowed to dominate. Secondly, music is an integral and necessary part of our worship. If we can hold these two principles in balance then they will provide a foundation for the development of the musical life of our parishes.

Often in the past priests have invited me to come and teach some new music and thereby liven up the Mass. I understand their clear wish to enhance the joyfulness of the liturgy and to 'thaw out' some of God's 'frozen people'. However, such an approach remains superficial. The 'dance band on the Titanic' principle is being called into play. The ship is going down, but let us entertain the passengers as a distraction whilst we sink. A much more radical solution is required. Music has to be seen as a part of the ship that keeps us buoyant. If our music is one with the liturgy, one with the source and summit of our Christian lives, then it will not merely distract or entertain but will nourish and sustain us. It will keep the ship afloat.[18]

NOTES

[1]   *Constitution on the Sacred Liturgy*, trans. C. Howell, Cirencester: Whitegate

Publications, 1963, n. 10.

2 *ibid.*, n. 112.

3 J. Jungmann, in *Commentary on the Documents of Vatican II*, ed. H. Vorgrimler, New York and London: Burns Oates/Herder & Herder, 1967, vol. 1, p. 76.

4 *Constitution on the Sacred Liturgy*, n. 112.

5 American Bishops' Committee on the Liturgy, *Music in Catholic Worship*, The NPM Commentary, ed. V. Funk, Washington, D.C.: The Pastoral Press, 1983, n. 4.

6 *ibid.*, n. 6.

7 Dietrich Bonhoeffer, *Life Together*, London: SCM, 1976, pp. 43–45.

8 1 Pet 2:9.

9 *Constitution on the Sacred Liturgy*, n. 6.

10 Joseph Gelineau, *Voices and Instruments in Christian Worship*, Collegeville, Minnesota: The Liturgical Press, 1964, p. 27.

11 A. Bugnini, *The Reform of the Liturgy 1948–1975*, Collegeville, Minnesota: The Liturgical Press, 1990, p. 47.

12 A. Kavanagh, in *Music in Catholic Worship*, p. 60.

13 *Constitution on the Sacred Liturgy*, n. 7.

14 American Bishops' Committee on the Liturgy, *Music in Catholic Worship*, n. 26.

15 In Britain we have available some excellent resources composed by the Thomas More Group of composers, and in America GIA publications have issued some very fine liturgical music.

16 American Bishops' Committee on the Liturgy, *Music in Catholic Worship*, nn. 30–39.

17 Joseph Gelineau, *The Liturgy Today and Tomorrow*, London: Darton, Longman and Todd, 1980, p. 94.

18 This chapter is adapted from an article published in *Priest and People*, with permission.

12

Jazz – Lewd or Ludens?

Bill Hall

'He's constantly renewing himself through the music'[1] was a Billy Strayhorn assessment of Duke Ellington, the colossus of twentieth-century music. Strayhorn, as Ellington's co-composer and arranger, was certainly well placed to make such an assessment. Ellington was constantly renewed through his phenomenal creativity. By drawing on the creations of artists such as Ellington, we too are renewed, or re-*created*.

EARLY DAYS

For as long as I can remember, music in general – not least jazz – has been for me an important source of that process of renewal, of re-creativity. As a teenager with an evangelistic fervour to share my enthusiasm for jazz, I sought permission from my headmaster to form a jazz club. At the time there was an interest in revivalist jazz. It was largely of minority interest, but in the words of Francis Newton, 'there were probably few grammar schoolboys, attenders of youth clubs, and other youth organisations who had not become familiar with it.'[2] In Britain the focus for this interest centred largely on our own so-called 'trad bands' with vocalists often modelling themselves on earlier jazz pioneers. My aim was to create a forum in which, without the ideal of being able to play, we could at least explore this passion beyond the exigencies of the British commercial offerings.

I believe my headmaster entertained a colourful if somewhat disturbing image of jazz, arising from his knowledge of the environment out of which much of it had developed. Certainly he did not share my enthusiasm. To him the image projected by jazz was incom-

patible with that of the respectable grammar school. All school societies had to be supervised by a member of staff. He was confident that
no member of staff would supervise a jazz club. I was prepared for
this: the art master played drums in a local band and, given official
approval, he had already agreed to accept responsibility. His back to
the wall, the headmaster then insisted that it must be called 'The
Modern Music Society', and that we should not restrict ourselves
solely to jazz.

Here was an irony I later savoured. The proposed change in title
was in tune with the thinking of some of the luminaries of this art
form, one which by this time had become an international musical
language. 'Jazz' as a category has long been recognised as too restrictive. Saxophonist Ornette Coleman classified himself 'as a composer
who also performs music'.[3] In a radio broadcast in 1968, Duke
Ellington made a similar observation. 'We've all worked and fought
under the banner of jazz for many years, but the word itself has no
meaning. There's a form of condescension in it.'[4] To Ellington there
were only two categories of music: good and bad. There is no doubt-
ing the category into which his music is classified. Igor Stravinsky,
Percy Grainger, Constant Lambert and Leopold Stokowski are among
those who, in different ways and at different times, acclaimed him one
of the greatest living composers.

While agreeing that problems arise from its use, I will continue to
use the word 'jazz', solely for ease of description.

CLUB AND CHURCH

The north-east of England was the birthplace of a minor social revolution in entertainment provision in the early 1960s. Increased holiday
travel abroad had widened the horizon of people's expectations of
entertainment. A test case in Newcastle upon Tyne made it possible
to extend licensing hours. The revenue generated by this change, and
by the new ancillary gaming facilities, provided the fees for the most
expensive of cabaret artists. Out of this combination of social expectation and changed legislation the cabaret club was born. In 1965 I
became chaplain to the newest – and one of the grandest – of these
clubs.

The origins both of the cabaret club and of chaplaincy work of this
nature can be found in the nineteenth century: the former in the
variety theatre and the northern workingmen's club, and the latter
with the birth of the Actors' Church Union in 1898/9. The ACU is
the body now responsible for the appointment of some 200 chaplains

to those who are engaged professionally in the performing arts in film, television and theatre – on-stage, backstage and front of house.

Each cabaret club had its own house band of musicians who played for dancing and invariably had the additional responsibility of accompanying the cabaret. Many able musicians were attracted to the North-East for regular and lucrative employment in these clubs. After playing from a printed score for cabaret and dancing, they would often seek stimulus through an after-hours' jazz session. This is a time-honoured tradition for generations of jazz musicians. Francis Newton has described such occasions as both collective experiment and contest, and in support he quotes two musicians of an earlier generation from Kansas City. First, drummer Jo Jones explained collective experiment. 'The guys did take the time to study, and when they had found something new they would bring it to the session and they would pass it round to the other musicians ... it was a matter of contributing something and experimentation. Jam sessions were our fun, our outlet.'[5] Pianist Mary Lou Williams, writing about the same town at the same time, described the competitive aspect: the 'cutting' or trying to outplay someone else. She recounted a specific occasion on which Coleman Hawkins, the leading tenor sax player of the time, made an appearance in Kansas City. He had not anticipated the stiff competition from the very able tenor men already present there, who included Lester Young and Ben Webster. Mary Lou was awoken by Webster at around four o'clock in the morning. He told her to get up; it had been a long session 'and all the pianists are tired out now. Hawkins has got his shirt off and is still blowing. You got to come down.'[6]

I am unable to match such a colourful story, but those elements of contest (albeit with less animosity) and collective experiment were also present in the north-east of England in the 1960s, and this made for some very exciting sessions. It was, though, a risky business. With each session, and especially when they improvised, the musicians' skills, reputation and pride were on the line. What is more, they would repeatedly create within each session and yet the creation, unlike that of some other art forms, was transitory, existing just for that glorious moment. As Ornette Coleman explained: 'Jazz is the only music in which the same note can be played night after night but differently each time.'[7]

My ministry gave me access not only to some excellent music and memorable moments but also to a lively community of musicians. Very quickly friendships were forged. Some of the musicians were living in the parish where I was working. When we met jazz was not the only subject we discussed, but it was a prominent one. The familiar references to the gospel roots of jazz developed at one time into an exchange of information on jazz musicians who had been explicit in expressing their religious faith through their music. We probably talked about the bassist Charles Mingus, who liked to think of the bandstand as something like a pulpit: 'You're up there ... trying to express yourself. It's like being a preacher in a sense.'[8] On another occasion Mingus emphasised: 'I believe in God ... And that's what the music is about, man.'[9] We might have talked about Coleman's belief that a dedicated performance was just 'showing that God exists.'[10] We certainly did talk about saxophonist John Coltrane and what he described as his 'spiritual awakening' in 1957.[11] There was much interest in his 1964 recording of *A Love Supreme*. It is a work in four parts, comprising 'Acknowledgement', 'Resolution', 'Pursuance' and 'Psalm'. Coltrane wrote: 'This album is a humble offering to Him. An attempt to say "Thank you, God" through our work, even as we do in our hearts and with our tongues.'

Although I cannot recall all the musicians who were mentioned in our conversation about jazz and faith, I know that we did not talk about Duke Ellington. I remember with great clarity being amazed many years later to learn that, at that very time and unknown to us, Ellington had accepted an invitation to play a concert of sacred music in San Francisco's Grace Cathedral. It was to be a contribution to the celebrations for the Cathedral's consecration. His autobiography, published a year before his death, bore the title *Music Is My Mistress*. Through what he came to call his 'Sacred Concert' he was introducing that 'mistress', his music, to the other 'mistress', his faith. That, entirely coincidentally, was an accurate description of what was developing out of our own conversations.

My original suggestion was that some of the pieces we had discussed might be performed in concert in church. The better suggestion came from the musicians themselves. They would play their own music if I would produce the words. With a little help from a friend, I did. The theme was 'God's actions in history and today'. It started with the Bible and progressed from there giving examples of the Holy Spirit at work in the world, with the final section – 'Alabama Today' – reflecting on the issue of racial harmony in 1966 America.

The music was to be provided by six very talented musicians then working in the cabaret clubs: alto saxophonist Ron Aspery, pianist Bob Stephenson, vibraphone player Jack Gibson, bassists Roy Babbington and Kenny Wright, and drummer Ronnie Pearson. Jo Jones' 'collective experiment' was a notable mark of this ensemble. When we met for practice, each individual would suggest themes to illustrate passages of the text. In an atmosphere of mutual encouragement, agreement would be reached, the music would be played and I would talk through the text. It could, however, never be a full rehearsal. Allowance had to be made for improvisation on the day.

The press coverage during the week leading up to the performance on the eve of Whitsunday 1966 was not encouraging. The church's sacristan, a respected member of the congregation, told a reporter she thought it was 'terrible'. 'I don't think jazz music is reverent. I don't think it blends in with the sacredness of the church ... Still, I shall be here ...'[12]

She was there on that sunny Saturday afternoon, along with an audience of about a hundred or so others. The atmosphere was charged; the musicians played as I could never have expected. We planned for an interval to follow the account of Jesus' crucifixion. This section would end with the familiar account of Jesus' death and the music would be tacit. On the day of the performance I spoke those words and then, totally unexpectedly, Ron Aspery grabbed his saxophone and released a piercing wail. I knew my movement from the church was to signal the start of the interval but, for what felt like several minutes, I could not move. When eventually I did, I walked outside the church into the sunlight and was soon joined by a hundred people walking around the church grounds in total silence, lost in their own thoughts, reflecting on what they had just experienced.

A rousing resurrection theme introduced the second part of the programme, and so on to Alabama. At the end of the performance, the vicar, a Fellow of the Royal College of Organists, rushed to the organ where he improvised as never before. It could have been an expression of relief that his young curate had not, after all, been the cause of a scandal in church! I prefer to believe, however, that he had been inspired by the afternoon's experience.

My assessment of the event can justifiably be dismissed as biased. Let me, then, quote from an account by Luke Casey, a journalist who was present. 'The jazzmen played music such as has never been heard in church before. It was sweet like the voice of angels, harsh like the cruci-fixion. It soared all the way to heaven and sank to the doors of hell.' Through it all there came the story: 'one that chilled, moved and inspired ... told ... as though it was the first time ever. Yet it was the old, old story of God.' Of the musicians he wrote: 'Like many other people they were not particularly strong Christians. Yet after the session they all declared that "something wonderful" had happened to them.' Drummer Ronnie Pearson told him: '[It] really happened here today. I wouldn't care if I didn't play at the club for another year, just to have experienced that.' Ron Aspery's description of the aim and experi-ence was reported as: 'to put over how God had revealed himself to men, and that is exactly what I think happened today. It was marvellous.'[13] One of the musicians told me that, far from 'cutting', he did not even think about impressing – the music just flowed through him. Almost word for word, he had articulated drummer Billy Higgins' experience that 'Music doesn't come from you, it comes through you.'[14] This is an experience common to all art forms.[15]

Luke Casey also interviewed the sacristan; or rather, she sought him out. She had the grace to tell him: 'It was magnificent. I don't mind admitting I was very wrong indeed.'[16]

THE ELLINGTON EXPERIENCE

In 1968 I was appointed full-time Chaplain to the Arts and Recreation in North-East England, which allowed more time for work with artists of all art forms. We converted a former rectory into an arts centre where those who were engaged professionally in the arts could meet and experiment. Musicians, skilled and adept at improvisation, played a leading part in some of the sessions, especially those with visual and performing artists.

There were more opportunities to develop what had been started on that Whit Saturday two years earlier. On one occasion the text came from *Markings*, the spiritual journal of Dag Hammarskjöld. The ensemble consisted of piano, bass, drums/percussion and one front line saxophone doubling on flute. Peter Ayton, who played bass, remembers well the experience as they responded 'through improvisation to some extremely profound spiritual writings. This was coupled with performing in church, complete with all its aesthetic and spiritual ambience, to offer further succour to the extemporisation.'[17] Once again the reaction of both musician and audience bore testimony to the power of this music in this setting.

One of the first entertainers I met as chaplain to the cabaret club was Will Gaines, a dynamic exponent of be-bop, the high speed style of tap dancing that has close associations with jazz. He had grown up in Detroit alongside some of the most important jazz musicians such as pianist Tommy Flanagan and guitarist Kenny Burrell. Among others Will had worked with were the saxophonists Lucky Thompson and Sonny Stitt. In 1969, a few years after we met, he worked with Ellington and his orchestra in a concert in Bristol – part of Ellington's Seventieth Birthday Tour. The piece which Will Gaines danced came originally from the major show *My People*, that Ellington had conceived and composed in 1963. The piece was called *David Danced*, and illustrated the reference in the Second Book of Samuel to David dancing before the Lord with all his might (2 Samuel 6).

It was not until 1982, eight years after Ellington's death, that I realised the significance of this. Will invited my wife and me to St Paul's Cathedral where, as part of the Festival of the City of London, there was to be a further attempt to present items from Ellington's sacred music, and Will was again to dance *David Danced*.

I was to learn there that Ellington's Sacred Concerts were very important to him. He had said, quite simply, 'This is personal, not career. Now I can say out loud to all the world what I've been saying to myself for years on my knees.'[18] His deep and abiding faith sprang from his mother. From her he derived his love of the Bible. He used to claim that he had had three educations: 'the street corner, going to school and the Bible. The Bible is the most important. It taught me to look at a man's insides instead of the outside of his suit.'[19] His was a simple faith, but a powerful one. Those who knew him knew this.

In the programme for the first Sacred Concert, in Grace Cathedral in 1965, Ellington wrote: 'As I travel from place to place by car, bus, train, plane ... taking rhythm to the dancers, harmony to the romantic, melody to the nostalgic, gratitude to the listener ... receiving praise, applause and handshakes, and at the same time, doing the thing I like to do, I feel that I am most fortunate because I know that God has blessed my timing, without which nothing could have happened – the right time or place or with the right people. The four must converge. Thank God.'[20]

That first Sacred Concert had two British performances: in 1966 in Coventry Cathedral and the following year at Cambridge's Great St Mary's Church. In 1968 all but one of the compositions were replaced for his second Sacred Concert which was performed at the Cathedral of St John the Divine in New York. His third Sacred Concert was premicrcd in Westminster Abbey in 1973, the year before he died.

The concert in St Paul's Cathedral in 1982 was organised by Derek Jewell. Then jazz critic of the *Sunday Times* and an Ellington biographer who knew him personally, Jewell brought to the task both a knowledge and an awareness of the importance of this music to Ellington. He chose carefully those who were to take part, just as Ellington had always done. The music was played by the Alan Cohen Big Band, which had the finest available musicians, including pianist Stan Tracey and saxophonist John Surman. It was hosted and narrated by actors Rod Steiger and Douglas Fairbanks Jnr respectively. Among the featured singers were Tony Bennett, Adelaide Hall and the Swingle Singers. Jazz fusionist Jacques Loussier took part, and the dancers included Wayne Sleep as well as Will Gaines dancing the mighty *David* piece.

For whatever reason, even this glittering array of talent was insufficient to ensure success. It is true that the Cathedral's acoustics merged badly with the amplification of television. Reviewing the event, Peter Vacher commented that 'therein lay the concert's ruin, with the combined evils of showbiz and Channel Four considerations overtaking its solemn and serious purpose. Sound failed and lights went down, a floor manager waved his arms and the ghost of Ellington got up and crept away.'[21] Of course these technical difficulties detracted from the performances, but I had a different theory to explain the failure. I admitted to Derek Jewell that I had been disappointed by the concert and was relieved to hear him agree. Ellington had always insisted that only the best talent should be engaged for his Sacred Concerts. Derek Jewell had applied this criterion. Why then had it not worked?

There followed a number of questions in quick succession to which I attempted some answers. I suggested that the Sacred Concerts were a personal statement or testimony. Without Ellington they lost their integrity. Perhaps the integrity could be found through the objective structure of the church's eucharistic liturgy? The liturgical invitation to confession, for example, could be replaced by Ellington's *Don't Get Down On Your Knees To Pray Until You Have Forgiven Everyone*. Employing items from the Sacred Concerts in this way might create the equivalent of an 'Ellington Mass'.

Derek was interested. We met the following day to explore further my suggestion. We also reached agreement on where it might be performed in this form and who might play. The main problem would be finance. The costs for arrangements, rehearsals and performance would be substantial, but there could be no charge for admission to an act of worship. Sadly, Derek Jewell died before I was able to raise the necessary money. But I was determined to carry forward the proposal.

I chose the items from recordings of the Sacred Concerts, and decided where they should fit into the Eucharist. I was pleased with the result, yet I was concerned that in performance the music might be a pastiche. To my mind only one musician could save it from this: Stan Tracey, one of the greatest jazz musicians to emerge from either side of the Atlantic. As well as leading almost every ensemble from duo to octet, he also leads a highly acclaimed big band which 'mirrors his piano work in its pungent dynamism'.[22]

In 1989, as an expression of his admiration for Duke Ellington, Tracey issued the record *We Still Love You Madly*. 'Duke Ellington', he told me, 'was for me one of the great musicians of the twentieth century and in the field of jazz beyond category.' The influence of

Ellington on Stan's music has been well documented, as have similarities in approach. His piano playing, for example, has been described as 'pungent, percussive and harmonically daring', influenced as it is by the piano styles of Ellington and Thelonius Monk.[23] Further, Felix Aprahamian, writing in the *Sunday Times* in the 1960s, described Tracey as the most individual harmonist since Frederick Delius. Thirty years earlier Ellington had himself enjoyed the same comparison, made by Constant Lambert in the *New Statesman*[24] and by Percy Grainger before Ellington had heard of Delius![25]

There could, then, be no one better qualified and more sensitive to the task than Stan Tracey. Will Gaines effected our introduction and I outlined my plan. Stan was immediately enthusiastic.

While still trying to raise the money, I sought the support of Peter Baelz, the then Dean of Durham, for the work to be premiered in Durham Cathedral with the Cathedral choir singing some of the items. His enthusiasm matched that of Stan himself. But the Master of the Choristers at first rejected the idea. For him this music was totally inappropriate for a church. Only after further discussions with the Dean did he reluctantly agree.

These preparations would have been quite futile without the necessary finance. A chance meeting with Lord Palumbo, then Chair of the Arts Council of Great Britain, provided the immediate impetus. He, too, was enthusiastic and passed on the information about the proposal to a friend who was a jazz aficionado. This led to the surprise arrival of a cheque for a substantial contribution to the costs. Additional support came from Northern Arts, and then, at the last minute, from Durham County Council. Stan immediately started work. First, the recordings had to be transcribed because there were no printed scores available. For jazz this is not unusual. As Francis Newton noted: 'Most jazz scores, if they exist at all, are ... rather simple and rough approximations, which leave at least the detail of tone, rhythm, inflexion, and the like to the jazz instincts of the players.'[26] This was a major task out of which Stan produced arrangements for his fifteen piece orchestra; arrangements which capture the spirit of Ellington without slavishly reproducing every note, so that the musicians can be engaged in 'a process of discovery, rather than a series of achievements'.[27] As such, the Mass was to be a living creative art form rather than a pastiche.

The musicians engaged by Stan Tracey always read like a who's who of British modern jazz, including both a range of major soloists and some of the foremost section players. The premiere in Durham Cathedral on 6 October 1990 was no exception. With Stan Tracey on piano were saxophonists Peter King, Jamie Talbot, Art Themen, Alan

Skidmore, with baritone saxophonist Dave Bishop; trumpeters Guy Barker, Henry Lowther, John Barclay and Alan Downey; trombonists Malcolm Griffiths, Chris Pyne and Geoff Perkins; bassist Dave Green and drummer Clark Tracey. The choir was augmented by jazz vocalist Tina May, who sang some of the solo parts, and, of course, Will Gaines was engaged to dance the *David* piece.

Two days before the event James Lancelot, the Master of Choristers, and I travelled to London for the rehearsal of the orchestra at the Black Bull in Barnes. Once James heard the orchestra he was fully converted!

On the afternoon before the evening Eucharist the orchestra performed Stan Tracey's own masterwork *Genesis*, a suite in seven parts based on the creation narrative from the Book of Genesis. Reviewing the work, Anthony Troon describes Tracey as 'one of our most abundantly inspired composers' and further comments: 'The curious thing is that, while it does not plagiarise Ellington in any way, the shade of the Duke sits somewhere in the middle of it, snapping his fingers and narrowing his eyes against the cigarette smoke. Ellington would have loved it madly; alternatively, he would have hated it because it was not his creation.'[28] Between each movement I inserted the relevant verses from the Book of Genesis together with poetry chosen by David Jasper, including works by Henry Vaughan, Dylan Thomas, William Blake, Gerard Manley Hopkins, Dante and Ezra Pound. Professional actors Edward Wilson and Val McLane were the readers. The original reason for the performance of *Genesis* was financial. As it was a concert we could charge for admission and any profits would help to defray some of the costs of presenting the Eucharist. In the event it was itself a great artistic success, 'in every way worthy of such a magnificent setting'.[29]

In his address at the Eucharist Peter Baelz,[30] by now Dean Emeritus, focussed on the importance of offering: 'There is something deep within the human spirit which wants to offer, to give of its utmost and best, not so much to celebrate human achievement as to signify the presence of ultimate mystery. More than once [Duke Ellington] made reference to God's juggler who, having no skills in music or in song, offered the only skill he had, and in the silence of an empty church stood before the high altar and juggled to the greater glory of God, and to the astonishment of a chance observer. In discerning, developing and sharing our gifts of nature and grace we align ourselves with the creative and redemptive purposes of the One whom we call God, and in offering them in worship we participate in his continuing work of making creation whole and holy.' Ellington's music was, he said, 'a music of memory and hope. Finding its own place at a particular time and in a particular culture, it nevertheless speaks universally to the human condition. And so speaking it takes its proper place in a universal sacrifice of praise and thanksgiving.'[31]

Peter Baelz had certainly captured the spirit of the occasion; the common experience that what was taking place encapsulated that spirit of praise and thanksgiving. It was, without doubt, both a profoundly spiritual experience and a musical triumph, as well as being a fitting tribute to the greatness of Duke Ellington.

Pete Martin reviewed the occasion for *The Guardian*: 'Critics of Duke Ellington's music have been rather hard on his extended pieces, and few have enthused over the Sacred Concert which became his preoccupation late in life. Such works, it is said, lack structure and development. . . . What this view neglects, however, is that Ellington's sacred music was conceived as explicitly functional – its purpose being to accompany and stimulate worship, to engender a sense of both humility and transcendence. The congregation of Durham Cathedral on Saturday night had a rare and precious opportunity to experience the power of Ellington's inspiration. The problem of structure was solved . . . by the simple but brilliant expedient of setting a selection of the Duke's sacred music in the context of a full-scale Mass . . . Stan Tracey arranged [the pieces] with evident respect, and the whole memorable event was realised by Tracey's orchestra with the Cathedral choir and soloists. The occasion seemed to draw a response from the musicians which surpassed even their usual impressive standards, as they evoked the spirit of the Duke while telling their own stories . . . I'm sure that there were many in the Cathedral on Saturday who felt Ellington was present among them.'[32] Another reviewer referred to the occasion as 'quite unforgettable', adding 'the Cathedral's eleventh-century Romanesque setting proved uncannily conducive for jazz, both when the orchestra blended with the Durham Cathedral Choir and when this great big band simply rocked in rhythm.'[33]

My aim of bringing together jazz and the cathedral choral tradition of music had worked well because of the high quality of each and through mutual respect. It was a triumph both for Stan and for James Lancelot, who by now was very enthusiastic and eager to repeat the experience. Over the next few days, we received very many letters of appreciation.

World-renowned saxophonist Peter King, whose 'glorious floating alto solo on *Come Sunday*'[34] lives on in the inner ear, expressed his immense admiration for Stan Tracey's achievement and told me that, for him, it was 'unlike any other occasion, both moving and awesome'. For Tracey himself, this opportunity to play Ellington's 'sacred music in Durham Cathedral was one of the most uplifting moments in my career'.

James Lancelot lent his voice to the demand for it to be repeated and, in May 1993, it was. The occasion was a combined celebration: the 25th anniversary of the Chaplaincy to the Arts and Recreation and part of the celebrations of the 900th anniversary of the laying of the foundation stones of Durham Cathedral.

Once again it was a great success. Of the many expressions of appreciation let one suffice. Professor Dick Watson, an expert on Victorian hymnody and a member of the Archbishops' Commission on church music, attended the performances both in 1990 and 1993: 'The first time I found the "Ellington Mass" to be extraordinarily exciting, and felt therefore that the second time I would be disappointed. In fact, I did find it less exciting because I knew what to expect, but I now found it deeply satisfying spiritually. It was on the second occasion that the integration of the music and the Mass particularly struck me.'[35]

Further performances followed, at Dewsbury and in Ely Cathedral. The Ely event was reviewed in *Jazz UK:*

> As a committed atheist, I had to keep reminding myself that the Anglican Eucharist service which took place in Ely Cathedral ... was not a jazz concert.... That this was a large congregation, not a jazz audience, was fascinating, for they were clearly responding to much of the music ... and when dozens of communicants filed up to take Bread and Wine while Stan ruminated in that unaccompanied Ellington solo style of which he is a master, I actually wished I could join in. The robes, the smiling faces, the incredible beauty of one of Britain's finest cathedrals, right down to dear old Will Gaines leading the Dean ... and all the rest down the aisle after the final *David Danced Before The Lord,* like some beatifically smiling Pied Piper, was pure joy. A wonderful, uplifting evening of rare beauty.[36]

This was a familiar expression of the experience from each venue. Each time, new ground was broken. Those who came for the music, and particularly to hear Stan Tracey, were caught up in the spirituality; while those who came because it was an act of worship were caught up in the music.

The Ely performance was recorded for BBC's Radio 4 to be broadcast as part of its programme of Sunday morning worship. Drastic editing was essential and was executed with great skill but, sadly, much was lost in the process. Nonetheless, the BBC received many letters of congratulations. They also, it should be added, received a few letters from some who felt that this music was inappropriate for church worship. *Déjà vu!*

THEOLOGICAL REFLECTIONS

On being asked to describe the effect of jazz in church, I instinctively reach to borrow from Miles Davis' words in dismissal of critics: 'Who can tell what love is?'[37] Through the occasion, the setting and the musicians with their skill, sensitivity and insight we have experienced what Ellington described as 'mystical moments': those occasions when performers' muses 'were all one and the same'.[38] The listener also has a part to play. As John Coltrane recognised, 'the audience in listening is in an act of participation ... And when somebody is moved as you are ... it's just like having another member of the group.'[39]

Words are inadequate to express this experience, but I am struck by the similarities between jazz and the church. Each has grown, for example, out of a liminal environment. In Neil Leonard's words, jazz for its part has existed 'on the fringes or in the cracks of the social structure ... flourishing in egalitarian, simply organised groups and guided mainly by peers, they operate at a remove from many ordinary responsibilities and preconceptions and freely question conventional standards of behaviour. Their climate is charged with potency and potentiality that encourages experimentation, spontaneity, improvisation and imagination in art and conduct.'[40] A deep sense of understanding and fellowship grew out of these circumstances.

Yes, 'improvisation and imagination'. Improvisation plays an important part in this because, as Francis Newton points out, 'it stands for the constant living re-creation of the music, the excitement and inspiration of the players which is communicated to us.'[41] Imagination is important as 'the ability by which human beings make present what is absent. It is at the root of the intellect ... It enables me to make present what is in fact not immediately present to me. It is also the ability to dream ... It is, too, the root of action. Because the imagination is a feeling and a feeling after, it is pre-conceptual. It allows images and symbols to do the work of communication before the intellect tries to order them and give them coherence and connection. Imagination is creative.'[42]

Similarly, it is out of a liminal environment, either actual or metaphorical, that many Christians have found what Miles Davis has described as 'a continuing process of discovery'.[43] This could be a description of the journey of faith, and for this improvisation and imagination are also necessary.

Pianist Dave Brubeck described improvisation in jazz as 'about the only form of art existing today in which there is freedom of the individual without the loss of group contact'.[44] As Christians, we are the players, improvising like the musicians by listening to the other players and making our contribution within the clearly-agreed rules by which we play.

This concept of *play* is rooted in the depths of our very being. Hugo Rahner argues that play is a neglected strand running through the Bible.[45] In the account of creation in the Book of Proverbs, for example, Divine Wisdom is depicted as 'at play' at the creation of the world. 'When he fixed the heavens firm, I was there, when he laid down the foundations of the earth, I was by his side, a master craftsman, at play everywhere in his world.'[46]

Divine Wisdom at play. This element of play has, then, to be seen as an essential element in God's nature. In fact, Psalm 104 speaks of God relaxing by romping in the sea with Leviathan,[47] and an old rabbinical tradition similarly depicts God as spending the last hours of daylight playing in the sea with this monster.

For Rahner, 'the picture of God rejoicing over the completion of the world still has about it something of the delight taken by the artist in his own free-roving fancy and so keeps alive the idea of play'.[48] At creation God established order, an order which is in marked contrast to the chaos of much human existence. Music gives a voice to that order and can also fuse together into a spiritual unity the joy and sadness of our human condition within creation. In all great music we can perceive an act of playing; one which includes a childlike awareness, just as the child at play combines celebration with a committed seriousness. This reminds us of Jesus' injunction that we become as little children.

God at play. This is our God in whose image we are made. *Deus sapiens. Deus ludens.* But we are *homo ludens* before we are *homo sapiens.* Sadly, in our work-based society that element of play is only allowed to be peripheral to what are often misrepresented as the essentials of life. The musician stands out in marked contrast to this, because music is a form of playing. It is no accident that in most languages the word used for play is the same word as the one used for playing a musical instrument. The jazz musician is in tune with this, employing the imagination and playing through the improvisation. In the eucharistic setting with Ellington's music, the combination of dance and music expresses this powerfully. This was highlighted in a letter to me from Edward Wilson, Director of The National Youth Theatre, who had been present at the 1990 performance. 'The Mass,' he wrote, 'so often a ceremony of great solemnity, should also be an occasion of great joy and exuberance. There can be no more potent an example of this than when the great jazz hoofer, Will Gaines, literally dances for joy at the conclusion of the Mass in the setting created from Duke Ellington's music.' The ending to the traditional Latin Mass, *Ite missa est* is thus replaced by *Ite et ludite* – Go and play.[49]

When we play jazz, or influence its playing by our receptive listening, we can be tuning in to something very precious and at the very depths of our being. When this takes place in church we can be consciously or unconsciously aware that *homo ludens* is truly made in the image of *Deus ludens*.[50]

NOTES

[1] Nat Hentoff, *Jazz Is,* p. 26, quoted in Neil Leonard, *Jazz: Myth and Religion,* Oxford: Oxford University Press, 1987, p. 58.

[2] Francis Newton, *The Jazz Scene,* Harmondsworth: Penguin, 1961, p. 245.

[3] John Rockwell, *All American Music,* p. 190, quoted in Leonard, *Jazz: Myth and Religion,* p. 33.

[4] Derek Jewell, *Duke,* London: Sphere Books, 1978, p. 25.

[5] N. Shapiro and N. Hentoff, *Hear Me Talkin' To Ya,* p. 264, quoted in Newton, *The Jazz Scene,* p. 72.

[6] *ibid.* Duke Ellington also referred to 'cutting contests where you defended your honour with your instrument' (Jewell, *Duke,* p. 213).

[7] Robert I. Fitzhenry (ed.), *Say it again Sam: A Book of Quotations,* London: Michael O'Mara Books, 1996, p. 311.

[8] Hentoff, *Jazz Is,* p. 64, quoted in Leonard, *Jazz: Myth and Religion,* pp. 47–48.

[9] Brian Priestly, *Mingus,* pp. 114, 192, quoted in Leonard, *Jazz: Myth and Religion,* p. 49.

[10] Nat Hentoff, *The Jazz Life,* London: Panther, 1964, p. 211.

[11] John Coltrane, *A Love Supreme,* notes from record sleeve (1964).

[12] As reported by Luke Casey, *The Northern Echo,* May 1966.

[13] *ibid.*

[14] Len Lyons, *The Great Pianists,* p. 127, quoted in Leonard, *Jazz: Myth and Religion,* p. 41.

[15] See Paul Klee's simile of the tree, in his essay 'On Modern Art', in Robert L Herbert (ed.), *Modern Artists on Art,* New York: Prentice Hall, 1964, pp. 76-77.

[16] *The Northern Echo,* May 1966.

[17] Peter Ayton in a letter describing the event, September 1997.

[18] Jewell, *Duke.* p. 181.

[19] *ibid.,* pp. 27, 33.

[20] *ibid.,* p. 182.

[21] Peter Vacher, *Jazz Journal International,* 1982.

[22] From *Jazz: The Essential Companion,* quoted by Chris Yates for programme notes in *Ellington in Durham 1990.*

[23] From *New Grove Dictionary of Jazz,* quoted by Chris Yates for programme notes in *Ellington in Durham 1990.*

[24] *New Statesman,* quoted by Jewell, *Duke,* p. 68.

[25] Jewell, *Duke,* p. 60.

[26] Newton, *The Jazz Scene,* pp. 20-21.

[27] *ibid.,* pp. 98-99.

[28] Anthony Troon, in *The Scotsman.*

29 Pete Martin, reviewing *Genesis* in *The Guardian* on Tuesday 9 October 1990.

30 Dean Peter Baelz and Canon Ronald Coppin had throughout been encouraging and supportive of my plans for the Ellington setting. Sadly Peter Baelz was to retire before the plans were realised, but John Arnold, his successor, continued to offer the same support and agreed to invite his predecessor back to preach at the premiere.

31 From Peter Baelz's address in Durham Cathedral on 6 October 1990.

32 Pete Martin's *Guardian* review of Tuesday 9 October 1990.

33 Chris Yates, 'Newcastle Notes', in *Jazz in the North East,* issue 18, jan/feb/mar 1991, p. 5.

34 *ibid.*

35 Quoted by Jon Williams, 'Cherished Ambitions', in *Choir and Organ*, April/May 1995, p. 27.

36 Item included in 'Scene and Heard', in *Jazz UK*, Jan. 1997.

37 Hentoff, *The Jazz Life,* p. 215.

38 Priestly, *Mingus*, p. 137, quoted by Leonard, *Jazz: Myth and Religion*, p. 54.

39 Frank Kofsky, *Black Nationalism and the Revolution in Music*, p. 226, quoted by Leonard, *Jazz: Myth and Religion*, p. 69.

40 Victor Turner, quoted by Leonard, *Jazz: Myth and Religion*, pp. 25-26.

41 Newton, *The Jazz Scene*, p. 130.

42 Peter Baelz, *A Serious Business: A Theatre-Church Consultation* (papers from a conference sponsored by the Actors' Church Union), 1989, p. 67.

43 Hentoff, *The Jazz Life,* p. 177.

44 Brubeck, quoted in Fitzhenry (ed.), *Say It Again Sam*, p. 311.

45 Hugo Rahner, S.J., *Man at Play,* tr. Brian Battershaw and Edward Quinn, London: Burns & Oates, 1965.

46 Proverbs 8:27-31 (Jerusalem Bible).

47 Psalm 104:24b-26 (Jerusalem Bible).

48 Rahner, *Man at Play,* p. 21.

49 *ibid.*, p. 61.

50 For the references to 'play', I owe much to the following: Rahner, *Man at Play*; Johan Huizinga, *Homo Ludens*, London: Paladin, 1970; Josef Pieper, *Leisure, the Basis of Culture*, tr. Alexander Dru, London: Fontana, 1965; Harvey Cox, *The Feast of Fools*, Cambridge, Mass.: Harvard University Press, 1969.

13

Music in General Education

Coral Davies

INTRODUCTION

A group of infants visited Durham Cathedral for the first time.[1] Despite careful preparation in school and sympathetic help from a verger, the truly awesome setting seemed to make them nervous and insecure. While recognising that being overcome with awe and wonder is part of religious experience, their teacher was concerned lest they be alienated by an experience they could not understand nor communicate. Then the children found one of the most recent additions to the thousand-year-old building: the North nave window by Mark Angus. They began to relax. Their faces showed their appreciation of the bright clear colours. But something was still missing, until a small voice began to sing: 'Red and yellow and pink and green, purple and orange and blue'. Then the whole group joined together singing, 'I can sing a rainbow, sing a rainbow, sing a rainbow too.' Through the song, which they had learnt in school, the children could celebrate and share their feelings in a way that they could not do in words alone.

This illustrates the two layers upon which we work in music and education. At one level, we teach skills, repertoire and musical knowledge; but we also seek to 'develop insight through music into areas of experience some of which cannot easily be verbalised' (DES, 1985, p. 2). As Langer suggests, music mirrors the forms of human feeling 'with a detail and truth that language cannot approach' (Langer, 1942, p. 235). But it is difficult to plan a curriculum in terms of the forms of human feeling. The National Curriculum Working Group recognised this and confined themselves in the main 'to those aspects of music education which can be taught and assessed, whilst acknowledging that its benefits will in practice be both wider and deeper' (DES, 1991, p. 4).

MUSIC EDUCATION IN HISTORICAL CONTEXT

In the first half of the twentieth century, music's benefits, seen as being to ennoble the mind through the contemplation of beautiful forms, were approached largely through the singing of 'good songs' (with carefully chosen words to express approved sentiments) and the hearing of 'good music'. The emphasis was on the acknowledged masterpieces of the western classical tradition, and educators were confident that they could define 'good' in this way.

This diet of listening and singing was for the majority. Those who could afford to pay and (later) those provided with tuition by LEA instrumental services could receive more intensive training in performance and music reading, take music examinations and play in orchestras; but these were selective activities, not part of the class music curriculum.[2]

By the 1960s, there were clear signs of tensions in music classrooms. Many children were finding class music 'useless and boring' (DES, 1968), and school inspectors could refer to the 'almost total rejection of "school music" by a vast majority of older pupils' (DES, 1970). It was not music itself which was being rejected; but rather that the gap between school music and music in everyday life had become too large for pupils to bridge, and schools were challenged to acknowledge and deal with this lack of coherence.

The resulting concern to re-examine music as a curriculum subject for all pupils – addressed, for example, in influential Schools Council projects at York and Exeter (Paynter, 1982; Ross, 1976) – focussed on the belief that the arts are important ways of knowing and experiencing our feeling lives (Langer, 1942) and on music's perceived rôle in the education of the feelings. In translating this into a music curriculum, helping pupils to compose their own music was seen to be important, a new idea in music classrooms. Composers such as Addison, Maxwell Davies, Dennis, Paynter, Schafer and Self became involved in music education and showed that 'it was possible to offer children a view of artistic endeavour from the inside [which was] valuable for its own sake [and] for the way in which it enhanced understanding of other artists' work' (Paynter, 1992, p. 5).

The children themselves wanted to engage in active music-making, instrumental as well as singing, and popular musicians as well as the composers already mentioned had shown that this could be done without the years of formal training expected in a classical music education. It became increasingly difficult to concentrate solely on the traditional musical heritage – western classical music – in school, and to ignore the dynamic musical culture outside. Contemporary 'classical' composers had, anyway, become increasingly dissatisfied with traditional forms, and their search for new forms of expression was reflected in titles such as *New Sounds in Class* (Self, 1967), *The New Soundscape* (Schafer, 1969) and *Sound and Silence* (Paynter and Aston, 1970).

It was also important to take account of what pupils were experiencing out of school. The challenges and opportunities offered by popular and non-western musics in education have been much discussed elsewhere (see, for example, Vulliamy and Lee, 1976, 1982; Scarfe, 1993). The vigorous protests (by, for example, O'Hear, 1991; Scruton, 1991) about the inclusion of non-classical examples in the National Curriculum proposals re-opened the debates of the 1970s and 1980s about both the rôle of schools in preserving 'our cultural heritage' and how such a heritage should be defined.

MUSIC EDUCATION TODAY

It is now generally accepted among music educators that there are 'many different styles of music, appropriate for different purposes and offering different kinds of satisfaction and challenge' and that 'excellence may be found in any style of musical expression' (DES, 1991, p. 7). Our concern is still with the pursuit of excellence, but not with arguing for superiority of any one style or culture over another, for this would deny the richness which has come into the music curriculum with popular and non-western musics and fail to value much that pupils will bring to their lessons.

The belief that music education should offer all children practical experience in the three main activities of musicians crystallised (in Swanwick, 1979) into a model for the music curriculum summarised as C(L)A(S)P. This put Composition, Audition and Performance at the centre, with Literature (of and about music) and Skills as important but subsidiary components.

Music education at the end of the twentieth century, then, concerns itself with trying to provide practical experience of and insight into performing, composing and listening, for all children, within the constraints of time and resources. It recognises that children are highly motivated to engage in music, and that they have their own cherished experiences of music from life outside school; these experiences can be a rich resource and starting point for development in classrooms, and need to be taken account of. It emphasises the practical, creative nature of music and seeks to provide opportunities for all children, not just those who have lessons outside the classroom, to make music for themselves as well as to listen to the music of others. It recognises that our job is to 'extend pupils' musical experience and knowledge and develop their appreciation of the richness of our diverse musical heritage' (DES, 1995, p. 2).

The changes in school music first received formal recognition in GCSE syllabuses and were then established in the National Curriculum. The National Curriculum teaching requirements for music at 'key stages' 1 and 2 (covering the primary school) specify that 'listening, and applying knowledge and understanding' be developed through 'the interrelated skills of performing, composing and appraising'. Among other things, pupils should be taught:

- how to control sounds through singing and playing (performing skills);
- how to create and develop musical ideas (composing skills);
- how to respond to, explore and explain their ideas and feelings about music (appraising skills); and
- how to listen to music with concentration, attention, knowledge and understanding.

National Curriculum attainment targets set out the knowledge, skills and understanding that pupils are expected to have at the end of each key stage. At the age of eleven, the majority of pupils may be expected to achieve 'level 4' of the attainment target in music:

Pupils identify and explore the relationship between sounds and how music reflects different intentions. While performing by ear and from simple notations they maintain their own part with awareness of how the different parts fit together and the need to achieve an overall effect. They improvise melodic and rhythmic phrases as part of a group performance and compose by developing ideas within musical structures. They describe, compare and evaluate different kinds of music using an appropriate musical vocabulary. They suggest improvements to their own and others' work, commenting on how intentions have been achieved. (DFEE/QCA 1999)

It can be seen that the National Curriculum gives prominence to activities. But music education also involves knowledge and understanding. Teachers have developed an active approach and learnt to manage practical activities involving sound in crowded classrooms, to organise group music-making and encourage social skills and to tolerate attendant noise levels. There is still much to learn about how to engage and educate children's musical minds more fully. An interest in the study of music as an act of mind has been reflected in a steady outpouring of writings: e.g., Witkin, 1974, Sloboda, 1985, Serafine, 1988, and Swanwick, 1988 and 1994.

What can pupils know in relation to music? What is, or should be, the knowledge content of the music curriculum? As we have seen already, the National Curriculum confines itself to aspects we can teach and assess; but it actually gives little detailed guidance even here, for the Working Group's brief was to advise on a statutory framework which would be 'sufficiently broad and flexible to allow schools wide discrimination in relation to the matters to be studied' (DES, 1991, p. 67). Teachers still have the responsibility to decide content, so long as knowledge and understanding are developed through practical engagement.

The central focus of musical knowledge and understanding is seen to be the musical elements of pitch, duration, dynamics, tempo, timbre and texture, and their use within musical structure (DFE, 1995). Music teaching has moved away from a study of set works, the rudiments of theory and the rules of composition to focus on processes, asking 'How does this piece work?', rather than 'Who wrote this and why is it great?' (Dunbar-Hall, 1993).

This focus allows pupils to recognise musical elements in their own, as well as in others' work. There is an emphasis now on understanding the musical elements in a wide range of music, studying specific examples from different cultures and styles, and becoming aware of 'their common elements as well as their differences' (DES, 1991, p. 51).

There is a danger in this approach, however, of listing elements and looking for pieces (or worse, bits of pieces) simply as illustrations of the element selected. We have to remember that 'elements' are not music. Music results when the elements are combined into musical structures; and some musical structures are more successful than others. So the important questions for pupils to address are 'How are the elements used?' and 'How does the piece work as music?' Appraising music deals with what the pupil can hear, so development of aural awareness and analysis (in performing and composing, as well as audience listening) is a key factor. The analytical study needs to be balanced by the interpretive side, what music means to its creators and listeners, and whether it fulfils its expressive purpose.

While helping their pupils to understand what music is and what it means to us, teachers must also continually remind themselves why they engage in and teach music at all and be prepared to justify its place in schools. Although there is a National Curriculum for music, the inclusion of music in the curriculum for all children has again been called into question (in 1997–8). Many primary school teachers lack the musical education and confidence to teach music, and resources continue to be inadequate in some schools. The reduction in free instrumental tuition as funds were devolved to schools seems certain to have a detrimental effect on the rich musical activities which, though never available to all students, have nevertheless been a valuable part of British musical education since the 1950s.

MUSIC EDUCATION IN PRACTICE

The following examples show the richness and variety of the National Curriculum in practice.

Example 1. A year 8 class (age 12–13) had been composing pieces for the voice. In this lesson, they were introduced to a recording of Berio's *Sequenza III*. A worksheet with a series of sharply focussed questions helped pupils to analyse what they were hearing. After hearing the music several times, the pupils used graphic scores with a view to adopting similar structures in their own work (DES, 1992).

This example illustrates the National Curriculum reference to the interrelated skills of performing, composing and appraising.

Example 2. Secondary pupils, working with a professional musician from the Japanese *shakuhachi* tradition, 'have worked on creating "single line" music of extreme expressiveness using the two pentatonic scales of *shakuhachi* music ... as pitch material. Structural devices have included "breath phrase" ... and "mountain form", where the music increases in pitch, speed, volume and intensity towards the middle and decreases in all of these at the end (a form based on the shape of Mount Fuji). Ornamentation has also been explored' (Moore, 1992a).

This illustrates the important contribution that professional musicians have made in enriching the curriculum, and the possibility that 'magic can happen when the previously separated worlds of professional musician and school music collide' (Moore, 1992b).

Example 3. In a suburban infant school the reception class is led by the teacher in a game of 'Pass the tambourine.' The instrument is passed around a circle to musical accompaniment. When the music stops, the child with the tambourine improvises a short solo. The teacher encourages pupils to explore the instrument's capabilities, concentrating on variations in timbre and dynamic. Such games help children to 'refine their listening skills and to expand their span of concentration [and] to listen with care to the sounds around them' (DES, 1991, p. 85).

Much of the work in infant schools tends to focus on careful listening to, and exploration of, sound. Indeed, as already mentioned, this has been a feature of music education for all ages from the 1970s onward, reflecting the preoccupation of adult composers. As children get older, they can explore more sophisticated instruments and electronic sound sources.

Technology has made a revolutionary contribution to music education, though its full potential is still unexplored in many classrooms where it tends to be used only for traditional ends – e.g. keyboard tuition and the teaching of notation and aural skills. Though it is used for composing, many pupils are still working in terms of what we could compose on traditional instruments. At least technology has brought such activity within the reach of many more people. But music technology, especially when combined with exploration into musics of non-western cultures, can open up whole new worlds of sound and experience for contemporary composers. For example, Stockhausen 'became aware that the Javanese have an expanded time-scale with much slower and longer events than usual in the west'. Under this influence, and through technology, he has increasingly become concerned with rhythms not previously perceptible, intensifying micro-rhythms, 'devising – through sound – projects and models for a future world' (Stockhausen, 1989, p. 21).

Ellis (whose *Designing Sound*, 1991, encouraged innovative sound exploration in the classroom) points out that education, as well as dealing with the richness of the past, is concerned with 'leading people towards the future, ... generating new knowledge ... revealing new possibilities with unknown boundaries'. Technology will enable us to 'discover and create new worlds of sound'. In this way, too, we may 'encounter and explore areas of experience otherwise denied to us; an inner or spiritual experience which may enrich our everyday life' (Ellis, 1993, pp. 109–110).

Which brings us back to that class of infants needing – and finding in music – a way to 'enrich' their experience of a cathedral. They used a known song to express their response; but children's own compositions may also show how, through music, they can organise and give form to aspects of their feeling lives (Loane, 1984; Davies, 1992, 1993). Such is this *Spring Song*, by Sarah, aged 6 (from Davies, 1993):

NOTES

1   I am grateful to Rita Harris, the class teacher of the children referred to at the beginning of this chapter, for sharing this story with me.
2   This is an important point and one which was seemingly overlooked by critics of the National Curriculum (e.g. Scruton, 1991) who compared the proposals for class music unfavourably with the music education only ever available to the minority.

REFERENCES

Davies, C. V. (1988), 'Music – a Curriculum Subject?', *Curriculum*, 9, 3, pp. 135–139.
Davies, C. V. (1992), 'Listen to My Song: A Study of Songs Invented by Children aged 5 to 7 years', *British Journal of Music Education*, 9, 1, pp. 19–48.
Davies, C. V. (1993), *Young Children as Song-Makers*, unpublished D.Phil thesis, York University.
DES (1970), *Creative Music in Schools*, Report on Education No. 63, London: HMSO.
DES (1985), *Music from 5 to 16*, London: HMSO.
DES (1991), *Music for Ages 5 to 14: Proposals of the Secretary of State for Education and Science and the Secretary of State for Wales*, London: HMSO.
DES (1992), *Music in the National Curriculum*, London: HMSO.
DFE (1995), *Music in the National Curriculum*, London: HMSO.
DFEE/QCA (1999), *The National Curriculum Handbook for Primary Teachers in England: Key stages 1 and 2*, London: HMSO.
Dunbar-Hall, P. (1993), 'Designing a Teaching Model for Popular Music',

International Journal of Music Education, 21, pp. 16–24.

Ellis, P. (1991), *Designing Sound* (Computer Program), Coventry: NCET.

Ellis, P. (1993), 'Resonances of the Future – A Contemplative Computer', in D. Starking (ed.), *Religion and the Arts in Education*, Sevenoaks: Hodder and Stoughton, pp. 106–117.

Langer, S. (1942), *Philosophy in a New Key*, Cambridge, Mass.: Harvard University Press.

Loane, B. (1984), 'Thinking about Children's Compositions', *British Journal of Music Education*, 1, 3, pp. 27–36.

Moore, G. (1992a), 'Gaining Access', *Music Teacher*, June, pp. 34–35.

Moore, G. (1992b), 'Take Your Partners', *Music Teacher*, November, pp. 12–13.

OFSTED (1993), *Music, Key Stages 1, 2 and 3. First Year, 1992–3*, London: HMSO.

O'Hear, A. (1991), 'Out of Sync with Bach', *Times Educational Supplement*, London, 22 February, p. 28.

Paynter, J. and Aston, P. (1970), *Sound and Silence*, Cambridge: Cambridge University Press.

Paynter, J. (1982), *Music in the Secondary School Curriculum*, Cambridge: Cambridge University Press.

Paynter, J. (1992), *Sound and Structure*, Cambridge: Cambridge University Press.

Ross, M. (1976), *Arts and the Adolescent*, Schools Council Working Paper 54, London: Evans/Methuen Educational.

Scarfe, J. (1993), 'Music Education: Whose Music? Whose Education?', in P. Pumphrey *et al.* (eds), *The Foundation Subjects and Religious Education in Secondary Schools*, London: Falmer, pp. 135–147.

Schafer, M. (1969), *The New Soundscape*, London: Universal Edition.

Schools Council (1968), *Enquiry One: Young School Leavers*, London: HMSO.

Schools Curriculum and Assessment Council (1994), *Music in the National Curriculum*, Draft Proposals (Dearing Review), London: HMSO.

Scruton, R. (1991), 'Rock Around the Classroom', *The Sunday Telegraph*, London, 10 February, p. 19.

Self, G. (1967), *New Sounds in Class*, London: Universal Edition.

Serafine, M. L. (1988), *Music as Cognition: The Development of Thought in Sound*, New York: Columbia University Press.

Sloboda, J. (1985), *The Musical Mind*, Oxford: Clarendon Press.

Stockhausen, K. (1989), *Towards a Cosmic Music*, translated T. Nevill, Shaftesbury: Element Books.

Swanwick, K. (1979), *A Basis for Music Education*, Windsor: NFER Nelson.

Swanwick, K. (1988), *Music, Mind and Education*, London: Routledge.

Swanwick, K. (1994), *Musical Knowledge*, London: Routledge.

Vulliamy, G. and Lee, E. (1976), *Pop Music in School*, Cambridge: Cambridge University Press.

Vulliamy, G. and Lee, E. (1982), *Pop, Rock and Ethnic Music in School*, Cambridge: Cambridge University Press.

Witkin, R. (1974), *The Intelligence of Feeling*, London: Heinemann Education Books.

14

Music and Christian Learning

Jeff Astley and Mark Savage

'With the possible exception of architecture,' wrote van der Leeuw, 'music of all the arts stands the closest to religion'.[1] There is also a close relationship between education in religion and (education in) the musical experience,[2] and that is our concern in this final paper. Our focus here is primarily on Christian education understood in terms of the processes that facilitate the learning of those attitudes, values, beliefs, and dispositions to act and experience that may properly be described as 'Christian'.[3]

MUSIC AS ANALOGY FOR CHRISTIAN EDUCATION

The Composer/Performer/Listener Analogy

When working with groups of adult learners we have found the complex interrelationships between the composer, performer and listener, as illustrated in Part One of this book, to be a powerful analogical tool.[4] It illuminates some of the themes of hermeneutics and a number of other important theological issues, and sheds light on the nature of Christian education itself. The analogy is particularly helpful in explaining how learners are affected by the content and processes of Christian learning.

Keith Swanwick has argued that 'the ability to respond adequately to another person, an object, a life experience or whatever is a fundamental and crucial human attribute. To feel a lack of it is to go hungry, to find the world grey and bleak ... An aesthetic experience is primarily and always an intensified response raised into full consciousness. Aesthetic means to feel more powerfully, to perceive more clearly. Its opposite is *anaesthetic*.'[5] This aesthetic experience is analogous to experience in religion. In both music and religion there is creation, expression and response. Reflecting on the act of listening shows that responsiveness is at its heart. It is also an integral part both of the learning act and of religious experience. Responsiveness includes an ability to be open, to wonder and to believe that life can be different. These are some of the central features of religious spirituality, and therefore among the most welcome outcomes of effective Christian education, in addition to being commonly expressed reactions to the experience of listening to great music. And in religion, as in music, listening – rather than being the end-point of a process – can become the starting point for new questions, new learning and a quest for new experiences. Listening can therefore be creative.

More generally, the composer/performer/listener relationship parallels that between tradition, educator and learner. Even when one is 'learning on one's own', by reading a book for example, a 'performer-teacher' is not absent. Rather, the reader serves as both performer and listener, as does the music buff sitting alone silently reading a musical score. One element of dissimilarity is that in the educational relationship the rôles of teacher and learner may be more readily reversed than those of performer and listener, especially in those species of Christian education where a dialogue between the two is encouraged.[6]

Cognitive and Affective Dimensions

'Structuring Reality'

Nietzsche argued that music may function for some people as an alternative to religion as a way of structuring reality, giving expression to their hopes and fears in an ordered form, and enhancing life as it reconciles them to it.[7] We may thus identify a cognitive rôle for music in providing in this way a perspective that makes sense of life; such a perspective will inevitably also encompass and direct our affections.[8]

Music certainly structures our sense of *time* (see Jeremy Begbie's paper, chapter 4, above). It can create its own virtual time, forming different patterns of time within a single, coherent structure. It may also ensnare people in a strange and not always welcome time-frame. Hence those descriptions of what appear to be interminable periods of listening to Wagner operas, when only fifteen minutes have actually elapsed. Timothy Hone argues that music may even be said to structure *space*, both 'horizontally' and 'vertically', operating like a 'multi-faceted object' moving in space (chapter 9, above). Much music is clearly illustrative of *movement*. This often includes an emotional movement, as with the 'financial symphony' suggested by Bernard Shaw to Elgar: '*allegro*: impending disaster; *lento maestoso*: stony broke; *scherzo*: light heart and empty pocket; *allegro con brio*: clouds clearing'.[9] At another level, the effect of the creation and release of tension has been recognised as highly significant in explaining the human brain's reaction to music (see Sloboda, chapter 7, above).

Such reflections provide an educational analogy, in that Christian formation may also be said to involve the development of a new way of structuring reality, as we learn the skills, dispositions and conceptual apparatus that enable us to view the world as God's world, other people as God's children and historical events as the story of the acts of God. This 'experiencing-as', as an epistemological as well as a psychological phenomenon, has been characterised as central to religious experience, spirituality and faith.[10]

Music and the Emotions

The place of emotion, and more generally of feeling or 'affect', in religion and religious education can hardly be overstressed. Jonathan Edwards' classic claim that 'true religion lies much in the affections'[11] is supported by more recent analyses of the nature of religion and the place of 'sacral sentiments' within it.[12] Such accounts imply that both the content and the processes of religious formation should be understood as affective in nature, at least in part.[13]

This emphasis on the formation of emotions in education is not to be seen as anti-rational, not least because emotions (and to some extent other affects, particularly attitudes) may be analysed as having cognitive aspects, components or implications. These are the beliefs, 'apprehensions' or 'thoughts', including appraisals or evaluations,[14] that allow us to judge emotions to be either reasonable or unreasonable.[15] Thus an emotion is unreasonable if it incorporates an unreasonable apprehension: a false belief or unjustifiable evaluation. Some would argue that *critical education in religion* is largely a matter of our learning to be more reasonable about the targeting of our religious emotions and attitudes. This will be the result of our asking ourselves, for example, whether it is rational to worship a God of this sort of character, or to feel guilt for a situation that we cannot change.[16] Others have argued that 'artistic appreciation and creation are fully objective' in that they are based on criteria of value that are objective (though not necessarily absolute) in the sense that it is possible to give 'supporting reasons by reference to one's understanding of qualities of the object'.[17]

There are, however, severe limits to these claims about the rationality of emotions and attitudes, and therefore to educational techniques of rational persuasion in this area. For example, it should be recognised that some emotions, such as being in love, cannot be adjudged reasonable or unreasonable. This is because of the personal character of the evaluations that undergird them.[18] Further, encouraging rational (cognitive) reflection on a person's own emotions may be less important than actually evoking a particular emotion in the first place, if the possession of that affect is deemed to be an intrinsically good thing. David Cooper makes this claim about those musical emotions that are elicited through musical experience.[19] Many Christian educators would wish to make the same point about some of the Christian affections.

There is a considerable literature on the place of emotion in, or the 'feelingfulness' of, music.[20] Music is often (but not always) an expression of emotion, and valued in part on account of this. However, there are real problems with the various philosophical accounts that have been given of the relationship of music to the emotions,[21] and it has been rightly argued that the value of music is intrinsic and cannot therefore be merely the value of the (separable) emotional effect of the music.[22] Nevertheless, educationalists cannot ignore the fact that music usually does have an intimate relationship with the life of the emotions. Even if we could – and should – strip music of all its associations of memory or 'emotional character', 'music would still be an intensely emotional experience'.[23]

Educators are interested in effects, not least where the effects are affects! Indeed, education – as Aristotle insisted – is partly an education of the emotions, teaching us what and how to feel.[24] Musical experience does more than encapsulate emotion. It helps us to 'explore feelings', and 'at its most powerful, reformulates the ways in which we feel life', influencing our perspective on living.[25] Christian educators are also very often engaged in educational processes in which the learning outcomes are similarly related to certain feelings and emotions. In such cases the analogy between religious and musical education can be very close.

The Musical Brain
Electro-encephalogram evidence about hemispherical specialisation within the human brain indicates that (at least for right-handed people) the left hemisphere is primarily concerned with cognition, language and logic – the linear processing that includes musical sequence and rhythm. The right lobe, however, processes non-verbal skills, and the perception of intuitive insight and of the intensity and tonal qualities

of music.[26] Anthony Storr describes an experiment that neatly illustrates the relationship of the two hemispheres in response to music. When he listened to Mozart while under sedation of the left hemisphere, he found the music almost unbearably charged with emotion, but frustratingly unsatisfying. Its appeal was fleeting, and he was unable to perceive any sense of form or purpose.[27] This offers us a striking analogy of the importance of the interrelationship between the cognitive and affective dimensions in Christian education. If education in religion is concerned with the integrity and wholeness of the individual, then it must also be concerned to engage both sides of the brain, and not (as is often the case) only the intellectual left hemisphere.[28] To satisfy the learner in both music and religion it is necessary to keep a balance between the two sides of the brain. This should also prevent our viewing music merely as a corrective to our tendency to engage in theologising that is skewed too much in a cognitive direction.

Paul Robertson contends that composers with a left hemisphere dominance tend to write more dissonant music than those with a right hemisphere dominance. He identifies the right limbic system within the brain not only as the centre of our perception of 'emotional arousals', but also as the centre of religious experience. Arguing that music that provokes a strong emotional arousal from a background of a 'flat' emotional state is felt by many people to have a strong 'spiritual' dimension, he seeks to explain the huge popular appeal of the music of contemporary composers such as John Tavener, Arvo Pärt and Henryk Górecki,[29] whose work has been alluded to on several occasions in this collection.

Musical education has always stressed the rôle of music in stimulating and guiding the (creative) imagination,[30] a function of the right lobe. Helping learners express what they feel or imagine or intuit, areas of experience that cannot be easily verbalised because they are located in the right brain, is a significant task both for musical education and for religious education.[31] Interestingly, although speech has been found to function primarily in the left cerebral hemisphere, song is located primarily in the right. The Augustinian dictum, *qui cantat, bis orat* ('whoever sings, prays twice') may thus have a biological basis, in that hymns, liturgies or 'sung prayers' engage both parts of the brain: lifting up both the mind and the heart to God so as to allow real contemplation and full religious experience.[32] The truly important feature of hymns, as has been noted in a number of earlier papers, is that they are sung and normally sung together. They cannot be properly understood merely in terms of their words, whether as snatches of theology or as (often indifferent) poetry.

The 'fusion theory' asserts that a musical passage is appropriate to, and coherent with, a verbal discourse sung to it 'when it has itself some qualities referred to in that discourse'.[33] Monroe Beardsley writes that the musical substance of a song may well be an exemplification of 'qualities of mind that would already be there to some extent in the tone and timbre of the voice if the poem were read aloud'.[34] Singing is here represented as a modification of speaking – a very human activity that expresses and communicates the whole of a person, and not just her ideas. Others have claimed that in singing 'language itself is transcended', as the words are taken up into heightened expression without being stripped of their ordinary meaning,[35] or that a complex relationship is established between the words and the music in which it may be said that the words 'heighten' the music in creating the 'final product', 'its own integrated work of art'.[36]

Much has been made of the educational (in the sense of formative) rôle of worship in evoking, as well as expressing, religious affections and beliefs.[37] Such a view is consonant with the claim that Christian education is properly an holistic activity that integrates both sides of the brain.[38] Affective Christian education enables individuals to understand and express their emotions. This is not just an individualistic thing, for these emotions themselves contribute to community. 'The power of shared emotion to create oneness or unity between individuals cannot be denied.'[39] As the rest of this volume shows, music's religious relevance is by no means limited to 'church music'. Nevertheless, hymnody and liturgical music are of particular significance as ways of bringing people together: 'by being of one voice, [they] learn to become of one heart and one mind' – that is, a congregation rather than just a collection of individuals.[40] The place of music in the ministry of communal Christian formation that builds up the body of Christ is one that we neglect at our peril.

The Aesthetics and Ethics of Music

The evocative power of music is double-edged, however, for music has the ability to evoke evil emotions, attitudes and beliefs as well as good ones. It is noteworthy that music can have a frightening capacity to impose a common discipline on a crowd, as exemplified by Hitler's huge and tightly choreographed rallies. Perhaps it is for reasons such as these that it has often been feared by the church; or at the very least, distrusted. The untranslatability of musical form into ordinary language has also sown seeds of doubt, as has the emotional ambiguity that music often expresses.

It is therefore difficult to argue that any music is wholly and purely good. But goodness, like beauty, is not just to be found ready-made. In musical terms, as in life, they are sometimes best discovered through struggle with conflict and disorder and its eventual resolution. Evil and discord may then be said to be needed in order to create and reveal their opposites. Christian educators must explore with care the extent to which evil might be incorporated for this purpose into their own proper procedures. For example, although the struggle with disorder may be of central value, does it permit us to include porno- graphic or violent images or narratives within the content of Christian learning? There is no doubt that some form of implicit censorship takes place within most Christian education, as it does in the promo- tion of forms of music. The question is, What are the criteria being employed here? Some would claim that both music educators and Christian educators have a duty to stand out against the premature narrowing of experience that is prevalent in much contemporary secular education.

We have noted that a full education properly includes something that may be described as 'an education of the emotions'. For John Macmurray this must be 'primarily an education of our sensibility', developing an 'emotional knowledge' of the world as it is – experi- enced for its own sake, without any ulterior, utilitarian purpose.[41] On this view the emotions do not work against knowledge, but rather enable a certain way of knowing, with the affective contributing to the cognitive. Such an experiencing-for-the-sake-of-experiencing sounds close to the activity that Simone Weil labelled as 'attention', a form of experience which she portrayed as underpinning both academic study and true devotion.[42] Music may certainly contribute to this 'education for proper seeing', which is an education for seeing things sensitively, as they truly are – even God. It has been argued that a work of art itself is of aesthetic value only 'to the extent to which it is capable of stimulating and sustaining intense and prolonged aesthetic attention'.[43]

Music as Mantra

Historically, particularly in those cultures that have been labelled 'primitive', music has been associated with the power to take over the listener, sometimes creating states of trance or possession. We should take these claims seriously, and examine them critically. In recent years a number of composers have created music that uses simple but striking textures, makes considerable use of repetition, and in which rhythms and harmonies develop with a slow underlying pulse. Allowing for the differences in social structures, such music seems to produce a mood somewhat akin to these more primitive reactions to music. John Tavener describes the effect of listening to music as being like 'soothing pain'. He adds that 'at the age of 53 ... I can finally understand why. Because I see it as a form of prayer ... The act of writing puts me almost in a trance state, where I feel enormously close to God.'[44]

The philosophical theologian (and bishop) Ian Ramsey argued that one of the primary functions of religious language was to evoke religious revelation and experience (in his terms, 'disclosure' and 'discernment'). Ramsey claimed that the 'main merit' of certain theological terms was to provide a 'kind of technique for meditation' that induces religious awareness.[45] Prayer is a prime example of such an evocative use of religious language.[46] In hymnody and a great deal of liturgy these evocative words are complemented by evocative music. This, we may note, is similar to the way in which powerful language, which is evocative of certain feelings and insights, is made even more effective in film and TV drama by the addition of some appropriate 'background music' or film score. Theological education has much to learn from worship about the proper context in which discourse about God is naturally situated and most effectively learned,[47] a context in which music is often central.

We are reminded here of the importance some would place on 'trusting the liturgy', and their insistence that clergy should not worry over much about explaining 'what is going on' in worship, but should instead allow the symbolic and evocative power of the words and actions to speak for themselves. The same may certainly be said for music. The effect of a piece can easily be destroyed by detailed preliminary 'explanation'. Both music educators and religious educators often need to be more reluctant to speak.

Music as a Form of Life

Following Wittgenstein, some philosophers speak of cultures, or communal patterns of behaving and speaking, as 'forms of life'. According to Richard Wollheim, art is such a form of life.[48] Others would prefer to say that art, like (and including) language, originates *in* forms of life, arguing that art has what biblical scholars and others – following Wilhelm Dilthey – call a *Sitz im Leben* ('situation in life'), as it is always created in a specific cultural world and is subject to that culture's own particular conventions.

A number of contemporary philosophers of religion have viewed religion itself in terms of a form or forms of life, which incorporates its own language-game or games with its own distinctive logic or 'grammar'.[49] It is possible to argue that to learn to understand religion fully, and to understand art fully, is to *enter* such a way of action and expression. Neither can be properly grasped from the outside. Those Christian educators who stress the notion of 'lifestyle education' as the central plank of the process of being educated into a religion offer accounts of what education into a form of life might be like. For James Michael Lee, religious formation is essentially a matter of learning this particular way of living. This bears some resemblance to induction into musical creativity, interpretation and expression. Music might even be said on occasions to illustrate the twin and interrelated dimensions of Lee's concept of a 'lifestyle', or pattern of our human life activity, namely totality (incorporating other aspects of human functioning into this way of life) and integrativeness (meshing them together into some sort of order and harmony).[50]

In religious learning, as in music, the interplay within the form of life between the individual and the social is significant. 'Music', it has been said, 'serves to synchronise and socialise':[51] creating both integrity of the individual and participation in community. The work of the individual in composing, performing and listening only makes sense in the light of a wider communal context, in that, however 'private' the experience, it is dependent on skills, traditions and expectations that are shared and passed on within a society. Religion and religious formation function similarly. Even when religion is 'what the individual does with his own solitariness',[52] this religion – as (or as within) a form of life – is a *shared* faith that is properly learned only from and in community. This is true even on those occasions when the religious community is incarnated solely in a pupil and her teacher.

BRIDGING THE GAP: ANALOGY TO PRACTICE

Hermeneutics and Music

If music, like other forms of art, is an instrument of communication and revelation, then questions of meaning and interpretation properly arise for it. These questions are similar to those raised in theology and Christian education.

There has been much debate as to whether the author's intention, including his or her intention to express and communicate emotion, is relevant to our appreciation of a piece of music. It may seem that the author's intentions in music and literature are normative (even perhaps her/his 'unrealised intentions'). But listeners and performers routinely uncover meanings in music that go beyond what the composer intended, as the reader does in literature. Osborne notes that works of art are not like legal documents which are created so as to exclude alternative meanings, but rather are analogous to human verbal and non-verbal communicators. A work of art thus 'carries more meaning than is apparent on the face of it and more meaning than was consciously intended by the artist'.[53]

Theology has recently tended to move away from the historical hermeneutical task, as interpreted by Schleiermacher and others, of unearthing the author's intention as *the* meaning of a (biblical) text. Today it is more usual to claim that meaning is given in a creative process in which the intentions and pre-understandings of the interpreters (listeners, performers) also play a part in a hermeneutical dialogue.[54] This species of interpretation involves a confluence of text and listener, a fusion of their 'two horizons',[55] that enables a revised, renewed tradition of interpretation which is continuous both with the past text and with present cultural experience. Thus, although we are challenged, criticised and changed by the text, we are never absorbed by it. Rather, what emerges from our encounter with the text is 'a new creation of the understanding'.[56] A number of Christian educators have proposed such a dialogical or dialectical account of interpretation as the appropriate model for Christian learning. Thus Thomas Groome argues for a dialectical hermeneutic between the learners' present experience (their 'story' and 'vision') and the past Christian tradition as the proper locus for Christian education. On this view, we learn to be Christian as we select, appropriate, modify and are changed by the conversation between our story and *the* Story (or, better, Stories).[57]

The analogy of the relationship between a musical score and its performance is often used to illustrate the importance of both fidelity to foundations and (constrained and contextualised) re-creativity in the work of the theologian and religious educator. Their rôle is like that of the performer, who brings music to life 'not simply by the technical competence of his playing but even more by his shaping, phrasing and general interpretation, so that there is something of himself in addition to the original vision of the composer'.[58]

This account of the situation may be developed. Paul Kline writes that 'hermeneutic analysis is unquestionably appropriate for the arts or for subjects which form closed systems and do not impinge on other systems in the world.' He quotes Sharpe's claim that there are several interpretations of a Beethoven sonata some of which, in the hands of maestri, will be of equal value; and notes that if an interpretation is regarded as inferior it is often in terms of the 'coherence of the whole piece and in terms of aesthetic beauty'. He goes on: 'It is almost nonsense to talk of a correct or incorrect interpretation, providing the player has not violated the instructions of the composer. Classical composers expected the player to interpret the score of which, quite deliberately, only the essentials were made explicit.'[59] Again the argument is that every text has a surplus of meaning 'within' it, and may give rise to a plurality of plausible interpretations. Nevertheless, Frances Young argues that there are some criteria for 'authentic performances', both in music and in religion.[60] The Christian educator, particularly the teacher and preacher of Scripture, needs to attend to this important debate. (See the discussion by Gordon Giles, chapter 5, above.)

Music as Theological Metaphor and Medium

As has been noted elsewhere in this volume, there is much in music that illuminates the *content* or subject-matter of Christian education, as well as its *processes* or *methods*. Music is the structuring of sound in patterns of rhythm, harmony and melody. While unstructured sound may have its own beauty, it remains unpredictable, haphazard and unsatisfying. In order for music to have 'meaning' it must have structure. Anthony Storr's experience of listening to Mozart when his brain was partially sedated (see above) illustrates this. Music sheds light on the profound human need for order; but it also shows how disorder may be transformed and transcended.

Richard Harries points out that Barth was drawn to Mozart because of that composer's extraordinary capacity 'never to hear the negative except as taken up into the positive'.[61] Music has this almost unique ability, as Harries puts it, to 'do justice to the dark and tragic, whilst at the same time transfiguring them into joy and delight'.[62] It can be argued that it is the duty of Christian artists to face up to the disorder of the world in their art: both to give us an insight into the human world as it really is, and to attempt to show that it can be better. This creative struggle is, perhaps, a parable for salvation, or even a sharing in redemption itself.

Salvation is a process of healing,[63] located in the battle with the forces of darkness and despair. Music often operates in the same way, in the same place. Music can certainly assist the healing process, and not just in the narrow sense of music therapy. Even musicians who would claim no conventional religious faith insist, as Michael Tippett has done, that music can put us in touch with important aspects of ourselves and make us whole again.[64] The duty to face up to the world as it really is does not always have to be explicit in the music itself.

We would argue that the heavenly visions of John Tavener are not diminished just because their composer has chosen not to reveal the struggle which brought them to life. The temptation to select only the beatific, the lovely and the good is dangerous only if it is an attempt to escape and deny the harsher realities of existence.

In the Nazi concentration camp of Terezin, through which 140,000 Jews passed on their way to Auschwitz and the other death camps, music played a vital part in many lives. One survivor, Zdenka Fantlova, admits that music made people forget their situation, but she also says that it gave them hope and helped them to live 'some kind of normal life under abnormal conditions'. The enthusiasm for music in Terezin was astonishing, and the quality of works composed there by Viktor Ullman, Hans Krasa, Pavel Haas and Gideon Klein was of the very highest order. Works such as Ullman's satirical opera *The Emperor of Atlantis* directly addressed the twisted world of 1944, and faced up to the great themes of life and death. Other works, especially *Brundibar*, Krasa's opera for children, had a different function. Enormously popular, it was described by one prisoner as 'sun brought into our dark world'.[65] In Terezin it seems on balance that music was not so much a form of escapism as a means of putting the grim world 'veiled in darkest shadow' into context. In *The Emperor of Atlantis* Ullman enabled his audience to see more clearly the sickness and depravity of the Nazi regime and offered them an allegory for its destruction, while still recognising that they themselves would first have to face death. The opera therefore functioned very much like an apocalyptic text such as the biblical books of Daniel and Revelation.

Music can also surely shed light on the nature of revelation. The interrelationship between composer, text, performer and listener can be a helpful point of reference in understanding the dynamics of revelation.[66] The relevance of this for Christian education, which has often been construed as part of a process of contemporary divine revelation, is patent.[67] The conviction that music *is* itself revelatory of God is as hard to explain as it is commonly stated. As John V. Taylor puts it, 'music comes out and meets (us) as a "Thou", not an "It".'[68] But a word of warning is sounded by Gerd Theissen in his claim that we cannot be sure *what* music reveals. He adds that 'a piece of music can on one occasion be experienced as "revelation" and on another as no more than a structured mass of sound', and notes that 'for many people God does not exist outside a particular "mood". It is therefore a concern of religion to reach out beyond this dependence on fleeting moods.'[69] Nevertheless, Swanwick's description of the aesthetic experience illustrates the value of those 'revelatory' moments which can transform the rest of our lives. And David Tracy has argued that in the greatest classics (he cites Mozart and Beethoven as examples) 'the form ... does express, can communicate a world disclosive of a radical sense of both participation and non-participation in the incomprehensible mystery that is our existence, the mystery which we can now feel, not merely affirm.'[70]

Music can thus be a window onto the divine, a glimpse of the transcendent. Certainly, many composers have felt that their own work has been influenced by a reality quite beyond themselves. An example would be Schoenberg, who set Balzac's line 'I feel an air from another planet', a phrase which Michael Tippett thought to be 'the key to all his being'.[71] But this experience has to be internalised if the composer is to translate it into music, and the listener must also internalise that music – which is for her or him 'out there' – in order to hear it and respond to it. Perhaps this could be a helpful starting point in theological education for an exploration of the relationship between transcendence and immanence.

MUSIC IN THE PRACTICE OF CHRISTIAN EDUCATION

Music has been declared by one Christian educator as having the capacity, more than any other art, of taking a person out of herself, and plunging her 'into a world which may be characterised as divine'.[72] Many have discovered this power of music when it is used within the practice of Christian religious education. 'Listening to the learners' here is instructive. The response to the question 'What does music mean to you?' often elicits such strong statements as 'I couldn't live without music' and even 'Music reveals God to me.'

Types of Christian Education

Christian education may be most broadly understood as including both (i) the *formation* of Christian attitudes, beliefs, emotions, skills and dispositions to experience and action ('formative education'), and (ii) the *critical evaluation or self-criticism* of such a Christian culture, world-view and lifestyle using the tools of logical or moral evaluation ('critical education'). While we have noted some examples of critical education in religion, we recognise that music's main contribution is as an element in formative Christian education. Within such Christian formation or nurture we may distinguish *formal* and *explicit* Christian education, where the intentional facilitation of Christian learning by educators or teachers is acknowledged and recognised, from *implicit*

Christian learning that takes place without such intention and/or intimation – often through the 'hidden curriculum' of worship and church life.[73] Music is clearly a most effective ingredient in this latter form of learning, but it can also be used in more explicit species of Christian education.

Creation and Salvation in Christian Education

We return here to the interrelationship between composer, performer and listener. The composer is able to have direct involvement with the new materials of creation and to explore at first hand the relationship between form and content. To do this is to participate very directly in God's own continuing act of creation, a claim that Jeremy Begbie has explored.[74] The performer re-creates and incarnates the composer's work, but so also does the listener. If responsiveness is at the heart of listening, then far from being a passive and uncreative activity, listening is an essential part of the creative actualisation of the music. We need not all be composers or performers; there are many occasions when simply to listen is enough. In all these rôles people may learn directly about the nature of the act of creation.

Improvisation has been mentioned in earlier papers as a particularly interesting special case of creativity, because it effectively combines all three rôles of composer, performer and listener in one.[75] To improvise effectively some knowledge of musical form is required. But experiments with both children and adults show clearly that even the untrained can find considerable value in improvised music-making. A great deal of such work, for example, has been carried out through the national programme of the Association of British Orchestras, enabling people from the widest possible range of client groups to achieve the highest standards. One project run in a prison was described as a 'kind of collaborative melting pot that influenced the lives of composers, players and inmates permanently'.

Another observation that comes out of this programme of education, this time from work with children with special needs, is particularly relevant to the claim that in both music and religion the activity of creation and that of salvation are essentially bound together: 'If therapy can be defined as an attempt to make us feel more at ease with ourselves, then all music making has the potential to be therapeutic.'[76]

Listening to music can teach us much that is profoundly religious about what it means to receive and appropriate a mysterious phenomenon that is other than and outside ourselves, but which moves and motivates us so intimately. Listening to music can provide a valuable counter-point to our excessively logical and linguistic theologising in religious learning, and encourage a more healthy balance between the cognitive and affective domains. By listening we may come to realise that we can know intuitively just as surely as we can know rationally. The listener's ability to be surprised and to be open to a sense of awe and wonder are capacities that are of considerable value in the development of the religious psyche.

All of which tends to show how musical experience, even if it is only the experience of listening to music, may properly be a piece of Christian education, if the learner learns through it the skills, openness, creativity and transcending vision that are essential aspects of that which is truly religious. If the claims about the healing, salvific function of music and its power to enable us to see differently are also well grounded, then they provide us with further powerful reasons for including music in our pastoral programmes, both educational and liturgical.

Musical experience can feed, excite and challenge people, but it can best do this when the music is allowed to speak for itself. Should our word-based education and liturgy permit this, we will surely add an invaluable extra dimension to our ecclesial endeavours. Music is not just enormously worthwhile in itself and a powerful and revealing analogy for our theologising, it can also serve as raw material for our religious lives. As such, it is a proper part of the substance and style of Christian education.

Some Examples of Practice

Two illustrations from our own experience may serve to show how music may play an effective part in the Christian formation of adults.

Example 1. A group was invited to listen to a number of pieces of music that explored a specific theme, in this case Jesus's words from the cross. Purely instrumental or orchestral settings by Haydn and Sofia Gubaidulina were contrasted with vocal settings by James MacMillan and Edmund Rubbra.

The first objective of the exercise was to surprise the listeners into the possibility of experiencing awe and wonder, but more particularly, and following from this, to enter more profoundly into the mystery and meaning of the event of the cross itself. In this way the exercise served as an act of formative Christian education. The second objective was to enable the listeners to explore the validity of the 'dialectical hermeneutic' described by Groome (see above), by shedding new light on the event of the cross as integrating affective and cognitive understandings, and thus to explore issues of authenticity. This second objective falls more under the description of critical education.

Other exercises invited a group to listen to more extended reflections of the Passion theme. These included Bach's *Matthew* and *John Passion*, alongside MacMillan's extraordinarily powerful *Triduum* (1996/7), as well as – more abstractly, but hardly less significantly – orchestral music that seeks to express or describe love. Berlioz, Scriabin and Messiaen are among the composers that provided suitable material for such reflection.

Example 2. A 'singing group' was formed in a parish to enable people, some of whom professed little or no musical expertise, to perform together once or twice each year in public. The first task was to build the confidence of those who were unfamiliar with musical notation and to teach them sufficient singing (and listening) skills so that any performance would bring enjoyment, and with it a sense of satisfaction and achievement.[77] The group learned quickly, although the technical challenge of some works pushed them very much to the limit.

This limit seemed to have been breached when the group began rehearsals for Britten's *Ceremony of Carols*. The difficulty of learning the notes clearly contributed to a dislike of the music expressed by some members of the group. The leader patiently persisted, however, and very gradually the group began to grow in confidence. The eventual performance, while far from perfect, had such vigour and engagement that even a number of those who had been most vociferous in their condemnation of the piece felt a keen sense of disappointment when it was over, and expressed a wish to be able to sing it again as soon as possible. It was for them, as for many of the audience, a Spirit-filled experience of what Hardy and Ford have called 'sober drunkenness'.[78]

For many people, singers and audience alike, that performance was the highlight of the whole Christmas season. The sense of commitment and struggle to create the music was tangible. It drew performers and audience together; indeed without the audience it would have not been possible. Many things were learned, some of which could not be adequately expressed in words. For a number of participants, the strangeness of Christ's incarnation was undoubtedly made more real. The icy crispness of the music, so much like the weather on the evening it was performed, combined with its passionate evocation of expectation to furnish new insights into the mystery of incarnation and its extraordinary interplay of awful mystery and intimate closeness, of God's transcendence and immanence.

Here was a musical experience of some depth, teaching theology at its most profound.

NOTES

1. Gerardus van der Leeuw, *Sacred and Profane Beauty: The Holy in Art*, Nashville: Abingdon, 1963, p. 225.
2. Cf. Timothy Arthur Lines, *Systemic Religious Education*, Birmingham, Ala: Religious Education Press, 1987, p. 152; Gabriel Moran, *Religious Education as a Second Language*, Birmingham, Ala.: Religious Education Press, 1989, pp. 231–232.
3. See Jeff Astley, *The Philosophy of Christian Religious Education*, Birmingham, Ala.: Religious Education Press; London: SPCK, 1994, ch. 1; Jeff Astley and David Day (eds), *The Contours of Christian Education*, Great Wakering: McCrimmons, 1992, ch. 1.
4. The comments on practice in this paper are informed by experience of over twenty diverse seminars and workshops using music, which took place over a period of about five years and included university extra-mural students, ordinands, Anglican and ecumenical groups of adult educators, Anglican Readers in training, and other lay and clergy groups.
5. Keith Swanwick, *A Basis for Music Education*, London: NFER-Nelson, 1979, p. 112.
6. Cf. Jeff Astley and Leslie J. Francis (eds), *Critical Perspectives on Christian Education: A Reader on the Aims, Principles and Philosophy of Christian Education*, Leominster: Gracewing Fowler Wright, 1994, p. 6 and section 5 *passim*.
7. Friedrich Nietzsche, *The Will to Power*, London: Weidenfeld & Nicolson, 1968, p. 452; Nietzsche, *Beyond Good and Evil*, Harmondsworth: Penguin, 1973, p. 93.
8. See Anthony Storr, *Music and the Mind*, London: HarperCollins, 1992, chs. VIII and IX.
9. Quoted in Evan Eisenberg, *The Recording Angel: Music, Records and Culture from Aristotle to Zappa*, New York, 1987, p. 154.
10. John Hick, *God and the Universe of Faiths*, London: Macmillan, 1973, ch. 3 and *An Interpretation of Religion: Human Responses to the Transcendent*, London: Macmillan, 1989, ch. 10.
11. Jonathan Edwards, *Treatise Concerning the Religious Affections*, London: Banner of Truth, 1961 (original ed. 1746), pp. 23–53.
12. Cf. Kai Nielsen, *An Introduction to the Philosophy of Religion*, London: Macmillan, 1982, p. 75; Robert Solomon, *The Passions*, Notre Dame, Ind.: University of Notre Dame Press, 1983, p. 73, cf. p. xvi; Ninian Smart, *The Science of Religion and the Sociology of Knowledge*, Princeton, N.J.: Princeton University Press, 1973, p. 15.
13. See also James Michael Lee, *The Content of Religious Instruction*, Birmingham, Ala.: Religious Education Press, 1985, ch. 5; Lee, *The Flow of Religious Instruction*; Birmingham, Ala.: Religious Education Press, 1973, pp. 98–106; Astley, *The Philosophy of Christian Religious Education*, pp. 131–149 and ch. 9. Cf. John Macmurray, *Reason and Emotion*, London: Faber & Faber, 1962; Francis Dunlop, *The Education of Feeling and Emotion*, London: Allen & Unwin,

1984, ch. 5.

[14] William Lyons, *Emotion*, Cambridge: Cambridge University Press, 1970, pp. 70, 179 and *passim*. See also Andrew Ortony *et al.*, *The Cognitive Structure of Emotions*, Cambridge: Cambridge University Press, 1988.

[15] See R. S. Peters, 'Education as Initiation', in Reginald D. Archambault (ed.), *Philosophical Analysis and Education*, London: Routledge & Kegan Paul, 1965, p. 99; Peters, 'The Education of the Emotions', in R. F. Dearden *et al.* (eds), *Education and Reason*, London: Routledge & Kegan Paul, 1975, pp. 76–93.

[16] See, e.g., John Wilson, *Education in Religion and the Emotions*, London: Heinemann, 1971, and 'First Steps in Religious Education', in Brenda Watson (ed.), *Priorities in Religious Education*, London: Falmer, 1992, ch. 1.

[17] David Best, 'Values in the Arts', in J. Mark Halstead and Monica J. Taylor (eds), *Values in Education and Education in Values*, London: Falmer, 1996, pp. 82–83.

[18] Lyons, *Emotion*, p. 80; G. Pitcher, 'Emotion', in R. F. Dearden *et al.* (eds), *Reason*, London: Routledge & Kegan Paul, 1975, pp. 232–233.

[19] David Cooper, *Authenticity and Learning*, London: Routledge & Kegan Paul, 1983, p. 65.

[20] Keith Swanwick's word, see *A Basis for Music Education*, ch. 2. Swanwick uses the term very broadly, as a synonym for consciousness and the 'life of feeling' which includes both emotion and thinking (cf. p. 31).

[21] See especially Malcolm Budd, *Music and the Emotions: The Philosophical Theories*, London: Routledge, 1985 and Monroe C. Beardsley, *Aesthetics: Problems in the Philosophy of Criticism*, New York: Harcourt, Brace & World, 1958, pp. 325–332. Such theories include Susanne Langer's cognitive claim that music is an (untranslatable) language of human feeling, whereby formal patterns in subjective experience (motion, rest; tension, release; conflict, resolution; etc.) are articulated in musical forms, so that 'music is a tonal analogue of emotive life' (Susanne K Langer, *Philosophy in a New Key*, Cambridge, Mass.: Harvard University Press, 1978, ch. VIII; Langer, *Feeling and Form*, New York: Scribner's, 1953, p. 27).

[22] Budd, *Music and the Emotions*, pp. 124–5, 175 and *passim*.

[23] John Sloboda, 'Music – Where Cognition and Emotion Meet', *The Psychologist*, 12, 9, 1999, p. 453.

[24] Cf. Roger Scruton, *An Intelligent Person's Guide to Modern Culture*, London: Duckworth, 1998, pp. 15–16.

[25] Swanwick, *op. cit.*, pp. 112, 54.

[26] Sally P. Springer and George Deutsch, *Left Brain, Right Brain*, New York: W. H. Freeman, 1989, espec. pp. 205–206.

[27] Storr, *Music and the Mind*, pp. 39–40.

[28] Paul E. Bumbar, 'Notes on Wholeness', in Gloria Durka and Joanmarie Smith (eds), *Aesthetic Dimensions of Religious Education*, New York: Paulist, 1979, p. 64.

[29] Paul Robertson, 'The Great Divide', *BBC Music Magazine*, May 1993, pp. 23–26.

[30] Cf. *Music for Ages 5–14: Proposals of Secretaries of State*, London: DES/ Welsh Office, 1991, pp. 7–8.

[31] See HMI, *Music 5 to 16*, London: HMSO, 1985, pp. 2–3; Jean Holm, *Teaching Religion in School*, London: Oxford University Press, 1975, p. 120.

[32] Bumbar, *op. cit.*, pp. 65–66; cf. Ken Meltz's article in the same collection, p. 96 and Lee, *Content*, p. 647.

[33] Beardsley, *Aesthetics*, p. 342, cf. p. 344.

[34] *ibid.*, p. 345.

35 Daniel W. Hardy and David F. Ford, *Jubilee: Theology in Praise*, London: Darton, Longman and Todd, 1984, p. 15.

36 William Edgar, *Taking Note of Music*, London: SPCK, 1986, pp. 63–64. For further reflections on the relationship between words and music, see chapters 9, 10 and 11 in the present volume.

37 John A. Berntsen, 'Christian Affections and the Catechumenate', reprinted in Jeff Astley, Leslie J. Francis and Colin Crowder (eds), *Theological Perspectives on Christian Formation: A Reader on Theology and Christian Education*, Leominster: Gracewing Fowler Wright, 1996, ch. 7.1.

38 Jeff Astley, 'The Role of Worship in Christian Learning', in *ibid.*, ch. 7.2.

39 Bumbar, *op. cit.*, p. 64.

40 Meltz, *op. cit.*, p. 97.

41 Macmurray, *Reason and Emotion*, pp. 34–37, 44–46, 71. These are the traditional marks of a liberal education.

42 Simone Weil, *Waiting on God*, London: Collins, 1959, pp. 66–76. Cf. Richard Harries, *Art and the Beauty of God: A Christian Understanding*, London: Mowbray, 1993, pp. 41–42, 51.

43 Harold Osborne, 'Introduction' to H. Osborne (ed.), *Aesthetics*, Oxford: Oxford University Press, 1972, p. 15.

44 From an interview by Nicholas Roe in *The Independent*, 18 September 1997.

45 See, for example, Ian T. Ramsey, *Christian Discourse,* London: Oxford University Press, 1965, pp. 67–71; Ramsey, *Models for Divine Activity*, London: SCM, 1973, p. 37.

46 Ian T. Ramsey, *Our Understanding of Prayer*, London: SPCK, 1971.

47 Cf. Dean M. Martin, 'Learning to Become a Christian', reprinted in Astley and Francis (eds), *Critical Perspectives on Christian Education*, ch. 4.2.

48 Richard Wollheim, *Art and Its Objects*, Harmondsworth: Penguin, 1970, pp. 120–156.

49 See especially the works of Dewi Z. Phillips: for example, *Faith and Philosophical Enquiry*, London: Routledge & Kegan Paul, 1970; *Religion without Explanation*, Oxford: Blackwell, 1976; *Belief, Change and Forms of Life*, London: Macmillan, 1986. Phillips argues that religion is not itself a form of life, but 'it is impossible to imagine a religion ... without imagining it *in* a form of life'. D. Z. Phillips, 'Belief, Change and Forms of Life', in F. Crossan (ed.), *The Autonomy of Belief*, Notre Dame, Ind.: University of Notre Dame Press, 1981, p. 60.

50 Lee, *Content*, ch. 9.

51 Peter Brown, *The Hypnotic Brain*, New Haven: Yale University Press, 1991, p. 60.

52 A. N. Whitehead, *Religion in the Making*, Cambridge: Cambridge University Press, 1926, p. 16.

53 Osborne, *op. cit.*, p. 22.

54 Hans-Georg Gadamer, *Truth and Method*, New York: Crossroad, 1982; Vincent Brümmer, *Speaking of a Personal God*, Cambridge: Cambridge University Press, 1992, ch. 1; but contrast Basil Mitchell, 'Theology and Philosophy', in G. J. Hughes (ed.), *The Philosophical Assessment of Theology*, Georgetown: Georgetown University Press, 1987, pp. 3–14.

55 See Anthony C. Thiselton, *The Two Horizons*, Exeter: Paternoster, 1980; *New Horizons in Hermeneutics*, London: HarperCollins, 1992.

56 Gadamer, *op. cit.*, pp. 347, 419, 430.

57 Thomas H. Groome, *Christian Religious Education*, San Francisco: Harper &

Row, 1980; *Sharing Faith*, San Francisco: Harper Collins, 1991.

58 R. M. Rummery, *Catechesis and Religious Education in a Pluralist Society*, Sydney: Dwyer, 1975, p. 195.

59 Paul Kline, 'Objective Tests of Freud's Theories', in Andrew M. Colman and J. Graham Beaumont (eds), *Psychological Survey 7*, London: Routledge, 1989, pp. 128-129. The reference to Sharpe's work is to R. Sharpe, 'Mirrors, Lamps, Organisms and Texts', in P. Clarke and C. Wright (eds), *Minds, Psychoanalysis and Science*, Oxford: Blackwell, 1988.

60 Frances Young, *The Art of Performance: Towards a Theology of Holy Scripture*, London: Darton, Longman and Todd, 1990, pp. 104-105 and *passim*. Here Young explores what is involved in musical performance 'so as to illustrate the process of appropriating the Bible in the modern world' (p. 3). In particular, she examines the call for authenticity in performance and argues that any good performance has an authenticity of its own. She concludes that, like music, God's word is *realised* in performance, a performance that has the power to energise and change those who listen. Cf. Nicholas Lash, *Theology on the Way to Emmaus*, London: SCM, 1986, ch. 3 and Trevor Cooling, 'Education is the Point of RE - not Religion?', in Jeff Astley and Leslie J. Francis (eds), *Christian Theology and Religious Education: Connections and Contradictions*, London: SPCK, 1996, ch. 10.

61 Harries, *Art and the Beauty of God*, p. 146.

62 *ibid.*, p. 145.

63 The New Testament understandings of 'healing' and 'salvation' share the same linguistic root.

64 Michael Tippett, *Moving into Aquarius,* London: Paladin, 1974, pp. 16–18.

65 Quoted by Simon Broughton in 'Terezin: Music Behind Bars', *BBC Music Magazine*, October 1993, pp. 28-31.

66 See Young, *The Art of Performance*, especially ch. 8 on 'improvisation and inspiration'.

67 Cf. Gabriel Moran, *God Still Speaks*, London: Burns and Oates, 1967; Moran, *Interplay*, Winona, Minn.: St Mary's Press, 1981; Harold W. Burgess, *An Introduction to Religious Education*, Birmingham, Ala.: Religious Education Press, 1975, ch. IV.

68 John V. Taylor, *The Christlike God*, London: SCM, 1992, p. 31.

69 Gerd Theissen, *Biblical Faith: An Evolutionary Approach*, London: SCM, 1984, p. 76.

70 David Tracy, *The Analogical Imagination*, London: SCM, 1981, p. 200.

71 Tippett, *op. cit.*, p. 48.

72 Lee, *Content*, p. 395, cf. p. 647.

73 See Jeff Astley, 'Christian Worship and the Hidden Curriculum of Christian Learning', in Astley and Day (eds), *The Contours of Christian Education*, ch. 10.

74 See, for example, Jeremy Begbie, 'The Gospel, the Arts and Our Culture', in Hugh Montefiore (ed.), *The Gospel and Contemporary Culture,* London: Mowbray, 1992, pp. 74–76.

75 Improvisation is discussed in this volume in chapters 2, 4, 9 and 12.

76 Something of the scope of the educational work undertaken by the Association of British Orchestras can be seen in Fiona Lockwood (ed.), *The Workbook: The Central Written Resource for the ABO National Education Programme 1997*, London: ABO, 1997.

77 See also Timothy Hone, 'When in Our Music God is Glorified', chapter 9, above.

78 Hardy and Ford, *Jubilate*, p. 15.

Afterword:

Music and Theology

Timothy Hone, Jeff Astley and Mark Savage

Although this volume does not include a systematic theology of music, it does have a wide theological reference, both explicit and implicit. This final section simply draws together some of these theological themes, and outlines some additional ways in which music can act as a metaphor in theological understanding.[1]

(i)   An understanding of creativity with reference to the composer (the primary creator), the performer (re-creative and incarnational), and the listener (imaginative and spiritual) is of fundamental importance. This composer-performer-listener relationship may offer an insight into the *trinitarian nature of God*. Thus the activity of the composer draws on and reveals the primary creative energy of God the Father, while the incarnational rôle of the performer is analogous to the realisation of the divine will in the person of Jesus Christ. The act of listening to music is less explicit, yet is essential to the completion and realisation of the musical process, in a way that may shed some light on the operation of the Holy Spirit.[2]

(ii)   Music can help in other ways to illuminate the *doctrine of creation*, and a better understanding of the composer's task may suggest insights into both human and divine creativity as such. Music-making itself brings order out of chaos, and utilises skills of selecting, shaping, adapting and combining raw materials. All creation is grounded in the expression of value, and the creative musical choices made by the composer reveal a great deal about what is 'beautiful', 'striking', 'meaningful' and 'interesting' in the world of sound.[3]

(iii)   The performing musician knows and shows a particularly close relationship between the processes of thought and of hand-controlled craftsmanship that is reflective of a profound integration between the spiritual and physical aspects of personality,[4] contributing to a holistic *understanding of human nature*. Close attention to the ways in which we react to music may lead to a greater awareness of the inner life of feeling and emotion, and in this way a contemplation of music may lead to a deeper contemplation of self. There are obvious connections here with the way in which prayerful Christians seek to develop an inner spiritual life, which may lead to a greater personal integration as well as a greater understanding of the voice of God within.

(iv) The theological relationship between *law and freedom* in the religious (and, indeed, human) life might be compared with the relationship between the demands in music of a style or system, e.g. of functional tonality, a 12-note serial technique, or a formal procedure such as fugue, over against the choices that have to be made by the composer.

(v) Music is often described as communicating an awareness of otherness. Because, for the listener, the music that is 'out there' has to be 'internalised' in order to be heard, music can act as a profound illustration of the metaphors of both *transcendence* and *immanence*. Music is radically alien and different from our nature, and yet it profoundly 'fits' the contours of the soul. Such reflections relate to fundamental debates about the subjective and the objective within theology.

(vi) Music may also serve as an appropriate model for divine *revelation*, giving us glimpses of 'other worlds' and a sense of the ineffable, while communicating truths that are often too deep for words and even disclosing aspects of God.

(vii) Debates over the issue of authenticity in musical interpretation also connect with reflections on the relationship between composer, performer and listener. Such conversations can be helpful in clarifying *the hermeneutical task* that is faced by anyone who wishes to appropriate the Christian tradition today.

(viii) Music has a unique contribution to make to our understanding of the concepts of *time, space and motion*.[5] Through music we may perhaps experience realities that otherwise rarely enter human understanding, connecting music with scientific and theological thinking at their most abstract. The hope music offers of being able to understand time in a sense other than the purely chronological is of considerable relevance to a theological perspective.

(ix) Because music seems to be in motion, it has often been felt to have a nature similar to, or symbolic of, organic life processes.[6]

Through music, then, there is the possibility of understanding more fully *what it means to be alive*. Processes of growth, transformation, transition and development are widely found in musical expression; along with the contrasting state of stillness and music whose movement is so slow that it can seem static. A deeper exploration of these features might suggest many possibilities for those engaged in counselling and therapy, and in education, spiritual development and liturgy.

(x) Because music is a process evolving in time, and because it has evolved within our own culture a harmonic language that involves dissonance and consonance, conflict and resolution, music offers the ready possibility of engaging metaphorically with suffering, and allowing for that suffering to be resolved. Although this is primarily a figurative process, it can also bring about a changed perspective for those whose attitudes and situations are in some measure redeemed by music through processes of actual psychological change. Music may therefore offer a potent symbol and experience of both healing and *redemption*.

(xi) A more complete understanding of the ways in which music can enhance and intensify worship and ritual may lead to insights about the nature of our needs as worshipping creatures, and to a renewed awareness of elements central to the building of human communities. As a consequence, we may identify essential features of *church*, and of the relationship between belief and practice revealed in the Christian community as it gathers in obedience for the liturgical transaction between God and his people which we call worship.[7]

(xii) Ultimately music is a *gift*. [8] As with any gift, the more we learn to value, use and understand it, the more we may learn about the nature and preferred way of working of the one who has given it. Presents are expressive of the presenter; and for many people music is foremost among those gifts of creation that serve to render the character of God.

Whenever and however we engage in music, we are presented with the challenge of understanding the experience more thoroughly and more theologically. It is our hope that this collection of papers will suggest further avenues for fruitful exploration: journeys that will help us to revisit the musical experience with new insights, re-discovering it afresh. In music as in religion – and as in life – the end of our best explorations is a return to our point of departing, so as to know it 'for the first time'.[9]

NOTES

1   Cf. Timothy Hone, Jeff Astley and Mark Savage, 'Variations on a Theme: Towards a Theology of Music?', *Modern Believing*, XXXVII, 4, 1996, pp. 54–62, and our 'Introduction and Overview' in this volume.

2   A parallel analogy (drawing on literary creativity) is offered by Dorothy Sayers in *The Mind of the Maker* (1941), reprinted in The Library of Anglican Spirituality, London: Mowbray, 1994.

3   See Jeremy Begbie, *Music in God's Purposes*, Edinburgh: Handsel Press, 1989.

4   Compare the reflections of Martin Heidegger, as discussed in Victor Zuckerkandl, *Man the Musician*, Princeton, N.J.: Princeton University Press, 1976, pp. 274ff.

5   See Jonathan D. Kramer, *The Time of Music*, New York: Schirmer Books, 1988, and the papers by Begbie and Hone, above.

6   See, in particular, the work of Susanne Langer, *Philosophy in a New Key*, Cambridge, Mass.: Harvard University Press, 3rd Edition, 1956.

7   See Aidan Kavanagh, *On Liturgical Theology*, Collegeville, Minnesota: Pueblo (The Liturgical Press), 1984, in particular chapters 5 and 6.

8   See James Lancelot, 'Music as a Sacrament', in David Brown and Ann Loades (eds), *The Sense of the Sacramental: Movement and Measure in Art and Music, Place and Time*, London: SPCK, 1995, pp. 179–185.

9   T. S. Eliot, 'Little Gidding', pt. 5, *Four Quartets* (1942), in *Collected Poems 1909–1962*, London: Faber, 1963, p. 222.

Index

CPSIA information can be obtained
at www.ICGtesting.com
Printed in the USA
LVOW13s0608120218
566147LV00011BA/271/P